Rational Emotive Behaviour
Group Therapy

Rational Emotive Behaviour Group Therapy

Edited by

WINDY DRYDEN

Goldsmiths College, London

and

MICHAEL NEENAN

Centre for Stress Management, London

W

WHURR PUBLISHERS
LONDON AND PHILADELPHIA

© 2002 Whurr Publishers
First published 2002 by
Whurr Publishers Ltd
19b Compton Terrace, London N1 2UN, England and
325 Chestnut Street, Philadelphia PA 19106, USA

British Library Cataloguing in Publication Data

A catalogue record for this book is available from the British
Library.

ISBN 1 86156 253 5

Printed and bound in the UK by Athenaeum Press Limited,
Gateshead, Tyne & Wear.

Contents

Preface   **vii**

Contributors   **ix**

Chapter 1   **1**

Rational Emotive Behaviour Group Therapy: An Overview
Windy Dryden

Chapter 2   **30**

Rational Emotive Behavior Therapy (REBT) and Its Application
to Group Therapy
Albert Ellis

Chapter 3   **55**

Critical Incidents in Group Therapy
Albert Ellis

Chapter 4   **91**

Rational Emotive Behavior Therapy and Its Application to
Women's Groups
Kristene A. Doyle

Chapter 5   **106**

The Florence Nightingale Hospital CBT Group Therapy Programme
Windy Dryden

Chapter 6   **124**

Teaching the Principles of Unconditional Self-Acceptance in a
Structured, Group Setting
Windy Dryden

Chapter 7   **142**

Rational Emotive Behavior Therapy Intensives
Albert Ellis

Chapter 8   **176**

Problems in Living: The Friday Night Workshop
Windy Dryden, Wouter Backx and Albert Ellis

Chapter 9   **188**

The Use of the Group in REBT Training and Supervision
Michael Neenan

Index   **205**

Preface

This book centres on the practice of Rational Emotive Behaviour Therapy (REBT) in groups. In the opening chapter, Windy Dryden presents a brief overview of REBT and maps the field in which the following chapters can be located. In Chapter 2, Albert Ellis, the founder of REBT, outlines his approach to Group REBT and in Chapter 3 he deals with a number of critical incidents that can occur in group therapy. In Chapter 4, Kristene Doyle shows how REBT can be applied to women's groups, while in Chapter 5, Windy Dryden considers how REBT can be used as a foundation for a hospital-based CBT group programme for day- and in-patients.

REBT is a psychoeducational approach to therapy and this is highlighted in the next three chapters. In Chapter 6, Windy Dryden discusses how unconditional self-acceptance can be taught in a structured group setting; in Chapter 7, Albert Ellis details the REBT approach to 9-hour group intensives and in Chapter 8, Windy Dryden, Wouter Backx and Albert Ellis feature the Friday Night Workshop, a group-based experience that Albert Ellis has been running for many years at his New York Institute.

The book is brought to a close by Michael Neenan who shows how the group can be used in REBT training and supervision.

Windy Dryden
Michael Neenan

Contributors

Wouter Backx, Fellow of The Albert Ellis Institute and Director of The Institute of RET, Haarlem, The Netherlands

Kristene A. Doyle, Fellow and Training Coordinator, The Albert Ellis Institute, New York

Windy Dryden, Goldsmiths College, London

Albert Ellis, President of The Albert Ellis Institute, New York

Micheal Neenan, Centre for Stress Management, London

CHAPTER 1

Rational Emotive Behaviour Group Therapy: An Overview

WINDY DRYDEN

History of Rational Emotive Behaviour Therapy

In this opening section I will provide a brief general overview of the historical development of REBT and will also consider the development of REBT as an approach to group therapy.

Historical development of REBT: a general overview

Rational Emotive Behaviour Therapy (henceforth referred to as REBT) was originated in 1955 by Albert Ellis, an American clinical psychologist. Ellis was initially trained in psychoanalysis, but was disappointed in the efficacy of this method and its shorter, less intensive variants. After experimenting with other therapeutic approaches in the early 1950s, Ellis created a form of therapy that brought together a number of different strands and blended them into an integrative whole. The two major strands were:

1. the Stoic view of Epictetus (1890) enshrined in his famous dictum that: 'People are disturbed not by things, but by their views of things' (cognitive strand);
2. the behavioural view of John L. Watson (1919) and others that stressed that the best way to overcome fears is to act against them (behavioural strand).

These two strands showed that REBT (known at the time as Rational Therapy (RT)) was one of the first approaches within what is now known as the cognitive-behavioural tradition within psychotherapy. At first when Ellis presented his ideas to a field dominated by psychoanalytic thinkers and practitioners, he received strong criticism in the form of what can now be seen as predictable attacks from this quarter, namely that: his therapy was too superficial, it neglected the patient's past, it was too intellectual and diminished the importance of the emotions, and the relationship that REBT urged its therapists to adopt with their clients completely downplayed the transferential nature of this relationship. Undaunted, Ellis continued to promulgate his ideas in print and at conferences and gradually attracted a growing number of enthusiastic followers and collaborators. At the suggestion of one of these collaborators, Robert Harper, in 1961 Ellis changed the name of his therapeutic approach from Rational Therapy (RT) to Rational-Emotive Therapy (RET). He did this for two reasons: (1) to silence his critics who wrongly claimed that RT neglected clients' emotions and (2) to distance his approach from another, albeit lesser known, therapeutic approach known as Rational Therapy which was based on Marxist philosophy. The twin concepts of rationality and emotion were emphasized in Ellis's first major book-length work on REBT entitled *Reason and Emotion in Psychotherapy* (Ellis, 1962) which is generally regarded today as a classic work.

Ellis's work very much came to the fore in the late 1960s and early 1970s when behaviour therapists were discovering the importance of cognitive factors (e.g. Lazarus, 1971). However, because of different priorities, Ellis did not grasp an opportunity that could have taken REBT to the forefront of the cognitive-behavioural movement. Behaviour therapy has always stressed the importance of undertaking research to test both the validity of theoretical constructs and the efficacy of therapeutic methods, but because Ellis has never held a full-time academic appointment, he did not personally initiate and co-ordinate a research programme to test his ideas.

This opportunity was fully exploited by another pioneer in the cognitive-behavioural tradition, Aaron T. Beck, the originator of cognitive therapy. Based full-time in the Department of Psychiatry and the University of Pennsylvania and unencumbered by a clinical caseload, Beck, beginning in the 1960s and continuing into the 1970s and 1980s, initiated and co-ordinated a research programme to test his cognitive theories of depression and anxiety and to test the efficacy of cognitive therapy for these two disorders. As his work became more widely known, Beck also attracted first-rate young researchers to work with him and as a consequence, cognitive therapy has attracted far more research funds than REBT and its reputation within the academic community has advanced accordingly, attracting the scientific attention of some of the world's leading psychotherapy researchers.

By contrast, much REBT research has been conducted by American PhD candidates and when it has been carried out by established researchers, these scientists have lacked the research funds to carry out studies of the calibre of those being carried out by cognitive therapy researchers. Having said this, there is a substantial REBT research literature and this will be reviewed briefly later in this chapter.

While REBT failed to capitalize on the research opportunities provided by the growing interest in the cognitive-behavioural therapies that occurred in the late 1960s and early 1970s, its development during those years and subsequently has occurred therapeutically. Thus, REBT has been practised with children, adolescents and adults experiencing a wide variety of clinical and non-clinical problems in individual therapy, couple therapy, family therapy and of course, group therapy which is the focus of this present chapter. In addition, thanks to the training efforts of what is now known as the Albert Ellis Institute for, REBT is now practised throughout the world.

Another feature of the historical development of REBT has been Ellis's skill at showing how REBT contributes to popular trends of the day in the field of psychotherapy. For example, when the encounter group movement was riding high in the 1960s, Ellis outlined the REBT approach to encounter groups in general and marathon groups in particular (Ellis, 1969) and later when various quasi-therapeutic organizations like EST, Lifespring and Forum were running highly touted, large-group 'intensives', Ellis and his colleagues devised REBT intensives. In the 1980s when the psychotherapy integration movement was attracting much attention largely by the efforts of the Society for the Exploration of Psychotherapy Integration (SEPI), Ellis (1987) wrote an article showing that REBT was indeed an integrative psychotherapeutic approach. In the last decade, constructivist and post-modern perspectives on psychotherapy have come to the fore and true to form, Ellis (1997) wrote significant papers outlining REBT's contribution to both perspectives. Thus, while Ellis has never contributed significantly to the research literature on psychotherapy, he has, almost single-handedly ensured that the REBT presence was felt whenever a significant trend in psychotherapy took centre stage. Even when a trend emerged with which Ellis significantly disagreed (e.g. transpersonal psychotherapy) Ellis's, and thus REBT's, voice was to be heard lambasting the trend (Ellis and Yeager, 1989). Ellis refers to himself as a propagandist for REBT and this certainly becomes clear if one were to study his list of publications. He rarely turns down an invitation to write on this subject, no matter who asks him and he has responded to many published criticisms of REBT whether these criticisms have come from outside REBT (e.g. Bernard and DiGiuseppe, 1989) or from within its fold (e.g. Dryden, 1996).

Amidst all this activity, Ellis decided once again to change the name of his therapy. You will recall that originally the approach was called Rational Therapy (RT) and was changed in 1961 to Rational-Emotive Therapy (RET) to counter arguments that RT neglected clients' emotions. Suddenly in 1993, Ellis decided to change the name again to Rational Emotive Behaviour

Therapy (REBT) in order to silence critics who had claimed, wrongly, that RET neglected clients' behaviour.

As the above helps to show, one of the features of REBT's development over the years has been the indefatigable efforts of its founder Albert Ellis. Earlier, I argued that Ellis failed to initiate and co-ordinate a research programme into REBT theory and practice. Instead he has chosen to promulgate REBT and ensure that its views on significant trends of the day are known. In addition to maintaining a heavy clinical caseload over the years, Ellis has also travelled widely both in North America and throughout the world giving REBT workshops and presentations and he regularly serves on the faculty on the Albert Ellis Institute's many training courses both in New York and elsewhere. At the time of writing, Ellis is 88 and still is as active in promulgating REBT as he ever was. His prediction that he will 'die in the saddle' will probably come true.

Development of REBT as an approach to group therapy

As I will presently discuss, REBT has been practised in group therapy format in several different ways. But it was Ellis, predictably, who was the first person to run groups based on REBT principles. He did so in 1959 partly at the request of his patients, although at first he was reluctant to do so. His reluctance was based on his experiences of psychoanalytic groups which he saw as being both ineffective and inefficient. However, when he began to run REBT groups, he quickly saw that his initial reluctance was misplaced. He soon began to run several groups and has done so ever since. Ellis's early groups were what might be called ongoing, semi-open, outpatient groups that met once a week. Clients had to commit themselves to the group for a minimum period and had to give the group a reasonable period of notice before leaving the group. However, another client could join the group assuming that there was a vacancy and that the necessary commitment was given. Since those early days, REBT group therapy has developed through innovation and the following formats are currently employed by REBT group therapists.

1. The ongoing, semi-open, outpatient group (as described above)

While most of these groups are heterogeneous in group composition (in the sense that clients have a variety of different problems, some REBT group therapists do run these groups along homogeneous lines where clients share similar problems (e.g. anxiety or eating disorders).

2. The time-limited, closed, problem or theme-based group

By definition, these groups are homogeneous in nature because they are based on a client problem (e.g. anger) or a theme (developing self-acceptance). The membership of the time-limited group is closed for a number of reasons: (a) to encourage group cohesion. This is particularly the case when there is no set therapeutic curriculum and the group is, relatively speaking, more open-ended; (b) to ensure that the therapeutic curriculum (when the group is based on one) is followed without needless repetition. As I will illustrate in Chapter 6 when this type of group is based on a curriculum, it is important that all clients attend each session because crucial information is presented and applied to each member present. If the group were open, then whenever a new member joined the group, the group therapist would have to begin each group session presenting material that would be new to the joining member, but well understood by the established members.

3. REBT marathon encounter groups

In the late 1960s, Ellis (1969) pioneered and ran REBT marathon encounter groups which shared many of the features of other marathon encounter groups at the time (with their emphases on experiential exercises and person-to-person encounter), but also focused on (a) processing participants' beliefs about the many emotion-laden situations they faced during the marathon group, disputing group members' irrational beliefs when they were uncovered; and on (b) encouraging participants to take risks based on rational thinking

4. REBT women's groups

REBT women's groups were pioneered by Janet Wolfe (1995) who, with sex educator Peggy Kellogg, began to run REBT sexuality groups for women in the early 1970s at the then named Institute for Rational Living. Later that decade Wolfe teamed up with Iris Fodor to run REBT assertiveness training groups for women and since then has run herself and inspired others to run a host of different REBT women's groups (see Chapter 4).

5. The hospital-based group REBT programme

In the hospital-based group REBT programme, in-patients and day patients attend a group therapy programme run on REBT principles. I am associated with one such programme and we offer two REBT-oriented groups a day for patients (see Chapter 5). Groups are either problem- or theme-based (with specific groups on anxiety, depression, anger/assertion and dealing with relationships), skills-based (where patients are taught how to (a) assess their problems using the ABC framework (to be discussed in the next section); (b) dispute their irrational beliefs; (c) use a variety of imagery, behavioural and emotive techniques to weaken their conviction in their irrational beliefs and to strengthen their conviction in their rational beliefs and (d) to confront and overcome obstacles to psychotherapeutic change) or agenda-based (where patients are all given an opportunity to discuss and deal with specific aspects of their problems).

6. 'Problems of living' large-scale groups

For many years, Albert Ellis has run, and continues to run, what has become known as his 'Friday night workshop' (Dryden and Backx, 1987). During this experience, Ellis interviews (one at a time) two volunteers from the audience of 50, 100 or even more people on one of their 'problems of living'. After Ellis has worked with the person for about 30 minutes, he invites the audience to comment on the process and to share relevant experiences from their own lives. A lively, but surprisingly therapeutic, debate often ensues (see Chapter 8).

7. Rational Emotive Behavior intensives

In 1983, Ellis devised and began to run nine-hour long intensive groups run along REBT lines. These groups are highly structured, divided into the following six learning modules each lasting 1 hour 15 minutes:

(a) The ABCs of REBT and the Disputing of Irrational Beliefs
(b) Perfectionism and Unconditional Self-Acceptance
(c) Dealing with Anger and Rage
(d) Dealing with the Dire Need for Love and Approval
(e) Dealing with Low Frustration Tolerance
(f) Goal Setting and Homework

Each learning module begins with a lecturette, followed by an experiential exercise and is concluded by a period of sharing and feedback on the lecturette and the exercise. At the end of the intensive, participants will have been given much valuable information on psychological disturbance and its remediation, been taught a number of REBT's major cognitive, emotive and behavioural techniques and helped to devise an individualized self-help programme based on what they have learnt during the intensive (see Chapter 7).

In addition REBT has been used in group-based education programmes in educational, workplace and non-clinical settings as will be shown in the fourth section of this chapter.

Theoretical Constructs on which REBT is Based

Rational Emotive Behaviour Therapy is based on a number of theoretical principles which for present purposes can be divided into (1) principles that account for psychological disturbance and its perpetuation and (2) principles that account for therapeutic change and which guide the practice of the therapy.

How REBT construes psychological disturbance and its perpetuation

I mentioned in the opening section that REBT has roots in Stoic philosophy and quoted Epictetus's famous dictum: 'People are disturbed not by things, but by their views of things.' At the core of the REBT conceptualization of psychological disturbance is a reformulation of this Stoic view. The REBT version is as follows: 'People are disturbed, not by things, but by their rigid and extreme views of things.' Let me now consider the rigid and extreme beliefs which REBT holds are at the core of psychological disturbance and which REBT group therapists encourage group members to challenge and change (known in the literature as irrational beliefs) and the alternative flexible and non-extreme beliefs which are at the core of psychological health and which REBT group therapists encourage group members to acquire and develop (known in the literature as rational beliefs).

Irrational beliefs and their rational alternatives

Irrational beliefs are evaluative ideas that have the following characteristics. They are: (1) rigid or extreme; (2) inconsistent with reality; (3) illogical or nonsensical and (4) yield dysfunctional consequences. On the other hand, rational beliefs have the following characteristics. They are: (1) flexible or non-extreme; (2) consistent with reality; (3) logical or sensible and (4) yield functional consequences. REBT theory posits four irrational beliefs and their rational alternatives.

Demands

Demands are rigid ideas that people hold about how things absolutely must or must not be. Demands can be placed on oneself (e.g. 'I must do well'), on others (e.g. 'You must treat me well') or on life conditions (e.g. 'Life must be fair'). Ellis's view is that of all the irrational beliefs, it is these demands that are at the very core of psychological disturbance. The healthy alternative to a demand is a full preference.

Full preferences

Full preferences are flexible ideas that people hold about how they would like things to be without demanding that they have to be that way. Full preferences can relate to oneself (e.g. I want to do well, but I don't have to do so'), others (e.g. I want you to treat me well, but unfortunately you don't have to do so') or life conditions ('I very much want life to be fair, but unfortunately it doesn't have to be the way I want it to be'). Again, Ellis's position is that of all the rational beliefs, it is these full preferences that are at the very core of psychological health.

Awfulizing beliefs

Awfulizing beliefs are extreme ideas that people hold as derivatives from their demands when these demands aren't met (e.g. I must do well *and it's terrible if I don't*; 'You must treat me well *and it's awful when you don't*' and 'Life must be fair *and it's the end of the world when it's not.*' An awfulizing belief stems from the demand that things must not be as bad as they are and is extreme in the sense that the person believes at the time one or more of the following: (1) nothing could be worse; (2) the event in question is worse than 100 per cent bad; and (3) no good could possibly come from this bad event. The healthy alternative to an awfulizing belief is an anti-awfulizing belief.

Anti-awfulizing beliefs

Anti-awfulizing beliefs are non-extreme ideas that people hold as derivatives from their full preferences when these full preferences aren't met (e.g. 'I want to do well, but I don't have to do so. *It's bad if I don't do well, but not terrible*'; 'I want you to treat me well, but unfortunately you don't have to do so. *When you don't treat me well it's really unfortunate, but not awful*'; and 'I very much want life to be fair, but unfortunately it doesn't have to be the way I want it to be. *If life is unfair, that's very bad, but not the end of the world.*' An anti-awfulizing belief stems from the full preference that I'd like things not to be as bad as they are, but that doesn't mean that they must not be and is non-extreme in the sense that the person believes at the time one or more of the following: (1) things could always be worse; (2) the event in question is less than 100 per cent bad; and (3) good could come from this bad event.

Low frustration tolerance beliefs

Low frustration tolerance beliefs are extreme ideas that people hold as derivatives from their demands when these demands aren't met (e.g. 'I must do well *and I can't bear it if I don't*'; 'You must treat me well *and it's intolerable when you don't*'; and 'Life must be fair *and I can't stand it when it's not.*' A low frustration tolerance stems from the demand that things must not be as frustrating or uncomfortable as they are and is extreme in the sense that the person believes at the time one or more of the following: (1) I will die or disintegrate if the frustration or discomfort continues to exist; (2) I will lose the capacity to experience happiness if the frustration or discomfort continues to exist; and (3) the frustration or discomfort is not worth tolerating. The healthy alternative to a low frustration tolerance belief is a high frustration tolerance belief.

High frustration tolerance beliefs

High frustration tolerance beliefs are non-extreme ideas that people hold as derivatives from their full preferences when these full preferences aren't met (e.g. 'I want to do well, but I don't have to do so. *When I don't do well it is difficult to bear but I can bear it and it's worth bearing*'; 'I want you to treat me well, but unfortunately you don't have to do so. *When you don't treat me well it's really hard to tolerate, but I can tolerate it and it's worth it to me to do so*' and 'I very much want life to be fair, but unfortunately it doesn't have to be the way I want it to be. *If life is unfair, that's hard to stand, but I can stand it and it is in my best interests to do so.*' A high frustration tolerance belief stems from the full preference that it is undesirable when things are as frustrating or uncomfortable as they are, but unfortunately things don't have to be different. It is non-extreme in the sense that the person believes at the time one or more of the following: (1) I will struggle if the frustration or discomfort continues to exist, but I will neither die nor disintegrate; (2) I will not lose the capacity to experience happiness if the frustration or discomfort continues to exist, although this capacity will be temporarily diminished; and (3) the frustration or discomfort is worth tolerating.

Depreciation beliefs

Depreciation beliefs are extreme ideas that people hold about self, other(s) and the world as derivatives from their demands when these demands aren't met (e.g. 'I must do well *and I am a failure if I don't*'; 'You must treat me well *and you are a bad person if you don't*'; and 'Life must be fair *and the world is bad if it isn't.*' A depreciation belief stems from the demand that I, you or things must be as I want them to be and is extreme in the sense that the person believes at the time one or more of the following: (1) a person can legitimately be given a single global rating that defines their essence and one's worth is dependent upon conditions that change (e.g. my worth goes up when I do well and goes down when I don't do well); (2) the world can legitimately be given a single rating that defines its essential nature and the value of the world varies according to what happens within it (e.g. the value of the world goes up when something fair occurs and goes down when something unfair happens); (3) a person can be rated on the basis of one of his or her aspects; and (4) the world can be rated on the basis of one of its aspects. The healthy alternative to a depreciation belief is an acceptance belief.

Acceptance beliefs

Acceptance beliefs are non-extreme ideas that people hold as derivatives from their full preferences when these full preferences aren't met (e.g. 'I want to do well, but I don't have to do so. *When I don't do well I am not a failure. I am a fallible human being who is not doing well on this occasion*'; 'I want you to treat me well, but unfortunately you don't have to do so. *When you don't treat me well, you are not a bad person, rather a fallible human being who is treating me poorly*'; and 'I very much want life to be fair, but unfortunately it doesn't have to be the way I want it to be. *If life is unfair it is only unfair in this respect and doesn't prove that the world is a rotten place. The world is a complex place where many good, bad and neutral things happen.*' An acceptance is non-extreme in the sense that the person believes at the time one or more of the following: (1) a person cannot legitimately be given a single global rating that defines their essence rated and one's worth, as far as one has it, is not dependent upon conditions that change (e.g. my worth stays the same whether or not I do well; (2) the world cannot legitimately be given a single rating that defines its essential nature and the value of the world does not vary according to what happens within it (e.g. the value of the world stays the same whether fairness exists or not); (3) it makes sense to rate discrete aspects of a person and of the world, but it does not make sense to rate a person or the world on the basis of these discrete aspects.

The effects of irrational beliefs and their rational alternatives

Holding irrational beliefs about life's adversities has a number of deleterious effects on a person's psychological functioning. First, they lead the person to have one or more unhealthy negative emotions such as anxiety, depression, guilt, shame, hurt, unhealthy anger, unhealthy jealousy and unhealthy envy. Secondly, irrational beliefs lead the person to act in a number of self-, other- and relationship-defeating ways. Finally, irrational beliefs have an impairing impact on the person's cognitive functioning: they lead the person to think unrealistically about self, others and the world. For example, irrational beliefs are often the breeding ground for what cognitive therapists call cognitive distortions. Thus, if you believe that you must perform well in public and you think that you haven't, then you are likely to think in a variety of distorted ways, for example mind-reading (e.g. 'I'm sure that the audience thinks that I made a fool of myself'), overgeneralization ('I'll always do poorly in public situations') and minimization ('There were no redeeming features to my presentation'). Irrational beliefs also have an effect on the person's attentional and memory systems. Thus, when there is a possibility that a threat may occur to something of value in an individual's personal domain and the person holds an irrational belief about the threat, then that person's attention will be drawn to the existence of the threat and she (in this case) may exaggerate (1) the chances that the threat will occur and (2) the nature of the threat itself. Also, when the person has experienced a significant loss to his (in this case) personal domain and holds an irrational belief about this loss, then he will tend to remember other losses rather than the gains that he has experienced in his life.

By contrast, holding rational beliefs about the same adversities has a number of productive effects on a person's psychological functioning. First, these beliefs lead the person to have healthy negative emotions such as concern, sadness, remorse, disappointment, sorrow, healthy anger, healthy jealousy and healthy envy. Secondly, rational beliefs lead the person to act in a number of self-, other- and relationship-enhancing ways. Finally, rational beliefs have a constructive impact on the person's cognitive functioning. Thus, they lead the person to think realistically about self, others and the world. In particular, this helps the person to accept that good, bad and neutral things can result from the adversity that she (in this case) is facing.

How the person perpetuates psychological disturbance

Once your client has made himself (in this case) disturbed then he may easily perpetuate his disturbance in the following ways:

1. by denying that he has disturbed feelings;
2. by failing to take responsibility for his psychological disturbance and thinking that other people or external events cause this disturbance;
3. by thinking that his past has caused his present disturbed feelings and that insight into his past is necessary to change these present feelings;
4. by not realizing that irrational beliefs are at the core of psychological disturbance and therefore not knowing that psychotherapeutic change is predicated upon changing these beliefs;
5. by acting in ways that reinforce his irrational beliefs;
6. by disturbing himself about his original disturbance;
7. by thinking that identifying his irrational beliefs is sufficient to change them;
8. by thinking that understanding why his irrational beliefs are irrational and why his rational beliefs are rational is sufficient to surrender the former and acquire the latter;
9. by thinking that disputing his irrational beliefs without acting in ways that are consistent with his rational beliefs is sufficient to promote psychological change;
10. by thinking that occasionally acting in ways that are consistent with his rational beliefs is sufficient to effect psychological change.

How REBT construes psychotherapeutic change

The Rational Emotive Behavioural view of the person is basically an optimistic one, because although it posits that humans find it easy to think irrationally about matters that are important to them, REBT also holds that humans have the capacity to choose to work towards changing this irrational thinking and its self-defeating effects, and that the most elegant and long-lasting changes that humans can effect are ones that involve the philosophical restructuring of irrational beliefs. Change at this level can be specific or general. Specific philosophical change means that individuals change their irrational absolutistic demands (musts, shoulds) about given situations to rational relative preferences. General philosophic change involves people adopting a non-devout attitude towards life events in general.

To effect a philosophical change at either the specific or general level, people need to do the following:

1. realize that to a large degree they create their own psychological disturbances, and that while environmental conditions can contribute to their problems, they are in general of secondary consideration in the change process;
2. recognize that they do have the ability to change these disturbances significantly;
3. understand that emotional and behavioural disturbances stem largely from irrational, absolutistic dogmatic beliefs;
4. detect their irrational beliefs and discriminate between them and their rational alternatives;
5. dispute these irrational beliefs using the logico-empirical methods of science;
6. work towards the internalization of their new rational beliefs by employing cognitive, emotive and behavioural methods of change; in particular, ensuring their behaviour is consistent with their rational beliefs;
7. continue this process of challenging irrational beliefs and using multi-modal methods of change for the rest of their lives.

When people effect a philosophic change at *B* in the *ABC* model, they are often able spontaneously to correct their distorted inferences of reality (overgeneralizations, faulty attributions etc.) which can be viewed as cognitions (Wessler and Wessler, 1980). However, they often need to challenge these distorted inferences more directly, as REBT has always emphasized (e.g. Ellis, 1962) and as cognitive therapists have more recently also stressed (Beck et al., 1979). Rational Emotive Behaviour therapists hypothesize that people are more likely to make a profound philosophical change if they first assume that their inferences are true and then challenge their irrational beliefs, rather than if they first correct their inferential distortions and then challenge their underlying irrational beliefs. However, this hypothesis awaits full empirical enquiry.

People can also make direct changes of the situation at *A*. Thus, rather than changing one's cognitions about a negative activating event, one could remove oneself from the event, directly change it in some way, or distract oneself from it by focusing on a different aspect of the event or on another event entirely.

A person can change his or her behaviour to effect inferential and/or philosophical change. Thus, one could change one's behaviour to elicit a different (more positive) response from someone who was acting in a negative way towards one. In this way the person could change the *A* and/or form a new more realistic inference about *A*. When the person changes his behaviour to promote philosophic change, it is important that he actually faces the negative event at *A* in order to give himself the opportunity of thinking rationally in the face of this negative event.

While Rational Emotive Behaviour therapists prefer to help their clients make profound philosophical changes at *B*, they do not dogmatically insist that their clients make such changes. If it becomes apparent that clients are not able at any given time to change their irrational beliefs, then REBT therapists would endeavor to help them either to change *A* directly (by avoiding the troublesome situation, or by behaving differently) or to change their distorted inferences about the situation.

How REBT construes the practice of therapy (with special reference to group therapy)

Rational Emotive Behaviour Therapy offers a very definite view on the practice of therapy with respect to therapeutic relationship, therapist style and therapeutic intervention. In dealing with this topic, I will refer specifically to group therapy.

View on the therapeutic relationship

The optimal relationship between therapist and patient in REBT as that between informed allies. Ideally the patient should be informed about REBT, its mode of practice in group therapy and her (in this case) role as a group member and, of course, the therapist should (ideally) be informed about his (in this case) role. As allies, they will share an understanding of and agree to pursue the patient's goals for change; they will undertake to implement their respective roles in carrying out activities to facilitate goal achievement and they will have a suitably well-bonded relationship to enable these activities to be carried out smoothly and skilfully. The hallmarks of this bond are that the patient experiences the therapist as (1) understanding of her feelings and of the roots of her problems; (2) genuine in the therapeutic encounter; and (3) accepting of her as a fallible human being. The REBT view is that these 'core conditions' are desirable, rather than necessary or sufficient for patient change to occur. They are important to the extent that they help both paries to engage productively in the tasks of REBT which in turn lead to goal achievement. This, of course, is an ideal picture and in reality, there will be many threats to this relationship which need to be dealt with if patient change is going to occur (Ellis, 1985; Neenan and Dryden, 1996). The picture is complicated in group therapy where it also matters that group members experience one another as empathic, genuine and accepting of one another and that they help one another engage in the tasks of REBT. When patient non-cooperation is apparent, then the group therapist will help particular patients to see the irrational beliefs that they hold which are interfering with their cooperative participation in the group process, but as will be discussed later, the dominant focus in the group is on members' problems in their daily lives outside the group, rather than on their relationships with one another within the group.

View on therapist style

The preferred therapist style in group REBT is active-directive. The therapist is active in her (in this case) interventions and directs group members to the irrational beliefs that underpin their disturbed feelings and unconstructive behaviour. REBT can be seen as an educational approach to psychotherapy in that the group therapist teaches group members the REBT model of disturbance and psychotherapeutic change and invites them to use this model to understand and address their psychological problems. As such, Ellis sees effective REBT group therapists as being authoritative (but not authoritarian) teachers who are clear communicators and help group members understand how they disturb themselves and what they can do to undisturb themselves. In doing so, effective REBT group therapists use either Socratic and didactic teaching methods or a mixture of the two depending on the learning style of individual patients.

REBT group therapists tend to favour an informal therapeutic style characterized by the discriminate use of humour and self-disclosure. However, they are prepared to vary their style according to the group member with whom they are working. Having said this, REBT group therapists take their role very seriously and this is demonstrated by the rigorous way that they stick to their main therapeutic task: to help group members to overcome their psychological problems by identifying, challenging and changing their irrational beliefs and to act in ways that are consistent with their developing rational beliefs.

View on group therapeutic intervention

REBT group therapy is a structured process in which the therapist ensures that all group members are given an opportunity to discuss their problems. Some REBT therapists take the lead from their cognitive therapy colleagues and set an agenda at the beginning of the group session in order to facilitate structured interaction and to help with time allocation. This emphasis on individual attention happens in all REBT groups with the exception of the REBT Intensives (see Chapter 8) which are both too large to permit such attention. Since every group member is given individual attention, the REBT view is that this process is best facilitated at the outset by the therapist. Thus, the early interaction is between the group therapist and the individual group member discussing her (in this case) problem. After a while, other group members make their points either of their own accord or at the suggestion of the group therapist who might say something like: 'Who would like to comment on what Bill has just said?' or 'What does the group think of what Brenda has just said?' Thus, much of the REBT group process is taken up by 'therapy in the group' interactions (between group member and group therapist) and 'therapy by the group' interactions (between the group member and other group members). However, even in the latter interactions the group therapist plays a gatekeeping role, ensuring that unhelpful interactions are kept to a minimum.

This gatekeeping role of the REBT therapist is a central one and warrants further consideration. It often happens, for example, when group members are endeavouring to help a particular member whose problem is under discussion that they either give that person practical advice of how to solve the problem or offer the group member a different perspective with which to view the situation. Assuming the gatekeeping role, the REBT group therapist listens carefully to the advice or perspective being offered and intervenes to correct bad or damaging advice and unhelpful perspectives (if other group members don't do this first). He then assists the whole group as well as the particular group member to see the belief core of the latter's problem while reinforcing the sensible aspects of the advice or perspective are being put forward. Here is an example of this last point (Stephen, one of the group members, has been discussing his feelings of guilt about hurting his mother's feelings):

Stephen:	So, that sums it up, I'm guilty about saying no to my mother because I might hurt her feelings.
Bruce:	But, you don't hurt your mother's feelings. She hurts her own feelings by the beliefs that she holds about you saying no to her.
Windy (after a pause to see who would take up Bruce's point):	That's a valid perspective, Bruce, but that won't help Stephen get over his problem of guilt.
Bruce:	Why won't it?
Windy:	Can anybody see why it won't?
Mary:	Because Stephen thinks that he can hurt his mother's feelings.

Bruce (jumping in):   When he can't, which is the point I made earlier.
Windy (deciding to make the point himself because he doesn't think that any
other group member will):

> But in REBT, we start by assuming temporarily that Stephen can and indeed has hurt his mother's feelings. We do this because doing so helps us to identify, challenge and change his underlying irrational beliefs that lead to his guilt. Then, Stephen will be over his feelings of guilt and in a better frame of mind to discuss whether he can or cannot hurt his mother's feelings.

I have made the point in this section that therapy takes place in the group (by the therapist) and by the group members working with one another (under the watchful supervisory eye of the therapist). In contrast, there is little emphasis on 'therapy of the group' interventions that tend to occur in some (but not in all) forms of psychodynamic group therapy. Here, the therapist's task is to observe the overall functioning of the group and to make interpretations of the observed phenomena based on a theoretical (psychoanalytical) understanding of what goes on in such groups. Here the focus is on the group as a whole and not on the problems of individual group members, whereas of course, in REBT group therapy, the definite emphasis is on these problems.

Methods of Assessment and Intervention in REBT Group Therapy

In this section, I will discuss methods and issues concerning assessment of patients who are suitable for different REBT groups and will outline exclusion criteria that help to ensure that unsuitable patients are not placed in these groups. I will also discuss the major interventions that are used in REBT group therapy.

Assessment

Assessment for REBT group therapy is done for two main purposes:

1. First, assessment is done for therapeutic purposes when the main issue concerns placing the patient in a group because it is considered that REBT group therapy (in one of its formats) is the treatment of choice for the individual concerned. Here, the emphasis is on inclusive criteria.
2. Secondly, assessment is done primarily for pragmatic purposes. Here, the main issue is that in the organization concerned, REBT groups are run largely for pragmatic purposes (e.g. for financial reasons or to reduce long waiting lists) and the emphasis is on exclusion criteria (i.e. patients

will be assigned to REBT group therapy unless there is a good reason not to do so).

The main way of assessing patients' suitability for REBT groups is by interview where the patient's problems are identified, his views on therapy are determined and the nature of REBT groups is explained. This interview is an assessment interview and not a therapy interview in that no therapeutic interventions are made. However, it is the practice of the Albert Ellis Institute to require that prospective group clients have at least one session of individual therapy to determine the individual's reaction to REBT interventions and likely reaction to these interventions when they are made in a group session. Whichever type of interview is preferred the purpose is to include or exclude that person from group REBT.

Inclusion criteria

The following are deemed to be sound criteria to include a patient in an REBT group:

1. *The person wishes to join an REBT group*. Here, the patient understands the REBT approach to his (in this case) problems and thinks that it will be helpful to him especially in a group session.
2. *The person is able to participate constructively in a structured group*. This means that the person is able and willing to (a) focus on specific problems and discuss these in a group setting; (b) share therapeutic time with other group members; and (c) help other group members as well as be helped by them.
3. *The person prefers a structured approach to their problems and wishes to have some time allocated every session to a discussion of her (in this case) problems*. In some other approaches to group therapy, time is devoted each session to a discussion of the problems of a small number of the group membership and this discussion is relatively unstructured. While this approach to group therapy suits some patients, it does not suit others and those who prefer a more structured approach to group therapy where they have an opportunity every session to discuss their problems are good candidates for REBT group therapy.
4. *The person's problems are particularly suited to a group approach*. If a patient is being assessed for a time-limited, closed, problem or theme-based group, then it is obviously important that that person has the target problem, for example, and wants help for it and is willing to put their other problems on the 'back burner' or deal with these problems in concurrent individual therapy. When the person is being assessed for an ongoing, semi-open, outpatient group, then he (in this case) can have a

variety of problems. Obviously, interpersonal problems lend themselves particularly to this type of group because such problems become manifest in the group interaction and can be explored in the here and now. Having said this, membership of a heterogeneous, ongoing, semi-open outpatient group is determined more by exclusion factors with respect to presenting problems (see below) than inclusion factors.

Exclusion criteria

The following are deemed to be sound reasons to exclude a patient from joining an REBT group:

1. *The person does not wish to join an REBT group*. It sometimes occurs that a patient is referred for REBT group therapy by a consultant psychiatrist who has made the referral without explaining to the patient the nature of this approach to REBT group therapy. When this group is explained to the person concerned, she (in this case) indicates that she does not wish to join such a group.
2. *It is predicted that the person will not be able to make therapeutic use of the structured nature of group REBT*. Thus, the person is deemed to be too undisciplined, talkative or manic to use the structured ABC framework of problem assessment or intervention, to respond to other group members or to listen silently and attentively when other group members are discussing their problems.
3. *The person is likely to be too withdrawn to participate*. Patients who are autistic, schizoid or severely socially anxious are all likely to respond to the interactive nature of REBT group therapy by withdrawing and thus will not participate in the group. If such a person does join the group they usually drop out when they are confronted (even gently) by other group members concerning their non-participation.
4. *The person is unable to share therapeutic time with other group members*. Sometimes, patients are too demanding of the therapist's time to participate constructively in a structured REBT group where the amount of time that can be allocated to any one group member is limited. Such patients often respond unconstructively to this fact of REBT group culture and are best seen in individual therapy until they can share therapeutic time with others.
5. *The person does not want to help others*. Membership of a therapy group is predicated on the notion that the members have some interest in helping others as well as being helped by them. Some patients, however, while interested in being helped by the group therapist and by the other group members, have no interest in helping others. Consequently, such

patients are not good candidates for REBT group therapy until they develop such an interest.

6. *The person is likely to be too hostile or too impatient to be a cooperative group member*. Patients whose anger problem means that they are likely to respond with overt hostility to attempts by the group leader or by group members to cooperate with the structured nature of the REBT group process are not good candidates for this type of group therapy. Neither are patients who are inordinately impatient and find it extraordinarily difficult to wait their turn to discuss a problem or to keep attentive when they have had their turn in group.

7. *The nature of the patient's problem means that group REBT is contraindicated*. Not all patient problems can be productively responded to in REBT group therapy. For example, patients with severe post-traumatic stress disorder (PTSD) are not good candidates for group REBT since they need extended sessions of individual therapy to ensure sufficient imaginal exposure to enable emotional processing to occur. The exception to this is where the group is devoted to the treatment of specific types of PTSD, in which case a group protocol can be devised for the treatment of this problem. For other patient problems, the presence of other group members may inhibit self-disclosure with the result that the therapist does not get a sufficiently full picture to help the person.

It may happen that the assessment does not reveal that a patient is unsuitable for REBT group therapy and this turns out to be the case after the person joins the group. If this happens they are shown how to be more effective members of the group, but if this does not work then they are told that they will have to leave the group and enter individual REBT until they can function effectively in the group setting.

Intervention

As I have stressed earlier, REBT group therapy interventions are largely therapist-led, at least until group members have learned how to use REBT with one another. Then the therapist increasingly takes a back seat, serving as a consultant to the group and intervening (a) when it becomes apparent that group members are off track in their attempts to help a particular member with his (in this case) problem; (b) when they give the member poor or damaging advice or suggest unhelpful homework assignments; and (c) when they just focus on the practical aspects of the person's problem, overlooking its psychological aspects (particularly the person's irrational beliefs).

When the therapist does intervene in REBT groups it is usually to direct a group member's attention to her (in this case) irrational beliefs and how she can challenge and change them. In doing so, the therapist uses the following methods.

1. ABC framework analysis

When a group member discusses a problem in an REBT group, the therapist will give her a brief time to discuss it in her own way, but will then encourage her to give a specific example of this problem and then to analyse this event using REBT's *ABC* framework:

A =   Activating event (the aspect of the situation that the group member was most disturbed about)
B =   Irrational beliefs about A
C =   Emotional, behavioural and thinking consequences of B

The *ABC* framework helps structure each group member's discussion of their problems and without this framework, the member might ramble which would be regarded as an unproductive use of group time.

2. Disputing of specific and core irrational beliefs

After helping the group member to assess her problem, the therapist takes the lead to help the member to dispute her irrational beliefs. Initially, the group member is helped to dispute specific irrational beliefs (held in specific situations about specific As, e.g. being rejected by a particular man in a particular situation), while later in the group process, the member is helped to dispute her core irrational beliefs (held about a variety of situations, e.g. whenever the group member thinks she has been rejected).

As DiGiuseppe (1991) noted, disputing irrational beliefs involves the group therapist (in the first instance) asking the group member whether her irrational beliefs (specific and core) are true or false, logical or illogical and functional or dysfunctional and to provide reasons for her responses. There then ensues a discussion where the therapist and other group members engage the member in a debate about her beliefs until she understands that her irrational beliefs are false, illogical and dysfunctional and her rational alternative beliefs are true, logical and functional.

3. Homework assignments

Unless the group member acts on her new rational belief, then she will not truly believe them and they will not influence her emotions, behaviour and thinking for the better. Consequently, a feature of REBT groups is the homework assignment, where the group member resolves to capitalize on the therapeutic work that she has done in the group session by doing something between group sessions. The following are common homework assignments suggested in REBT group therapy:

(a) Bibliotherapy – here the group member reads REBT-based self-help material to help her understand better a rational concept and how to implement it in her own life.
(b) Cognitive homework – here the group member uses one of a number of cognitively oriented written homework forms to practise disputing her irrational beliefs and to deepen her conviction into her rational beliefs.
(c) Emotive homework – here the group member practises one or more emotive techniques to deepen conviction in her rational beliefs (e.g. forceful rational self-statements, forceful disputing on audiotape where the client verbalizes rational arguments to strongly demolish her irrational defences of her irrational beliefs, rational emotive imagery where the client rehearses her rational beliefs while vividly imagining negative events at A about which she usually disturbs herself).
(d) Behavioural-cognitive homework – here the client rehearses her rational beliefs while acting in ways that are consistent with them. The conjoint use of behavioural and cognitive techniques, where the client faces negative activating events and practises thinking rationally in the face of such events while refraining from doing anything to feel comfortable in the moment is, in my view, the most potent homework assignment and one which I and other REBT group therapists particularly favour.

4. Correcting cognitive distortions

Cognitive distortions are negative unrealistic ways of making sense of situations that we face and the implications of facing them. They include distorted inferences of events at A (in the ABC framework) and distorted cognitive consequences at C of irrational beliefs at B.

Examples of cognitive distortions at A include 'My boss will fire me', 'People will laugh at me if I make a mistake in my presentation tomorrow', and 'My sister hates me for doing well in the test.' Now, of course, these inferences may be true, but they are distorted in the absence of evidence supporting them.

Examples of cognitive distortions (shown in italics) at C include:

(a) Always/never thinking ('*I will never get another job* when my boss fires me');
(b) Magnification ('People who laugh at my mistake at the presentation *will tell others and everyone will know that I made a fool of myself*') and

(c) Overgeneralization ('Because my sister hates me for doing well in the test, *everyone will hate me when I do well*')

Again, these thoughts are distorted in the absence of supporting evidence.

REBT argues that cognitive distortions at *A* and *C* largely stem from irrational beliefs and, thus, it is best to help group members to dispute their irrational beliefs before helping them to correct these distortions. Indeed, REBT group therapists often have to intervene with other group members who frequently rush in to correct their fellow group members' cognitive distortions instead of helping them first to dispute their irrational beliefs.

Correcting cognitive distortions involves asking group members to adopt an objective standpoint and provide evidence for and against their (distorted) thoughts at *A* and those at *C*. It also involves asking clients to form more realistic inferences at *A* and more realistic cognitive consequences at *C*.

I have stated that REBT group therapists first target irrational beliefs for change before disputing cognitive distortions. They do this because disputing group members' irrational beliefs helps them to adopt the objective standpoint necessary to correct their cognitive distortions. However, because REBT is a flexible approach to therapy, it argues that there may be times when the group therapist will target cognitive distortions for change before disputing irrational beliefs.

5. *Skill training and role play methods*

Skill training methods can be used when group members have various skill deficits. The group is particularly useful in this respect when these skill deficits are interpersonal in nature (e.g. assertion, dating and conversational skills) because other group members who are competent in these skills can give advice and can serve as good models in role play scenarios. Then the group member is given the opportunity to practise the *targeted* skill with one of the other group members playing a significant other.

Role play methods can also be used to encourage the group member to rehearse a behavioural-cognitive homework assignment before putting it into practise between sessions with other members playing relevant people in the group member's real life. While the main purpose of role play is to give group members practice at skill development and rehearsal or relevant behaviours, the feedback that group members give one another at the end of role plays and skill practice scenarios can be particularly therapeutic.

Throughout the skill practice sessions and role play scenarios the group therapist is alert for the presence of any irrational beliefs that may be impeding the group; when these are found they are disputed after the session or scenario has finished.

Role play methods can also be used to help a group member to strengthen her conviction in her rational beliefs. Thus, the group member can play the role of her rational 'self' while the other group members can, one at a time, play the role of her irrational 'self' and encourage her to think irrationally. The group member's task is to respond persuasively to these irrational attacks. The group therapist intervenes to keep the exercise on track and to prevent other group members from overwhelming the targeted group member with too many arguments.

6. Advice giving and problem-solving

Group members give much advice during the REBT group process. Indeed, if left to the members themselves, advice giving would be their most frequently used group intervention. Given this reality, the REBT group therapist is vigilant when such advice is given, and as I have already mentioned, intervenes to counter bad and potentially damaging advice. Instead, the group therapist helps the group member concerned to focus on identifying, challenging and changing the irrational beliefs that underpin her psychological problem, and then encourages the member to engage in practical problem-solving instead. This involves the group member clarifying the practical problem to be solved, brainstorming possible solutions, evaluating each solution, choosing the best one and overcoming obstacles to implementing the chosen solution. The other group members are encouraged to play an active role in this process which is overseen by the group therapist.

Major Syndromes, Symptoms and Problems Treated Using REBT Group Therapy

REBT group therapy is a useful therapeutic arena for patients with a variety of syndromes, symptoms and problems. To illustrate this variety, I will list in date order relevant articles on REBT group therapy that have been published in the journal sponsored over the years by the Albert Ellis Institute originally known as *Rational Living* (1966–83), subsequently called the *Journal of Rational-Emotive Therapy* (1983–87) and then the *Journal of Rational-Emotive and Cognitive-Behavior Therapy* (1988–present). It should be noted at the outset that this list is illustrative rather than comprehensive.

Rational Living

1966: Group therapy with hospitalized psychotic patients (Gullo, 1966)
1967: Group therapy with alcoholics (Sherman, 1967)
1972: Group therapy with unselected outpatient psychiatric patients (Maultsby, Stiefel and Brodsky, 1972)

1973: A structured approach to group counselling with couples with marriage problems (McClellan and Stieper, 1973)
1974: Group therapy with university students with speech anxiety problems (Straatmayer and Watkins, 1974)
1976: Group therapy with elementary school students with test anxiety (Warren, Deffenbacher and Brading, 1976)
1977: REBT group therapy with patients in a partial hospitalization setting (Lefkovitz and Davis, 1977)

Journal of Rational-Emotive Therapy

1984: Group therapy with non-assertive university students (Thorpe, Freedman and McGalliard, 1984)
1985: Structured group therapy with clients with low self-esteem (Ponzoha and Warren, 1985)
       Group therapy with high school females with bulimia (Harvill, 1985)
1987: Group therapy with a 'mixed' population of psychiatric inpatients – neurotic, psychotic and adjustment disorder (Jacobsen, Tamkin and Blount, 1987)
       Rational behaviour problem-solving as a group career development intervention for persons with mental and physical disabilities (Farley, 1987)

Journal of Rational-Emotive and Cognitive-Behavior Therapy

1988: Group therapy with women with mid-life transition or 'empty-nest' problems (Oliver, 1988)
       Group therapy with clients with divorce-related dysphoria (Malouff, Lanyon and Schutte, 1988)
       REBT in a group-based therapeutic community with patients with substance abuse problems (Yeager et al., 1988)
1989: Group therapy with women with premenstrual syndrome (Morse, Bernard and Dennerstein, 1989)
       Group therapy with university students with interpersonal anxiety (Vestre and Judge, 1989)
1990: Group therapy with clients with social anxiety (DiGiuseppe et al., 1990)
1992: An REBT group therapy-based inpatient programme with patients with major depression and a variety of personality disorders (Nottingham and Neimeyer, 1992)
1993: Education-based REBT training groups in the workplace (Grieger and DiMattia, 1993)
       Group therapy for preventing and coping with stress among safety officers (Kushnir and Malkinson, 1993)

Group therapy with conduct disorder and attention-deficit hyperactivity disorder adolescents (Morris, 1993)

1995:   A group-based parent education programme with non-clinical parents (Joyce, 1995)

REBT women's groups (Wolfe, 1995)

Group therapy with a variety of offenders (Bernard, 1995)

1997:   Group-based stress management with patients with chronic fatigue syndrome (Balter and Unger, 1997)

Group therapy with post-stroke patients (Alvarez, 1997)

Group-based parent education for stressed mothers of young children with Down's Syndrome (Greaves, 1997)

1998:   REBT group therapy and problem-solving with children with social skills deficits (Flanagan et al., 1998)

Group therapy to increase the performance of high-school students in mathematics (Shannon and Allen, 1998)

As can be seen from the above, group REBT has been used with a broad variety of problems and syndromes as well as with a broad client population. As with many other group treatments, REBT group therapy is best suited with those who are able to share time with the group therapist, can concentrate on the problems of others as well as their own and are willing to help others as well as receive help themselves. Effective REBT group therapy, then, requires clients who are free from severe psychiatric disturbance.

In the final section of the chapter, I will consider the empirical status of REBT as a therapeutic approach drawing upon research reviews on this model. Unfortunately, there are no reviews of the effectiveness of REBT group therapy, but since research shows that group therapy is at least as effective as individual therapy (Bergin and Garfield, 1994), there is no reason to suppose that this will be different for REBT.

Research on the Effectiveness of REBT

The first controlled study of REBT was published in 1957 and consisted of Ellis comparing the results he had obtained from using classical psychoanalysis, psychoanalytically oriented psychotherapy, and rational-emotive therapy (Ellis, 1957). It was hardly an unbiased study and its positive results are not to be taken too seriously. However, starting in the 1960s, and continuing into the 1980s, more than 1,000 outcome studies have been done on REBT and on closely related cognitive behaviour therapies. The great majority of these controlled studies have shown that, when compared to a control group, clients treated with REBT or with a form of cognitive behaviour therapy that is an essential part of REBT fare significantly better than those who are not so treated. Outcome studies have been reviewed by Hajzler and Bernard (1991), Hollon and Beck (1994), and Lyons and Woods (1991). Outcome studies testing the use of REBT and Cognitive Behaviour Therapy (CBT) derived from REBT continue to proliferate, most of them continuing to indicate that treatment methods that consist of REBT procedures help clients or subjects significantly more than control groups.

In addition to empirical studies that tend to back the main therapeutic hypotheses of REBT, literally hundreds of other controlled experiments have been published that tend to indicate that many of the main theoretical hypotheses of REBT – especially its *ABC* theory of human disturbance – now have considerable experimental backing. Also, hundreds more research studies present evidence that many of the REBT-favoured therapeutic techniques such as active-directive therapy, direct disputing of irrational ideas, the use of rational or coping statements, and the employment of psychoeducational methods have distinct effectiveness. Ellis (1979) has cited hundreds of these studies in his comprehensive review of the REBT-oriented literature. If his review were brought up to date it would now include hundreds of additional studies that present empirical confirmation of many of the most important REBT theories and therapeutic applications.

This is not to claim that REBT has undisputed evidence of the validity of its theories or the effectiveness of its practice. Like all other major systems of psychotherapy, it is still exceptionally wanting in these respects; considerable further research needs to be done to check on its major hypotheses. Although its treatment methods have been tested many times against the methods of other kinds of psychotherapy and against non-treated control groups and they have usually been proven adequate, they have not as yet often been compared to the procedures of other popular forms of cognitive-behaviour therapy. Considerable experimental studies could be done in this area, if appropriate funding was forthcoming.

Summary

In this chapter, I have presented the underlying theory of REBT, shown how it can be practised in a variety of different group therapy formats and presented a cautious review of its effectiveness. Given that REBT is a leading approach within the cognitive-behaviour therapy tradition it shares the strengths of that tradition. It is suitable for managed care, can be cautiously viewed as an empirically supported treatment (EST) and satisfies the current demand for brief outcome-based interventions. However, REBT has distinctive features within the CBT tradition and there is a need for more empirical research to be carried out on these distinctive features if REBT is to be regarded as an EST in its own right and not just because of its place within the broader cognitive-behavioural tradition.

References

Alvarez MF (1997) Using REBT and supportive psychotherapy with post-stroke patients. Journal of Rational-Emotive and Cognitive-Behavior Therapy 15: 231–45.

Balter R, Unger P (1997) REBT stress management with patients with chronic fatigue syndrome. Journal of Rational-Emotive and Cognitive-Behavior Therapy 15: 223–30.

Beck AT, Rush AJ, Shaw BF, Emery G (1979) Cognitive Therapy of Depression. New York: Guilford.

Bergin AE, Garfield SL (eds) (1994) Handbook of Psychotherapy and Behavior, 4th edn. New York: Wiley.

Bernard ME (ed.) (1995) Rational emotive and cogniitive behavioral therapy with offenders. Journal of Rational-Emotive and Cognitive-Behavior Therapy 13: 211–82

Bernard ME, DiGiuseppe R (eds) (1989) Inside rational-emotive therapy. San Diego: Academic Press.

DiGiuseppe R (1991) Comprehensive cognitive disputing in RET. In ME Bernard (ed.), Using Rational-Emotive Therapy Effectively (pp. 173–96). New York: Plenum.

DiGiuseppe R, McGowan L, Sutton Simon K, Gardner F (1990) A comparative outcome study of four cognitive therapies in the treatment of social anxiety. Journal of Rational-Emotive and Cognitive-Behavior Therapy 8: 129–46.

Dryden W (ed.) (1996) Rational emotive behavior therapy: critiques from within. Journal of Rational-Emotive and Cognitive-Behavior Therapy 14: 3–78.

Dryden W, Backx W (1987) Problems in living: the Friday night workshop. In W Dryden (ed.), Current Issues in Rational-Emotive Therapy (pp. 154–70). London: Croom Helm.

Ellis A (1957) Outcome of employing three techniques of psychotherapy. Journal of Clinical Psychology 13: 344–50.

Ellis A (1962) Reason and Emotion in Psychotherapy. Secaucus, NJ: Lyle Stuart.

Ellis A (1969) A weekend of rational encounter. In A Burton (ed.) Encounter (pp. 112–27). San Francisco: Jossey-Bass.

Ellis A (1979) Rational-emotive therapy: research data that support the clinical and personality hypotheses of RET and other modes of cognitive-behavior therapy. In A Ellis, JM Whiteley (eds) Theoretical and Empirical Foundations of Rational-Emotive Therapy (pp. 101–73). Monterey, CA: Brooks/Cole.

Ellis A (1985) Overcoming Resistance: Rational-Emotive Therapy with Difficult Clients. New York: Springer.

Ellis A (1987) Integrative developments in rational-emotive therapy (RET). Journal of Integrative and Eclectic Psychotherapy 6: 470–9.

Ellis A (1990) Is Rational-Emotive Therapy (RET) 'rationalist' or 'constructivist'? In W Dryden (ed.) The Essential Albert Ellis (pp. 114–41). New York: Springer.

Ellis A (1997) Post-modern ethics for active-directive counseling and psychotherapy. Journal of Mental Health Counselling 18: 211–25.

Ellis A, Yeager RJ (1989) When Some Therapies Don't Work: The Dangers of Transpersonal Psychology. New York: Prometheus Books.

Epictetus (1890) The Collected Works of Epictetus. Boston: Little Brown.

Farley RC (1987) Rational behavior problem-solving as a career development intervention for persons with disabilities. Journal of Rational-Emotive Therapy 5: 32–42.

Flanagan R, Povall L, Dellino M, Byrne L (1998) A comparison of problem solving with and without rational emotive behavior therapy to improve children's social skills. Journal of Rational-Emotive and Cognitive-Behavior Therapy 16: 125–34.

Greaves D (1997) The effect of rational-emotive parent education on the stress of mothers of young children with Down Syndrome. Journal of Rational-Emotive and Cognitive-Behavior Therapy 15: 249–67.

Grieger RM, DiMattia D (eds) (1993) RET in the workplace. Parts 1 & 2. Journal of Rational-Emotive and Cognitive-Behavior Therapy 11: 3–119.

Gullo JM (1966) Counseling hospitalized patients. Rational Living 1(2): 11–15.

Hajzler D, Bernard ME (1991) A review of rational-emotive outcome studies. School Psychology Quarterly 6: 27–49.

Harvill R (1985) Bulimia: treatment of purging via systematic rational restructuring. Journal of Rational-Emotive Therapy 2: 130–7.

Hollon SD, Beck AT (1994) Cognitive and cognitive-behavioral therapies. In AE Bergin, SL Garfield (eds) Handbook of Psychotherapy and Behavior Change, 4th edn (pp. 428–66). New York: Wiley.

Jacobsen RH, Tamkin AS, Blount JB (1987) The efficacy of rational-emotive group therapy in psychiatric patients. Journal of Rational-Emotive Therapy 5: 22–31.

Joyce MR (1995) Emotional relief for parents: is rational-emotive parent education effective? Journal of Rational-Emotive and Cognitive-Behavior Therapy 13: 55–75.

Kushnir T, Malkinson R (1993) A rational-emotive group intervention for preventing and coping with stress among safety officers. Journal of Rational-Emotive and Cognitive-Behavior Therapy 11: 195–206.

Lazarus AA (1971) Behavior Therapy and Beyond. New York: McGraw-Hill.

Lefkovitz PM, Davis HJ (1977) Rational-emotive therapy in a partial hospitalization setting. Rational Living 12(2): 35–8.

Lyons LC, Woods PJ (1991) The efficacy of rational-emotive therapy: a quantitative review of the outcome research. Clinical Psychology Review 11: 357–90.

McClellan TA, Stieper DR (1973) A structured approach to group marriage counseling. Rational Living 8(2): 12–18.

Malouff JM, Lanyon RI, Schutte NS (1988) Effectiveness of a brief group RET treatment for divorce-related dysphoria. Journal of Rational-Emotive and Cognitive-Behavior Therapy 6: 162–71.

Maultsby MC, Stiefel L, Brodsky L (1972) A theory of rational behavioral group process. Rational Living 1(1): 28–34.

Morris GB (1993) A rational-emotive treatment program with conduct disorder and attentional-deficit hyperactivity disorder adolescents. Journal of Rational-Emotive and Cognitive-Behavior Therapy 11: 23–134.

Morse C, Bernard ME, Dennerstein L (1989) The effects of rational-emotive therapy and relaxation training on premenstrual syndrome: a preliminary study. Journal of Rational-Emotive and Cognitive-Behavior Therapy 7: 98–110.

Neenan M, Dryden W (1996) Dealing with Difficulties in Rational Emotive Behaviour Therapy. London: Whurr.

Nottingham IV EJ, Neimeyer RA (1992) Evaluation of a comprehensive inpatient rational-emotive therapy program: some preliminary data. Journal of Rational-Emotive and Cognitive-Behavior Therapy 10: 57–81.

Oliver R (1988) 'Empty nest' or relationship restructuring? A rational-emotive approach to a mid-life transition. Journal of Rational-Emotive and Cognitive-Behavior Therapy 6: 102–17.

Ponzoha C, Warren R (1985) Self-acceptance techniques for structured groups. Journal of Rational-Emotive Therapy 3: 36–43.

Shannon HD, Allen TW (1998) The effectiveness of a REBT training program in increasing the performance of high school students in mathematics. Journal of Rational-Emotive and Cognitive-Behavior Therapy 16: 197–209.

Sherman SH (1967) Alcoholism and group therapy. Rational Living 2(2): 20–2.

Straatmeyer AJ, Watkins JT (1974) Rational-emotive therapy and the reduction of speech anxiety. Rational Living 9(1): 33–7.

Thorpe GL, Freedman EG, McGalliard DW (1984) Components of rational emotive imagery: two experiments with non-assertive students. Journal of Rational Emotive Therapy 2(2): 11–19.

Vestre ND, Judge TJ (1989) Evaluation of self-administered rational-emotive therapy programs for interpersonal anxiety. Journal of Rational-Emotive and Cognitive-Behavior Therapy 7: 141–54.

Warren R, Deffenbacher JL, Brading P (1976) Rational-emotive therapy and the reduction of test anxiety in elementary school students. Rational Living 11(2): 26–9.

Watson JL (1919) Psychology from the standpoint of a behaviorist. Philadelphia: Lippincott.

Wessler RA, Wessler RL (1980) The Principles and Practice of Rational-Emotive Therapy. San Francisco: Jossey-Bass.

Wolfe J (1995) Rational emotive behavior therapy women's groups: a twenty year retrospective. Journal of Rational-Emotive and Cognitive-Behavior Therapy 13: 153–70.

Yeager RJ, DiGiuseppe R, Olsen JT, Lewis L, Alberti R (1988) Rational-emotive therapy in the therapeutic community. Journal of Rational-Emotive and Cognitive-Behavior Therapy 6: 211–35.

CHAPTER 2

Rational Emotive Behavior Therapy (REBT) and Its Application to Group Therapy

ALBERT ELLIS

I began to do group therapy in 1949 with adolescents at the New Jersey State Diagnostic Center when I was still practicing psychoanalysis, and was able to help delinquent clients to open up and reveal themselves. I helped them to accept responsibility for their delinquencies, to work with other group members, to understand themselves, and to make some useful changes. But I soon discovered that psychoanalytic group therapy, like psychoanalytic individual psychotherapy, was woefully inefficient for several reasons:

1. It focused on people's past, especially their early life, mistakenly assuming that that made them disturbed.
2. It gave them dubious explanations for their disturbances, especially the idea that traumatic Activating Events (A's) or Adversities produced their distressed consequences, such as anxiety and depression, no matter what they Believed (B) about these A's.
3. It obsessively explored their 'transference' relationships with their therapists and other group members and assumed that these were caused by prior deep relationships in their childhood.
4. It deified the expression of group members' feelings and wrongly held that if they got in full touch with these feelings and honestly expressed them they would win the approval of others and minimize their serious panicking, depressing, and raging (Ellis, 1962; Ellis and Harper, 1961, 1997; Yalom, 1995).

For the first several years that I was in full-time practice in New York City, and even when I started doing REBT with my individual clients in 1955, I still avoided doing group therapy because of its usual inefficiencies. But I saw that one analyst had three of my individual clients in his groups, and that almost every time they attended his group sessions they became more disturbed, while after most of their individual sessions with me they became less disturbed. So I decided, in 1959, to start my first REBT group; I soon had four of these groups going – and going strong – every week; and I discovered that for most clients Rational Emotive Behavior group therapy was more effective, often in a brief period, than was my individual therapy – and much more effective than any form of psychoanalysis. Why? For several reasons:

1. In individual therapy, I mainly Dispute and show my clients how to Dispute their self-defeating Irrational Beliefs (IBs). But in group therapy, several other group members do active Disputing and thereby give better and stronger Disputations.
2. In individual therapy, clients rarely get practice in talking me out of my Irrational Beliefs (because we are mainly focusing on them and their IBs). But in group they have many opportunities to discover others' IBs, to actively Dispute them, and thereby receive excellent practice in Disputing their own irrationalities.
3. In group therapy, all the group members can, and often do, suggest bigger and better homework assignments for each of the other members.
4. When accepting homework, group members are more likely to carry it out than individual therapy clients, because they have to report back to the whole group as to whether or not they actually did it.
5. When people feel very upset during group sessions, which they often do, we can immediately zero in on what they are telling themselves to help them, right in the here and now, to undo their upsetness and to work at changing it.
6. Homework assignments and other emotive-evocative exercises, which are often used in Rational Emotive Behavior Therapy, can be carried out during group sessions, and not just outside of therapy. Thus, my groups are often given – or give themselves – shame-attacking, secret-revealing, hot-seat, risk-taking and other encounter-type exercises in the course of regular group sessions and are then able to express their feelings about these exercises and to receive feedback from the therapist and from other group members.
7. The many cognitive, emotive and behavioral methods that are commonly used in individual REBT can also be employed in group REBT – and, again, feedback from and interactions with other group members often add to their effectiveness.
8. Most people come to REBT (and other forms of therapy) with some signif- icant interpersonal and relationship problems. Because the group is a social situation, many such problems can be more easily assessed and worked on than they often can be in individual treatment.

Kinds of REBT Groups

Most of my groups are small, weekly held groups, lasting two and a quarter hours. They include a maximum of eight people, because REBT small group sessions are less rambling and more structured than other kinds of groups, and can include more than the six or seven members that other therapies usually set as their top limits. My own groups include males and females, usually ranging from 18 to 70 years of age, with many different kinds of problems.

However, at the psychological clinic of the Albert Ellis Institute in New York, we also have some same-sex groups, for men and women who prefer to open up only in such a group. In addition, we have time-limited groups – usually for only six or eight sessions – where all the members have a similar problem, such as procrastinating, overeating, rage, or relationship difficulties. Again, we regularly arrange all-day rational encounter marathons (with up to 16 people and large group intensives with 70 or more people).

We also have my famous Friday night workshop, 'Problems of Daily Living,' with as many as 200 people in the audience watching while I have public interviews with volunteer clients and then throw the discussion of the interview open to all the members of the audience who choose to participate (Dryden, Backx and Ellis, 1987; Ellis, Sichel, Leaf and Mass, 1989).

Finally, we have regular three and a half hour workshops, with from 10 to 80 participants, on special topics such as managing difficult people, creative personal encounters, panic disorders, post-traumatic stress disorders, and sexual problems.

Selecting Participants for Ongoing Groups

No one is usually allowed into any of my ongoing small groups at the Albert Ellis Institute unless he or she has had at least one individual therapy session. Often, potential members have a number of individual sessions at the Institute before joining a group; and if their individual therapist thinks that they are suitable for the group process, they can join one of my regular groups.

Almost all clients who desire to become group members are allowed to enter a group, even if they are seriously neurotic, have a severe personality disorder, or have some psychotic behaviors, as long as they are not considered to be disruptive or too combative. A few people may not be admitted into a group because they are compulsive talkers, have frequent angry outbursts at other group members, come to group under the influence of alcohol or other substances, cannot follow normal group procedures, or who would sabotage the regular group process. If these disruptive people do get into one of my groups, they are dealt with very firmly and trained to be more 'normal' group participants. If they are not trainable, they are told to enter individual therapy and only to return to group when their individual therapist advises that they are ready to do so.

A few members are also dropped from group when they violate its basic rules, especially the rule of confidence outside of group about anything that goes on during the group sessions. In conducting my regular groups steadily since 1959, and having many hundreds of different participants, I (in collaboration with other members of the group) have only insisted that less than ten people leave the group. However, several dozen more have participated so poorly in group that they have spontaneously seen that they are not suitable members and have quit on their own. Frequently, instead, they have gone into individual therapy with me or other therapists at the Institute.

Procedure of Small Group Regular Sessions

REBT group sessions can be arranged with different procedures and still be effective. I run my own weekly groups at the Institute as follows. I usually start each session by asking each member, one at a time, whether she or he has done the agreed upon last homework assignment (a list of which I have in front of me). 'If not,' I ask, 'why not?' I look for the dysfunctional, Irrational Beliefs (IBs) that probably stopped her or him from doing the homework, such as: 'It's too hard to do it. I should improve without doing it!' Or: 'I have to show myself and the group that I'll do it beautifully. Else, I'm a no-goodnik!' I and other group members Dispute this person's low frustration tolerance (LFT) and perfectionism, and encourage her or him to do the assignment next week or we modify it and add to it.

We then ask the member what main disturbances they felt this week, what Irrational Beliefs (IBs) accompanied upsets, what was done to Dispute their dysfunctional Beliefs, what other REBT techniques were used, what progress or lack of progress was made, what could best be done now. If the group is working well, I alone do not question, challenge and encourage each member, but several other members also do so, and there is much lively inter-action and interchange.

By the time each session ends, all the members present have usually been checked on their homework, led to discuss continuing or new disturbances, shown how their IBs are often remarkably similar to other members' dysfunctional beliefs, led to do some active Disputing of their IBs, helped to discuss other REBT methods they can use, encouraged to listen and to talk to other members and to try to help them, and asked if they will agree to take another homework assignment.

If time runs out before important issues can be discussed, they are put on the agenda for priority handling during the following session.

Useful REBT Group Techniques

As noted previously, nearly all the regular cognitive, motive, and behavioral REBT techniques that are used in individual sessions are also used in group therapy. In addition, sometimes used during group therapy sessions, some encounter-type exercises that are specially designed for group processes are employed. Here are some of the techniques that have been found to be most useful (Ellis, 1999, 2000a, 2000b, 2001a, 2001b; Ellis and Blau, 1998; Ellis and Dryden, 1997; Ellis and MacLaren, 1998).

Cognitive techniques of REBT

Active disputing

Members are all taught and re-taught the ABCs of REBT. They are shown how Adversities (A's) affect them but do not by themselves lead to disturbed Consequences (C's). Instead, their own Beliefs (B's) strongly influence their disturbed Cs. Therefore they feel and act dysfunctionally because of both A's and B's. In REBT language A x B = C. Clients largely upset themselves by Adversities (A's) *and* their Irrational Beliefs (EBs) *about* their Adversities. Time after time, group members are shown by the therapist, and *also* show each other, that when unfortunate A's occur in their lives – such as failure and rejection – they have a *choice* of making themselves *healthily* sorry and regretful or *unhealthily* anxious, depressed and raging. They can do this by telling themselves Rational Beliefs (RBs) – such as 'I don't like this Adversity. I wish that it didn't exist.' Or, they can strongly tell themselves Irrational Beliefs (IBs), such as, 'Because I don't like this Adversity, it absolutely must not exist! It's *terrible* and I *can't stand* it.'

Rational coping self-statements

In group and in their outside life, members are encouraged to prepare Rational *Beliefs* (RBs) and coping statements to substitute for their IBs, and to keep using them steadily until they consistently believe and act on them. Such self-statements can be factual and encouraging (e.g. 'I am able to succeed on this job, and will work hard to show that I can'). Or, preferably, they can be more philosophical (e.g. 'I'd like very much to succeed but I don't *have* to do so; and if I fail I am never a failure or a worthless individual').

Cost-benefit analysis

Group members can make a list of the real disadvantages of their harmful addictions (e.g. smoking) and a list of the real advantages of changing their dysfunctional behaviors (e.g. procrastination or avoidance of sex-love relationships). They can review and think about this list several times every day (Ellis and Velten, 1992).

Modeling

Participants are urged to model themselves after the healthy behavior of the leader, of another member, of friends or relatives, or of other good models they hear of or read about (Bandura, 1997; Ellis and Abrams, 1994).

Cognitive homework

Members use the ABCDEs of REBT, observe some of their unfortunate Adversities (A's), figure out their IBs, Dispute them (at D) and arrive at Effective New Philosophies (E). They do so either in their head or on one of the REBT Self-Help Forms.

Psychoeducational techniques

Group members use REBT books, workbooks, pamphlets, audio-video cassettes, and other self-help materials to understand and solidify their working at REBT cognitive, emotive, and behavioral methods.

Proselytizing

Members are encouraged to use REBT to try to help other members, as well as their friends and relatives, to overcome their IBs and thereby to practice helping themselves to overcome their own disturbances.

Recording therapy sessions

Participants may record the parts of their sessions where the other participants are largely trying to help them with their personal problems, and listen to these recordings in between the sessions.

Reframing

Members are shown how to look for unfortunate A's to see that they include good things as well. They learn to accept the challenge, when 'bad' A's occur, of making themselves healthfully sorry and frustrated, rather than unhealthily panicking and depressing.

Emotive techniques of REBT

Forceful coping self-statements.

REBT hypothesizes that group members (and other people) often hold their IBs quite strongly (with 'hot' cognitions) and that, therefore, they had better vigorously and powerfully think, feel and act against them. Among its emotive-evocative methods is the use of forceful coping self-statements – such as, 'I NEVER, NEVER need what I want. I ONLY prefer it!' 'I can ALWAYS accept *myself*, my personhood, even when I do stupid and wrong *acts*!'

Rational emotive imagery

Maxie Maultsby Jr, an REBT psychiatrist, created rational emotive imagery (REI) in 1971 and I added more emotive and behavioral elements to it (Ellis, 2000b; Maultsby, 1971). Group members do REI, both during group sessions and as homework, by imagining one of the worst things that could happen to them (e.g. steadily failing at an important project); letting themselves feel very upset about this image (e.g. panicking); keenly feeling this disturbed emotion; and then working on their feeling, to make themselves have healthy negative feelings (such as sorrow, disappointment or frustration). They can do this every day for 30 days (it usually takes only a minute or two each day to do so) until they automatically experience their healthy negative feelings when they imagine, or actually encounter, similar 'horrible' happenings.

Role-playing

Group members often role-play with other group members or with the therapist, as when one plays the interviewee for an important job and the other plays the interviewer. During this form of behavior rehearsal, the rest of the group critiques how well the member is doing in the role-play and suggests how she or he could improve. If either of the role-players shows anxiety, the role-play is temporarily stopped and this person is asked what he or she is thinking to create the anxiety and how he or she could think, instead, to allay it.

Reverse role-play

One group member takes another's Irrational Belief (e.g. 'So-and-so must always love me completely!') and holds on to it rigidly and forcefully while playing the irrational member's role. The person with the IB then has to talk the other role-player – actually himself or herself – out of this firmly held IB.

Forceful taped disputing

A group member tapes one of his or her main IBs as homework (e.g. 'Everybody always has to treat me fairly!') and vigorously Disputes it on the same tape. The other members listen to this Disputing to see if it is really rational and also to see how vigorous and forceful it is (Ellis, 1988).

Use of humor

Members are shown how to not take themselves and their mistakes too seriously, and encouraged to humorously challenge the IBs of other group members – but only to put down and laugh at the other's ideas and behaviors, and not to denigrate the person as a whole (Ellis, 1977a, 1977b). REBT group members at the psychological clinic of the Albert Ellis Institute in New York City are given a leaflet of rational humorous songs to sing to themselves when they panic, depress, or enrage themselves. The whole group, as an exercise, may also sing some of these humorous songs or other songs that they create. Two typical rational humorous songs are:

PERFECT RATIONALITY
(Tune: 'Funiculi, Funicula' by Denza)[1]
Some think the world must have a right direction,
And so do I – and so do I!
Some think that, with the slightest imperfection
They can't get by – and so do I!
For I, I have to prove I'm superhuman,
And better far than people are!
To show I have miraculous acumen
And always rate among the Great!

Perfect, perfect rationality
Is, of course, the only thing for me!
How can I ever think of being
If I must live fallibly?
Rationality must be a perfect thing for me!

LOVE ME, LOVE ME, ONLY ME!
(Tune: 'Yankee Doodle Dandy')
Love me, love me, only me
Or I will die without you!
O, make your love a guarantee
So I can never doubt you!
Love me, love me totally – really, really try dear;
But if you demand love, too
I'll hate you till I die, dear!

Love me, love me all the time
Thoroughly and wholly!
Living turns to slushy slime
Unless you love me solely!
Love me with great tenderness
With no ifs or buts, dear.
If you love me somewhat less,
I'll hate your goddamned guts, dear!

[1]New song lyrics by Albert Ellis. Copyright by the Albert Ellis Institute.

Relationship methods

Members are given unconditional other-acceptance (UOA) by the therapist, no matter how badly or selfishly they behave, and are taught how to give it to other group members and to people outside the group. They are helped to relate better to people in their regular lives and are often taught interpersonal and social skills training in the group.

Encouragement

Members are helped to encourage other troubled members to think, feel and act less disturbedly and more enjoyably; and to do their therapeutic homework, even when it is difficult to do.

Encounter exercises

Members are given group encounter exercises in their regular group and in special all-day marathons that are arranged for them regularly. Nine-hour intensives are also run by the Albert Ellis Institute in New York for group members (and other people) who want to participate in larger-scale group exercises (see Chapter 7).

Behavioral techniques of REBT

In vivo desensitization

Group members are encouraged to do a number of harmless acts, such as making a public speech or talking to strangers, that they are neurotically afraid to do, and also to use several other active-experiential behavioral methods of REBT. They are urged to expose themselves, through imagining or actually doing 'frightening' things so that they can face past or present traumatic scenes and work through their reactions of horror. Particularly if they have post-traumatic stress disorder (PTSD) or other forms of panicking, they are shown how to expose themselves to 'horrible' thoughts and images, so that they desensitize themselves to them.

Avoiding running away from obnoxious events

When group members find other members obnoxious or 'terrible' and overreact to them, they are encouraged not to leave the group until they modify their feelings of rage or horror – and to practice doing so in spite of the 'horrible' situation they encounter. Once they make themselves considerably less disturbed, they are advised to then decide whether it is more advantageous or disadvantageous for them to tolerate remaining with 'obnoxious' group members. Similarly, they are often encouraged not to completely avoid 'bad' people outside the group until they modify their rage or I-can't-stand-it-itis about these people.

Use of reinforcement

Being strongly behavioral, REBT shows group members how to suitably reinforce themselves by doing something enjoyable only *after* they have done something onerous – such as working on a term paper that they are avoiding. In group itself they may be allowed to speak up about their own problems only after they have tried to help other members with their difficulties.

Use of penalties

Many clients won't stop their addictive or compulsive behavior because it is too immediately pleasurable or reinforcing; and they will not change it for a normal reinforcement. Thus, they will not give up smoking or problem drinking by allowing themselves to read or enjoy television after they have not smoked or drank. Consequently, REBT encourages some group members to penalize themselves after their destructive indulgences – for example, to spend an hour with a boring person every time they gamble, or light every cigarette they smoke with a $50 bill. Clients also encourage other group members to enact suitable penalties and monitor their doing so.

Skill training

Group members often learn and practice particular important interpersonal skills in the group sessions, for example, learning to listen to others, accepting them with their poor behavior, communicating openly with them, and forming relationships with them. They are also urged to acquire suitable personal and interpersonal skills by taking courses and practicing them outside of group.

Relapse prevention

Members are shown how to ward off relapses, to accept themselves when they relapse, and to revert to self-helping thoughts, feelings, and behaviors when they fall back to dysfunctional behaving. To do this, they are taught the relapse prevention methods of Marlatt and Gordon (1989) and other cognitive behaviorists and the specific relapse-preventive methods of REBT – particularly monitoring and Disputing their own musturbatory philosophies that lead to relapse.

Processes of REBT Group Therapy

Transference

REBT views transference, first, as overgeneralization. Thus, because group members were once treated badly by their fathers and treated well by their mothers, they may tend to put other males in the same category as their father, and may feel hostile or indifferent to men and warm toward women.

They may – or may not! – also react to the therapist as a father/mother figure and to other group members as siblings. These are overgeneralizations but, unless they are extreme, may not lead to major emotional and behavioral problems. Because REBT is not preoccupied with this kind of transference (as psychoanalysis is), it does not obsessively look for it and consequently invariably 'find' it.

When normal, non-disturbed transference reactions are observed in my groups, I largely ignore them; but when they escalate into disturbed reactions in the group itself or in the members' personal lives, the other group members and I point to these reactions and show members how destructive they are and how to minimize them. Thus, if Miriam avoids sex-love relationships because her father kept rejecting her, we show her that all males are not her father, that she can sensibly choose a different type of man, and that if she makes a mistake and picks a partner who is as unloving as her father, that doesn't prove that she needs his love and that she is worthless without it, nor that she'll never be able to have a long-term loving relationship. The group and I dispute her disturbed overgeneralizing but not her normal generalizing.

Similarly, if a male member deifies or devil-ifies me, the group leader, and sees me as a loved or hated father figure, we point out his disturbed transference reactions, show him the distorted thinking that lies behind it, and encourage him to adopt less dysfunctional thoughts, feelings, and behaviors. Or if a woman fights with female group members just as she fights with her sisters, we point out her transference and the irrational cognitions behind it and show her how to break her rigid women-are-all-like-my-sisters reaction.

The term *transference* is also used in psychotherapy to denote the close relationship that usually develops between clients and their therapist. I find that such relationship factors do develop in my group, but not nearly as intensely as they do with my individual therapy clients. However, REBT actively espouses the therapist's giving all clients close attention, showing real interest in helping them solve their problems, and – especially – giving what Rogers (1961) calls unconditional positive regard and what I (Ellis and Harper, 1997) call *unconditional other-acceptance* (UOA). So, although I am often confrontational with group members, I try to show them that I really care about helping them; that I will work hard to hear, understand and empathize with them; that I have great faith that they can, despite their handicaps, improve; that I can poke fun *at their irrationalities* without laughing *at them*; and that I totally accept them as fallible humans, no matter how badly they often think and behave. I also use my *person* in my group sessions, and consequently am informal, take risks, reveal some of my own feelings, tell jokes and stories, and generally am myself as well as a group leader. In this way, I hope to model flexible, involved, non-disturbed behaviors.

Countertransference

I frankly like and dislike some of my group members more than I do others, and I especially tend to dislike members who often come late, act unhelpfully to others, fail to do their homework, and behave disruptively in group. When I see that I am feeling this way, I look for my possibly telling myself, 'They *shouldn't* be the way they are and are rotten shits for being that way!' I immediately dispute those damning beliefs and convince myself, 'They *should* act the poor way that they do, because it is their habitual nature to act that way right now. I dislike what they do but I can accept *them* with their unfortunate *doings*.'

By decreasing my *demands* on my clients, I largely (not completely) overcome my negative countertransference, and I am able to deal with 'bad' group members more therapeutically. I sometimes, depending on their vulnerability, confront them and honestly tell them, 'I try not to hate *you*, but I really do dislike some of your *behaviors*, and I hope for my sake, the group's sake, and especially your own sake, that you change it.' When I find myself prejudicedly favoring some members of my groups, I convince myself that they are not gods or goddesses, and I make an effort to keep liking them personally without unduly favoring them in group.

Methods of intervention

Most of my interventions take place with each individual member as he is telling about his homework, talking about his progress and lack of progress, presenting new problems, or returning to old ones. I speak directly to him, ask questions, make suggestions, ferret out and dispute his dysfunctional thoughts, feelings and behaviors, and suggest homework. My interventions are mainly about his personal problems, especially as they relate to his outside life, but also as they relate to what he says and doesn't say in group.

I often show a member that her actions (and inactions) in group may well replicate her out-of-group behaviors. Thus, I may say, 'Johanna, you speak so low here that we can hardly hear what you say. Do you act the same way in social groups? If so, what are you telling yourself to make yourself speak so low?'

My interpersonal interventions include commenting on how group members react to each other; noting that they often fail to speak up to, or interact with other members; noting their warm or hostile reactions to others, and encouraging the former and questioning the latter; giving them relationship exercises to do during group sessions; having a personal interaction with some of the members; and, especially, pointing out that their group interactions may indicate how they sabotage themselves in their outside relationships and giving them some in-group skill training that may help them relate better outside the group.

My intervention with the group as a whole largely consists of giving all its members cognitive, emotive and behavioral exercises to be done in the group; giving them all the same homework exercise, such as a shame-attacking exercise, to do before the next session; giving them a brief lecture on one of the main theories or practices of REBT; and explaining to them some of the group procedures and discussing with them the advantages and disadvantages of these procedures.

Most of the time, as noted above, I intervene on the individual level, but when interpersonal problems arise – such as two or more members failing to relate to each other – I often intervene with duos or trios. I also plan in advance group-as-a-whole interventions, or else I spontaneously promote them as I deem them advisable (or as the spirit moves me!).

Focusing on group processes

Most of the time in my group sessions I use an individualized content focus. I assume that the group members come to therapy to work on their own individual problems and mainly to help themselves in their outside lives. Therefore, I induce them largely to talk about the things that are bothering them in their personal and interpersonal relationships and, with the help of the group, try to show them how they are needlessly upsetting themselves in their daily lives and what they can do to think, feel and act more health-fully.

The purpose of REBT group (and individual) therapy is to show clients how they are not only assessing and blaming *what they do* but also damning *themselves* for doing it; to indicate how they are also evaluating others' behavior *and* damning these others for their 'bad' behaviour; and help them realize how they are confronting environmental difficulties and (externally and internally) whining about them, instead of constructively trying to change or avoid them. Therefore, whenever members bring up any undue or exaggerated upsetness, and feel unhealthily panicking, depressing, self-hating or raging (instead of feeling healthily sad, disappointed and frustrated) when unfortunate events occur, the other members and I focus on showing them what they are doing to upset themselves needlessly, how to stop doing this, and how to plan and act on achieving a more fulfilling, happier existence. When they are, as it were, 'on stage' in the group, almost everyone focuses on them and their difficulties and tries to help them overcome these in the group itself and in the outside world. So a majority of the time in each session is spent on dealing with individual members' problems.

When, however, any of the members displays a problem that particularly relates to the group itself, this is dealt with specifically and group-wise. Thus, if a member keeps coming quite late to group or is absent a good deal of the time, either I or other members raise this as an issue, and we speak to this member about it. We determine, for instance, why he comes late, what core philosophies encourage him to do so, how he defeats himself and the other members by his lateness, how he can change, and what kind of homework assignment in this respect he will agree to carry out. At the same time, the general problem of lateness – as it relates to group and also as it relates to the members' outside lives – is also frequently discussed, and it is shown how latecoming is disadvantageous to other members and how it interferes with a cohesive and beneficial group process.

Similarly, if a group member only speaks about her own problems and doesn't take the risk of speaking to the others, disputing their self-defeating thoughts and behaviors, and making some suitable suggestions for their change, she is questioned about this and shown how and why she is blocking herself in group, and how and why she probably behaves similarly in her outside life. But the general problem of members being too reserved – or, sometimes, too talkative – in group is also raised, and various members are encouraged to speak up about this problem and to give their ideas about how the group process would be more effective if virtually all the members talked up appropriately, rather than said too much or too little.

Also, if the group as a whole seems to be functioning poorly – for example, being dull, uninterested, apathetic, or overly boisterous – I raise this issue, encourage a general discussion of it, get members to suggest alternative ways for the group to act, and check on these suggestions later to see if they are being implemented. Once in a while I go over some of the general principles of REBT – such as the theory that people largely upset themselves rather than get upset – to make sure that the members as a whole understand these principles and are better prepared to use them during the sessions and in their outside affairs.

I keep looking for cues for underlying issues that are not being handled well in group. Some cues are the members only being interested in their own problems and not those of other members; not being alert during the group; being too negative to other members who may not be working at helping themselves improve; giving only practical advice to other members, rather than disputing their irrational philosophies; being too sociable, rather than being serious about their own and others' problems; not staying for the after-group session; and 'subgrouping' or talking privately to others during the group session. I usually intervene soon after these issues arise, and raise the issue either with the individual who is interfering with the group process or with the group as a whole.

My strategy of intervention is usually direct and often confrontational. Thus, I may say, 'Jim, you always bring up your own problems in group and seem to have no trouble speaking about them. But I rarely hear you say anything to the other group members about their problems. When you sit there silently, while the rest of us are speaking to one of the group members, I suspect that you are saying quite a lot to yourself that you are not saying to the group. Am I right about this? And if I am, what are you telling yourself to stop yourself from speaking up to the others?'

A more general intervention will also usually be direct and will go something like this: 'Several of you recently are not doing your agreed-upon homework or are doing it very sloppily. Let's discuss this right now and see if I am observing this correctly and, if so, what can we do about it to see that the homework assignments are more useful and to arrange that you follow them more often and more thoroughly.'

If the group process is going well and the members are fairly consistently bringing up and working on their problems, both in the group and outside the group, my interventions are relatively few in regard to the group process. But I frequently question, challenge, advise and confront members about their individual problems. I am an active teacher, confronter, persuader, encourager, and homework suggester, and I usually talk more than any of the other members during a given session. I try to make sure, however, that I do not give long lectures or hold the floor too long. My questions and comments, therefore, are usually frequent but brief.

Although I can easily run one of my groups by myself, without any assistance, because the Albert Ellis Institute in New York is a training institute and because we want all of our trainees to be able to lead a group by themselves, I am usually assisted by one of our trainees, a Fellow or Intern of the Institute. This assistant leader is with me and the group for the first hour and a half of each session and takes over the group by himself or herself for the after-group, which consists of another 45 minutes. The assistant leader is also trained to make active-directive interventions, but not to hog the floor at any one time, and to encourage the other members to keep making interventions, too. A few of the members in each group usually become quite vocal and adept at making interventions, but I tactfully correct them if they seem to go too far off base. The assistant leader and I particularly go after the non-intervening members and keep encouraging them to speak up more and more about other people's problems. If they are recalcitrant or resistant in this respect, we fairly often give them the assignment of speaking up a minimum of three times in each session about other members' problems.

I keep showing the members how their behavior in group often – but by no means always – mirrors their behaviors and problems outside the group. Thus, if one member speaks sharply to another member, I may say, 'Mary, you seem to be angry right now at Joan. Are you just objecting to her behavior, with which you disagree? Or are you, as I seem to hear you doing, damning *her* for exhibiting that *behavior*?' If Mary acknowledges her anger at Joan, I (and the other members) may then ask, 'What are you telling yourself right now to make yourself angry? What is your Jehovian *demand* on Joan?' If Mary denies that she is angrily carping at Joan, I may then ask the rest of the group, 'What do you think and feel about Mary's reactions to Joan? Am I just inventing her anger or do you sense it, too?'

We then get the group's reactions to Mary; and if several members agree that she probably is quite angry at Joan, we go back to the question: 'What are you telling yourself right now to *make* yourself angry?' The others and I will also try to get Mary to see that she is probably making the same kind of demands about people outside the group at whom she is angry as she is now making about Joan in the group.

Again, if Ted only offers practical advice to the other members and never helps them to see and to dispute their self-defeating philosophies by which they are upsetting themselves, I, my assistant therapist, or one of the group members may say to him, 'Look, Ted, you just ignored Harold's perfectionist demands that are making him refuse to work on the novel he is trying to write, and, instead, you only offered him some practical advice on how to take a writing course. You often seem to do this same kind of thing in group. Now isn't it likely that in your own life you don't look for and dispute your Irrational Beliefs, and that you mainly look for practical ways of your acting better with those irrationalities, so that you do not have to tackle them and give them up?'

Working with difficult group members

One kind of difficult group member is the one who interferes with the group process, such as Mel, who interrupted others, indicated that they were pretty worthless for not changing their ways, and often monopolized the group. Other members and I pointed this out to him several times, but he persisted in his disruptive behavior. So we insisted that he stop and consider what he was telling himself when, for example, he interrupted others.

His main musturbatory beliefs appeared to be (1) 'I *must* get in what I have to say immediately, or else I might lose it and never get to say it, and that would be *awful*!' and (2) 'If I don't make a more brilliant statement to the group than any of the others makes, I am an inadequate person and I might as well shut my mouth and say nothing at all!' We showed Mel how to dispute and change these ideas to *preferences*, but not *necessities*, that he speak and be heard and that he make brilliant contributions to the group. We also gave him the homework assignment of watching his interrupting tendencies and forcing himself for a while to speak up in group only after he had given some other member the choice of speaking up first. After several more sessions, he had distinctly improved his interruptive tendencies, and reported that he was doing the same thing in his conversations with people outside the group.

Another difficult type of member is the one who rarely completes the homework assignment he has agreed to do, or else completes it occasionally and sloppily. I (and other group members) then ask him to look for the irrational ideas that he is overtly or tacitly holding to block his doing these assignments, such as: 'It's hard to do this goddamned assignment; in fact, it's *too* hard and it *shouldn't be* that hard! I can get away with improving myself *without* doing it, even though other people have to do their homework to change. Screw it. I won't do it!' We keep after this member to look at the Beliefs he holds to block his doing the homework; to make a list of the disadvantages of not doing it and to go over this list at least five times every day; to dispute his Irrational Beliefs strongly and forcefully; to keep telling himself rational coping self-statements in their stead; to use rational emotive imagery to make himself feel sorry and displeased, but not horrified and rebellious, about having to do the homework; to reinforce himself whenever he does it, and perhaps to also penalize himself when he doesn't do it; and to use other suitable methods of REBT to undercut his dysfunctional thinking, feeling and behaving about doing the homework.

Another type of difficult group member is the one who is overly passive, polite, and non-participative. I usually do nothing about such a member until she has been in the group for several weeks and had a chance to acclimate herself to its procedures and to some of the principles of REBT. But then I directly question her about her passivity and lack of participation. If she acknowledges these behaviors, I encourage her to look at her blocking thoughts and actively to dispute them. Thus, one member, Josephine, kept telling herself, just before she thought of speaking up in group, 'What if I say something stupid! They'll all laugh at me! I'll be an utter fool! They are all brighter than I and know much better how to use REBT. I'll *never* be able to say something intelligent or to be helpful to the other group members. I'd better quit group and only go for individual therapy where it is much easier for me to speak up, because I only have to talk about myself and don't have to help others with their problems.'

In this case, the group and I did what we usually do: we disputed Josephine's unrealistic attributions and inferences and showed her that she wouldn't necessarily say something stupid; that the group might well not laugh at her even if she did; that all the members were not necessarily brighter than she; and that if she kept trying, she most probably would be able to say something intelligent and to be helpful to the other members. As usual, however, we went beyond this – as we almost always do in REBT – by showing Josephine, more elegantly, that even if the worst happened, even if she did say something stupid, even if she was laughed at by the group, even if all the others were brighter than she, and even if she never was able to say something intelligent or to be helpful to the others, she still would never be an inadequate or rotten *person*, but would only be a person who was now behaving poorly and who could always accept and respect herself while remaining unenthusiastic about some of her traits and behaviors.

This is what we usually try to achieve with difficult clients who continually down and damn themselves and who steadily, therefore, feel depressing, panicking and worthless. The group members and I persist in showing her that we accept her as a fallible human, and that she can learn to consistently do the same for herself. REBT group therapy, like REBT individual therapy, is particularly oriented toward helping all clients give themselves unconditional self-acceptance (USA): that is, to reject and to try to change many of their dysfunctional behaviors but always – yes, always! – to accept themselves as humans. Yes, *whether or not* they perform well and *whether or not* they are approved or loved by significant others.

This is one of the cardinal views of REBT; and one that often – though, of course, not always – works well with difficult clients. This aspect of REBT is probably more effective in group than in individual therapy, because all the members of the group are taught to accept both themselves and others unconditionally; so that when an arrant self-denigrator comes to group, she is not only accepted unconditionally by the therapist (who is especially trained to do this kind of accepting) but is almost always also accepted by the other group members, thus encouraging and abetting her unconditionally to accept herself.

Activity of the therapist and group members

In cognitive-behavioral therapy in general and in REBT group therapy in particular, the activity level of the therapist tends to be high. I am a teacher, who often shows my clients how they upset themselves and what they can do to change, but I also keep encouraging and pushing them to change. The romantic view in therapy is that if clients are provided with a trusting and accepting atmosphere, they have considerable ability to change, and will healthfully use this ability to get themselves to grow and develop. I take the more realistic view that they *can* but that they often *won't* choose to modify their thoughts, feelings and behaviors unless I actively and directively push them to do so. Consequently, as noted previously in this chapter, I speak more than any other group member during each session; I purposely and purposively lead the group in 'healthy' rather than 'unhealthy' directions; and I keep each session going in an organized, no-nonsense, presumably efficient way. I try to make sure that no one is neglected during each session; that no one monopolizes the group; and that sidetracking into chit-chat, empty discussion, bombast, endless philosophizing, and other modes of problem avoidance is minimized.

As leader, I try to maximize honest revealings of feelings, cutting through defensiveness, getting to members' core dysfunctional philosophies, Disputing of these philosophies. I also introduce behavioral assignments, such as getting members to accept present discomfort, and carry out difficult in-group and out-of-group experiential and behavioral exercises. For example, I (or the other members) may suggest that Sam, an unusually shy person, go around the room and start a conversation with every member who is present. I will then direct Sam to do so, will encourage him to keep going around the room, will ask him about his feelings as he does so, will get him to look at what he is thinking to create these feelings, will ask the other members for the reactions to his overtures, and will lead a general discussion on what has just transpired and how Sam and other members can gain from this exercise. Once, when we did this exercise with an exceptionally shy man, he not only became very much more active in group from that session onward, but also, for the first time in his life, began to approach people in his neighbourhood bar, where previously he had always waited for them to approach him. He noted that my actively persuading him and the group to participate in this exercise was a real turning point in his life.

The activity level of most of the members of my four weekly groups is usually quite high, not only in the expressing of their feelings and ideas, but in their disputing other members' self-defeating beliefs and helping them with their problem-solving.

In the section that follows, I provide a case example of how one particular client benefited from her participation in an REBT group.

Case Presentation of a Group Client

Barbara came to group because of her business and social unassertiveness. A 36-year-old secretary, she had always worked below her potential level because she nicely followed her supervisor's instructions but never took any initiative herself. She therefore failed to become a supervisor or office manager, although she definitely seemed to have the ability to do that kind of work. She married at the age of 21 and stayed with her alcoholic and irresponsible husband for eight years because of her horror of being alone. Although quite attractive, she practically never went to singles functions, but stayed in her apartment by herself most of the time, because she was afraid to socialize and be rejected by any 'good' men she might meet. She felt that she had 'nothing really to offer,' except to an inferior male. So she only, occasionally, dated unsuccessful, inadequate men whom she found 'safe' but too boring to stay with for any length of time. She had one close woman friend, Selma, who – like herself – was painfully shy and who only socialized with Barbara.

At first, Barbara talked freely enough about herself in group, especially about her unassertiveness at work and about her accompanying depression. But she would only give practical advice to other group members and never found or Disputed their Irrational Beliefs. When asked about this in group, she said that she did not know how to do REBT well enough to do good Disputing, even though she had read several REBT self-help books and pamphlets.

To show Barbara that she was able to do Disputing adequately, she was asked to fill out the REBT Self-Help Form; first, about one of her own problems; and, second, about another group member's unassertiveness with her husband. When Barbara did very well on these homework assignments and admitted that she could do adequate REBT Disputation, she was encouraged to do live Disputing of some other group members' Irrational *Beliefs* during several group sessions, and was again shown that she could do this well. After several weeks, she became one of the group's most frequent and persistent Disputers, and began to obviously enjoy the process. She also spontaneously began, outside of therapy, to teach REBT to her shy friend, Selma, and to considerably help Selma with some of her neurotic difficulties.

For several months, Barbara complained and put herself down for her unassertiveness with her supervisor at work. She saw that it stemmed from her dire need for this woman's approval, but did nothing to change her love slobbism or to act more assertively. After doing some assertiveness-training role-playing in group, and after being urged by all the other members to follow it up on the outside, she forced herself to speak up at work. Doing so, she soon arranged to get the promise of a raise in pay; also arranged to come in an hour earlier and to leave work earlier on Tuesdays and Thursdays, so that she could take a special word-processing course; and was able to ask for several other favors at work that she had been terrified to request for more than two years. Both Barbara and the group were delighted with her increased assertiveness, and she was encouraged to look for a better job – which, after four months, she finally attained.

Barbara's social anxiety proved more difficult to tackle than her unassertiveness at work, because she invented innumerable excuses to avoid going to singles affairs and to respond appropriately to males who tried to approach her at church, when she walked her dog, and at the other few activities in which she allowed herself to participate. She even refused to try a date with an eligible male cousin of Selma, who talked to this cousin and got him interested in seeing Barbara. She was sure that he would lose all interest in her if they actually met, and was terrified that he might have sex with her because he was only interested in her body and would then never want to see her again. She broke two tentative dates with him and perpetuated her perfect record of not having a single date in three years.

The group and I tried several REBT techniques to help Barbara overcome her extreme fears of rejection. We used cost-benefit analysis and had her list of many disadvantages of being socially reclusive and read these over many times to sink them into her consciousness. We tried to help her model herself after other group members who were overcoming their social shyness. We had her say several forceful coping statements to herself a number of times – such as, 'I *can* find some males who will like me for more than my body! And if any of them have sex with me and then reject me, that means something about *them* but never, never proves that *I* am an inadequate person!'

The group showed Barbara how to use rational emotive imagery by imagining that she did get rejected by one of the few men she really liked, letting herself feel very depressed and self-hating about this rejection, and then working on herself until she only felt quite sorry and disappointed but *not* depressed. Most of all, the group and I gave Barbara unconditional acceptance and showed her, by our attitudes, tone, and manner, that we always accepted *her*, as a person, even when she failed to work on herself, when she sabotaged our suggestions, and when she made up poor excuses for staying in her rut. In addition, of course, we consistently and vigorously taught her unconditional self-acceptance (USA) – that is, fully to accept *herself* no matter how badly, foolishly and self-defeating she often *acted*. After going over this important point many times, Barbara improved greatly at refusing to blame herself for her mistakes and failures; and she also helped talk several other group members into unconditionally accepting themselves even when they acted quite foolishly.

All this REBT work, by Barbara and by her therapy group, eventually began to pay off. After attending group regularly for five months, she finally agreed to do the paradoxical homework assignment of going to a dance and making sure that she got at least three rejections by suitable males. She was enormously afraid, at first, to carry out this assignment and for several weeks copped out on doing it. But she finally painfully forced herself to go to a 'safe' church dance, where three men refused to dance with her. After the first refusal, she almost ran shamefully back home. But she made herself stay, to her surprise got several acceptances, and just barely, by the end of the evening, got her required three rejections. She was elated with her social assertiveness – and so were the other members of her group.

From then onward, Barbara's battle with herself went almost swimmingly smoothly. She dated with increasing frequency, and was disappointed, but not depressed, when the 'good' men she occasionally met didn't turn out to be suitable for a long-term relationship. She became active in other ways – especially by participating in a regular discussion group. She became even more active in her therapy group and was voted, in one of the exercises we did, as being the most helpful member. She got a job as an office manager, liked it very much, and did more socializing at the new office in a few weeks than she had previously done in any of the previous jobs that she had held for years.

After being in group for a little over a year, Barbara decided to leave, partly because she now had so many other things to do in the evening that spending several hours once a week traveling to and from and being in group was getting too exhausting. But she mainly felt that she had achieved her goals of socializing better and becoming more assertive, and that she could continue therapy with intermittent individual sessions. She was still at times socially anxious, but was practically never severely depressed as she had often been previously.

The group members were very sorry to see Barbara leave and hoped she would invite them to her future wedding, which they were sure would not be too far away. Several of them continued to have personal friendships with her for quite a while after she left group. She herself was very happy about her group experience, remarked that she would have never benefited so much with just individual therapy sessions, and kept referring her friends and business associates to the Albert Ellis Institute, particularly for group therapy.

Not every member of my groups, of course, makes the dramatic and steady progress that Barbara made, and some take two or three years before they do significantly improve. But if people really work at it, and keep using REBT in group as well as in their outside lives, a large percentage of them make notable gains, minimize their anxiety, depression and rage, and begin to lead much more self-actualized lives.

Conclusion

Rational Emotive Behavior Therapy (REBT) and Cognitive Behavior Therapy (CBT) are efficient kinds of group therapy, because they involve people who regularly meet together with a leader in order to work on their psychological problems, they focus on the members' thoughts, feelings and behaviors, and they encourage all the participants to help each other change their cognitions, emotions and actions. Moreover, members usually give advice to each other, show how others' behavior had better be changed outside the group, and check to see if their homework suggestions are actually being carried out. Again, they normally interact with each other in the group itself, comment on each other's in-group behaviors, and give themselves practice in changing some of their dysfunctional interactions.

Even then, when a therapy group tries to follow a somewhat narrow theory of psychotherapy – for example, a psychoanalytic or a Jungian orientation – it tends to be much wider-ranging in its actions than in its theory, and often takes on a surprisingly eclectic approach (Yalom, 1995). The advantage of REBT group therapy is that it very consciously deals with its members as people who think, feel *and* act; who get disturbed, or *make* themselves disturbed, in all three interacting ways – cognitively, emotionally and behaviorally. Therefore, they had better consciously see how they largely *construct* their dysfunctioning and how they can reconstruct and improve their patterns of living (Ellis, 1999, 2000a, 2000b, 2001a, 2001b; Ellis and Dryden, 1997).

REBT and CBT group therapy, moreover, in principle accept the fact that humans are social animals and live interpersonally and in groups. It is therefore desirable, though not always necessary, that they work out their cognitive-emotive-behavioral problems together as well as in individual therapy. Group work also covers a wide variety of goals and problems. Thus, therapy groups may be homogeneous – e.g. all the members may be involved in skill training, overcoming alcoholism or overcoming procrastination. Or groups may be heterogeneous – e.g. the group may include several kinds of disturbed people. While one specific type of treatment is unlikely to be helpful to members of all these different kinds of groups, REBT includes so many different kinds of techniques that it can fairly easily be adapted to almost any kind of group process. With the use of group treatment, more opportunity for learning positive and unlearning self-defeating behaviour is provided than one therapist can provide in individual therapy and than one group therapist can provide in a one-sided form of group process.

From a research standpoint, Rational Emotive Behavior group therapy offers unique possibilities for exploring the effectiveness of group techniques. For it always includes many specific procedures – such as the Disputing of dysfunctional attitudes, the disclosure of 'shameful' feelings, and the assigning of homework activities. Each of these methods can be used and not used in controlled experiments, to determine how effective or ineffective they are in different kinds of groups and settings. If enough of this kind of experimentation is done, the wide variety of methods now used in REBT (and in CBT) may eventually be pared down to a relatively few effective ones.

For reasons such as these, then, I think that REBT and CBT group therapy will, first, become more popular as the years go by and, secondly, be increasingly incorporated into or merged with many of the other modes of group treatment. At the same time, cognitive-behavioral group and individual therapy will continue to change as the entire field of psychotherapy grows and develops. Some of its more popular present-day methods will wane and other methods, including some not yet invented, will flourish. Like its sister, behavior therapy, and unlike many of today's other treatment methods, CBT favors scientific experimentation and already has led to literally hundreds of controlled studies (Hollon and Beck, 1994; Lyons and Woods, 1991). If this characteristic continues, as I predict it will, REBT and CBT will continue to change and develop.

References

Bandura A (1997) Self-efficacy: The Exercise of Control. New York: Freeman.

Dryden W, Backx W, Ellis A (1987) Problems in living: the Friday night workshop. In W Dryden (ed.), Current Issues in Rational-Emotive Therapy (pp. 154–70). London and New York: Croom Helm.

Ellis A (1962) Reason and Emotion in Psychotherapy. Secaucus, NJ: Citadel.

Ellis A (1977a) Fun as psychotherapy. Rational Living, 12(1), 2–6. Also: Cassette recording. New York: Institute for Rational-Emotive Therapy.

Ellis A (Speaker) (1977b) A Garland of Rational Humorous Songs (Cassette recording and songbook). New York: Albert Ellis Institute.

Ellis A (1988) How to Stubbornly Refuse to Make Yourself Miserable about Anything – Yes, Anything! New York: Kensington Publishers.

Ellis A (1999) How to Make Yourself Happy and Remarkably Less Disturbable. San Luis Obispo, CA: Impact.

Ellis A (2000a) How to Control Your Anxiety before it Controls You. New York: Citadel Press.

Ellis A (2000b) Rational emotive imagery. In ME Bernard, JL Wolfe (eds) The REBT Resource Book for Practitioners (2nd edn) (pp. II 8–II 10). New York: Albert Ellis Institute.

Ellis A (2001a) Feeling Better, Getting Better, Staying Better. Atascadero, CA: Impact Publishers.

Ellis A (2001b) Overcoming Destructive Thinking, Feeling and Behaving. Amherst, NY: Prometheus Books.

Ellis A, Abrams M (1994). How to Cope with a Fatal Illness: The Rational Management of Dying. New York: Barricade Books.

Ellis A, Blau S (1998) (eds) The Albert Ellis Reader. New York: Kensington Publishers.

Ellis A, Dryden W (1997) The Practice of Rational Emotive Behavior Therapy. New York: Springer.

Ellis A, Harper RA (1961) A Guide to Successful Marriage. North Hollywood, CA: Wilshire Books.

Ellis A, Harper RA (1997). A Guide to Rational Living. Rev. ed. North Hollywood, CA: Melvin Powers/Wilshire Books.

Ellis A, MacLaren C (1998) Rational Emotive Behavior Therapy: A Therapist's Guide. Atascadero, CA: Impact Publishers.

Ellis A, Sichel J, Leaf RC, Mass R (1989) Countering perfectionism in research on clinical practice. 1: Surveying rationality changes after a single intensive RET intervention. Journal of Rational-Emotive and Cognitive-Behavior Therapy 7: 197–218.

Ellis A, Velten E (1992) When AA Doesn't Work for You: Rational Steps for Quitting Alcohol. New York. Barricade Books.

Hollon SD, Beck AT (1994) Cognitive and cognitive-behavioral therapies. In AE Bergin, SL Garfield (eds) Handbook of Psychotherapy and Behavior Change, 4th edn (pp. 428–66). New York: Wiley.

Lyons LC, Woods PJ (1991) The efficacy of rational-emotive therapy: a quantitative review of the outcome research. Clinical Psychology Review 11: 357–69.

Marlatt GA, Gordon JR (eds) (1989) Relapse Prevention: Maintenance Strategies in the Treatment of Addictive Behaviors. New York: Guilford.

Maultsby MC, Jr (1971) Rational emotive imagery. Rational Living 6(1): 24–7.

Rogers CR (1961) On becoming a person. Boston: Houghton-Mifflin.
Yalom ID (1995) The Theory and Practice of Group Psychotherapy. 4th edn. New York: Basic Books.

CHAPTER 3

Critical Incidents in Group Therapy

ALBERT ELLIS

Editors' Introduction

This chapter presents Albert Ellis's responses to six critical incidents in group therapy that were put to him and other group therapists in the second edition of an excellent book entitled *Critical Incidents in Group Therapy* by Donigian and Hulse-Killacky (Brooks-Cole, 1999). In this chapter we present each critical incident and Ellis's response as it appears in that book (material reproduced with permission from the publishers).

Critical Incident 1: The Initial Session

You are a counselor at a university counseling center. You have been acutely aware of the difficulty a number of freshmen students have been having in adjusting to college life. You offer to organize a counseling group to help students contend more effectively with their new environment.

Your group consists of nine volunteers (five men and four women), whom you have screened. Each has expressed a willingness to participate in the group you are forming. It is meeting today for the first time. All nine members are present as you enter the room and sit down. You introduce yourself, and the members introduce themselves. Then they each turn and look at you expectantly. There is an initial period of silence.

Albert Ellis's response

This is an ideal situation for the use of Rational Emotive Behavior Therapy (REBT) because the group starts off from scratch and has not been allowed or encouraged to flounder in any non-directive manner, nor to acquire a preju-dice in favor of becoming absorbed in its members' early history, in their 'family' relationship to each other, in their attachment to the group leader, in their obsessive-compulsive interest in the group process itself, or in various other kinds of theories that are dear to the heart of most leaders and are therefore willy-nilly crammed down the gullible gullets of most therapy group members. For a change, the prejudices of REBT will be able to prevail! In my thinking about the group and what form I would like to see it take before I actually begin working with it I would examine the general and specific goals of REBT and how they might best be implemented in this particular group.

Doing so, I see REBT as designed to help virtually all humans, and particularly intelligent ones, cope with their regular life problems and with their own tendencies to disturb themselves. I assume that virtually all college freshmen, in particular, are born and reared with a huge propensity to cause themselves needless emotional pain and turmoil, but they also have several significant innate healthy or rational tendencies, including the tendency to think, think about their thinking, be curious, learn, become aware of their own emotional disturbances, desire to change and actualize themselves, and be able to choose much of their future emotional and behavioral destiny. I therefore assume that just about all members of the present group will benefit from REBT and that some of them can be shown how to make profound changes in their thinking, emoting and behaving by learning and practicing its principles.

I would open the first session of the group by stating my goals in forming the group and would try to discover whether all or most of the members are willing to go along with these goals. I would say something like, 'Let me explain my main motives in forming this group. I think that all of you, as you have told me already in my individual talks with you, would like to contend more effectively with your new college environment and that you have the ability to learn to do so. As humans, you have some degree of free will, or choice, in the things you do – though let's not run this idea into the ground and piously claim that you are totally free! You, as humans, are somewhat limited by your heredity and your environment. You can't do anything you wish to do – even though you can do much of what you would like to carry out.

'One of your important limitations is that, in many ways, you often tend to think crookedly and behave dysfunctionally, and you do so mainly because that's the kind of creature you are – limited. Despite your intelligence and education, you still tend to think irrationally: to use absolutistic modes of thought; to believe in nonexistent magic; to observe poorly and often make anti-empirical conclusions about your observations; to make fairly frequent use of illogical cognitions, such as non-sequiturs, arbitrary inference and circular thinking; to deify and to 'devil-ify' yourself and other humans; and often to override your straight thinking with dogmas, overgeneralizations, bigotries, prejudices and superstitions.

'In terms of the form of psychotherapy and group therapy that I am going to employ with you in our subsequent sessions, all of you, like virtually all the rest of the human race, strongly tend to be intense *must*urbators. You mistakenly and quite self-defeatingly often think that, first, you absolutely must do well and be approved by others; second, that you *should* and *must* be dealt with considerately and fairly by the other people with whom you closely associate; and, third, that the world *ought to* and *must* provide you with conditions that give you, fairly easily and quickly, whatever you dearly want and refrain from giving you the things and situations that you consider highly obnoxious.

'Perhaps you can manage, because some of you are talented in this respect, to upset yourself emotionally without any use of imperatives like *must, should, ought, got to, have to* and *need*. Perhaps, but I doubt it. So far, whenever I have come across a disturbed person during almost 50 years of doing REBT, I have immediately been able to spot his or her *musts* that largely lead to this person's disturbance. And I have also found that the three main derivatives that people have as irrational ideas actually seem to stem from their basic *musts*. These derivatives are:

1. Since I *must* do well and be approved of by all the people I consider significant, it's *awful* if and when I don't!
2. I can't *stand* failing and being disapproved of by others, because I *must* not fail and *must* not be disapproved of!
3. Because I have failed and been disapproved of by my significant others, as I *must* not be, I am a *rotten person* who is not likely to do well at anything in the future and who really does not deserve good things.

'Now what we are going to do, in the course of these group therapy sessions, is to zero in on any or all of the things that bother you – or, in REBT terms, about which you choose to bother yourself. If you have problems in school, in your social affairs, in your love life, with your parents, or in any other area, I want you to bring them in – and we will work on them together. But, even more important, we will be interested in your problems *about* your problems. Thus, if you are doing poorly in your schoolwork, we will not only concern ourselves with ways in which you can do better but will also look at your feelings about this schoolwork – especially feelings of anxiety, depression, inadequacy, hostility or apathy. In REBT we define such feelings as unhealthy – meaning they do not help you to live happily and get more of what you want and less of what you don't want.

'This doesn't mean that we want you to be unfeeling and unemotional. Rational, in REBT, doesn't mean unemotional, calm, indifferent or passive. It means, usually, quite emotional – that is, vitally concerned with your own and others' well-being and feeling keenly sorry, regretful, disappointed, annoyed and irritated when things are not going well for you and those for whom you care. Rational also means strongly determined to change what you don't like in the world, including your own self-defeating feelings and acts; and it means willing to work for a happier, more fulfilled kind of existence.'

I would stop at this point and give the group members a chance to speak up and express themselves: to argue with me, to bring up other ideas, and especially to say what they would like to get out of the group sessions. I would have all of them try to bring up at least one problem that seems to be bothering them most at the present time: something on which they would like to work. I would have them briefly tell something about themselves – where they are from, why they came to college, what some of their main goals in life are, and the like.

I would then ask a member who is particularly bothered about something now – such as the problem of being relatively alone and friendless in this new college situation – to bring this up for discussion. I would also ask how many of the others felt similarly bothered. I would illustrate REBT to the group members, largely using this first individual's problem: showing her, for example, that she felt lonely at point C (emotional and behavioral conse-quence) after being in a situation at point A (activating experience) and that her new college situation, A, *did not* make her feel lonely, although it may have *contributed* to this feeling. I would try to show her (and the other group members) that she mainly chooses to upset herself, at point B (her belief system about what is happening at A), by *demanding* and *commanding* that a better situation exists, rather than merely *preferring* and wishing that it be better.

As I revealed to this group this woman's own irrational beliefs (at point B) with which she was creating her inappropriate feelings (of self-downing, hostility, and self-pity) at point C (consequence), I would also quickly start challenging these ideas and disputing them, at point D. Thus, I might show her that she was telling herself, at B, 'People *should* be more friendly to me in this new college environment! I *can't bear* their curtness and indifference! What a *terrible place* this is compared with the way things are at home!' I would try to help her dispute these irrational beliefs by asking her, 'Where is the evidence that people *should be* as friendly as you'd like them to be? In what way can't you *bear* their curtness and indifference? Assuming that things really are more difficult here than at home, how does that difficulty make this a terrible place? And I would try to get her, at least temporarily, to give up these self-defeating ideas.

While doing this, I would try to involve the other group members in disputing and challenging the member who brought up a specific problem.

In other words, I would get the group members immediately started on REBT problem-solving, discussing both of its aspects. First is discussing one's problem *about* a problem, or one's feelings of emotional upset when one experiences this problem; trying to see how it arises from one's own thinking or attitude toward the problem; and then making some concerted attempt to change that attitude and eliminate or minimize the emotional disturbance. The second aspect is, as the disturbance seems to be getting under one's control, going back to the original practical problem and trying to see how it can be solved. Thus, in the young woman's case, once she began to stop hating herself, hating others, and thinking of the school as a terrible place, the group would discuss with her what she could do about making more friends and being alone less. For example, she could speak more to the other students in her dormitory, meet with some of those in her class to study together, join some of the college clubs, and the like.

Before the session ended, I would hope that I had presented the main elements of REBT, and some of its usual goals, and illustrated some of its techniques by applying them to at least one major problem brought up in the group. I would also suggest an activity-oriented homework assignment to the member(s) whose problems we are trying to resolve. Thus, our lonely members might take the homework assignment of opening a conversation with at least three new people in the course of the next week. All members of the group might also be given a shame-attacking assignment, such as doing something they consider foolish, shameful or embarrassing, and working on their belief system so that they would not feel the usual degree of shame that they normally feel when doing this 'embarrassing' thing.

In this manner, I will be setting the stage for the group to have an ongoing experience of Rational Emotive Behavior Therapy. I would suggest that the members give it a chance for at least four or five sessions, to see what they can learn from it. However, if any members object seriously to the procedures that are used, they could discuss these objections from time to time and also choose to quit the group. If several of the group members want a quite different kind of group experience – such as a psychoanalytically oriented or an encounter-type experience – I would suggest that they still try this REBT group for a while and, if they are still dissatisfied, that they then try to find a group more amenable to their desires. I would not fall into the trap of seriously modifying the procedure that I usually follow in an REBT group because I personally believe in the effectiveness of that procedure. And if several or most of the group members really want to do something else, I think they should work with a leader who believes in that alternate kind of procedure.

Critical Incident 2: Group Attack of the Therapist

The group is made up of five couples. Initially, each couple had been seeing you separately. However, as you came to realize that their areas of concern had much in common, you asked each couple if they would be interested in joining a couples' group. You explained the rationale supporting your consideration for establishing the group, including the added value and benefits for recognizing behaviors that groups provide beyond meeting individually. They all volunteered to give it a try.

Briefly, the members are described as follows:

Couple 1   Nicholas and Lauri have been married for 15 years. They have two children, ages 10 and 13 years old. Nicholas is 35 years old, has a degree in engineering, and is employed as a design engineer. Laurie is 33 years old and has been a homemaker since they were married after graduating from. high school. Laurie has expressed a desire to go to college and has stated that she is not sure she wants to remain being just a homemaker. Nicholas is confused over this sudden turn in events.

Couple 2   Larry and Pamela have been married for two years. They have no children. Larry is 26 years old, has an associate degree, and is an associate with an ophthalmologist. Pamela is 25 years old and is employed as a registered nurse at the local hospital. When they first came to you, they stated that they were unhappy with their marriage but were not sure why.

Couple 3   Paul and Joan have been married for eight years. They have three children, ages 4, 6 and 7 years old. Paul is 34 years old, a high school graduate, and a self-employed plumber. Joan is 33 years old, has a master's degree in education, and teaches fourth grade at a local elementary school. Joan initiated their contact with you. When you first met them, the presenting issue was Joan's concern that Paul seemed to be avoiding her, and Paul had expressed that he was not happy.

Couple 4   John and Helen have been married for 10 years. This is Helen's second marriage. They have two children, ages 11 and 13 years old, both of whom are from Helen's first marriage. John is 40 years old, had attended college for three years, and now operates a printing company. Helen is 39 years old, a high school graduate, and is employed as a teacher's aide. She has stated that she wants to go to college. John has voiced opposition to this, and they have reached an impasse.

Couple 5   Peter and Doris have lived together for 10 years. They have two children, ages 4 and 6 years old. Peter is 31 years old and owns a florist shop. Doris is 31 years old, is a cosmetologist, and is employed by a department store. They came to you because they felt their relationship was not the same as it used to be.

The first two sessions had a great deal of activity. Member-to-member interaction seemed to develop easily. Early in session 2, the members engaged in a significant amount of disclosure and confrontation. It came about as a result of Nicholas's disclosure of his confusion about why his wife should want to go to school. He stated he felt that once she got a taste of it, she might want to go to work, and he questioned where this would all lead. As far as he was concerned, he felt their marriage was just fine the way it was, and he could not understand why it should change. As you listened to him, you observed how his wife was responding. She was sitting with her feet crossed in front of her and her arms and hands resting on her lap, with eyes looking toward her hands. Her face was expressionless. Your eyes shifted to the rest of the members. You could see John nodding as though he was agreeing with or understanding Nicholas's comments. His wife was looking at Laurie. Larry, Pamela, Paul and Joan were listening intently to Nicholas. He no sooner had completed his statement when Doris, with her voice sounding tense, stated, 'That sounded just like a man! All they ever think about is that because their wives are working, they might end up running around!' Before she was able to continue, her statement drew responses from the rest of the group. You observed (to yourself) that Laurie had not participated in the ensuing interaction. You determined it was perhaps too early to make this observation known and that perhaps Laurie would, in her own time, present herself. The emotional level of the group was still relatively high as you moved the session to termination.

At session 3, you notice that the members are very jovial and quite verbal as they enter the room. As a matter of fact, they continue to discuss a number of issues such as dieting, politics, and sports throughout the first 15 minutes of the session. You finally offer that you think this level of discussion is not dealing with the issues or purposes of the group and ask the members if they are aware of the direction their discussion has undergone. There is a brief silence in the group. Then one of the members attacks you for seeming to appear cool, distant and uncaring. With that, another states that she is beginning to question your qualifications as a therapist. The others join in the attack, each in turn questioning, in one form or another, your credibility as a therapist.

Albert Ellis's response

In terms of Rational Emotive Behavior Therapy (REBT), the situation is partly that of a cop-out: The members of the group are probably doing what they naturally and easily do – avoiding difficult problems and avoiding the issues or purposes of the group, for two reasons. First, it takes less effort on their part and second, it is easier for them to discuss whatever comes up and not get down to business. REBT sees this as the normal tendency of humans to have low frustration tolerance and to go for immediate satisfactions rather than long-range gains.

Therefore, as a group leader I expect this kind of thing to occur and to keep occurring. By luck, and probably not because I was doing very well myself as a leader during the first two sessions, Nicholas got to something important in his relations with his wife and showed that he was confused; and by luck, Doris reacted emotionally to Nicholas and showed her strong feeling about men dominating women in marriage and being over-concerned about their wives running around, rather than concerned about what their wives really want to do in life. This issue was not fully discussed, however, because time ran out so I would raise it again at session 3. More than one couple has expressed a problem with the wife's career goals conflicting with the husband's desire for the woman to stay with the old ways.

By session 3, I would realize that I had not structured the group process sufficiently and explained to the members that we are neither merely interested in their expression of feelings nor are we too interested in their discussing unimportant topics or questions irrelevant to therapy, such as politics and sports. I would therefore explain to the members the basic purpose of an REBT group: The group is here to bring out practical problems and emotional problems about these practical problems. I would also explain that the goal usually is to understand and resolve the emotional problems first and then to work, simultaneously, on the resolution of the practical marital and personal problems of the participants.

I would emphasize that one of the main purposes of the group is to help the members solve their marital difficulties as well as their personal difficulties and that because they all have somewhat similar problems in this respect we will try to explore those difficulties common to most of them and see what general, as well as individual, solutions can be arrived at. I would emphasize that this is an REBT-oriented group and that as leader, I expect to help all group members see that when they have practical marital problems, they almost always have an emotional problem or problem *about* the practical problem. The goal of group REBT is to help them see that they have some basic irrational beliefs directly causing or creating their disturbed emotional reactions. I would hope, therefore, that they disclose their emotional problems, look for the irrational beliefs that lie behind these problems, and dispute and surrender these beliefs.

I would then address the specific member who has attacked me for appearing cool, distant and uncaring in the following manner: 'Yes, John, you may well be right in accusing me of appearing cool, distant and uncaring. I think that I definitely care about your and the other group members' problems and disturbances, and I am very concerned about helping you with these difficulties. But that doesn't mean that I care, personally, about *you* – that I like you or love you or would want to have you as one of my close friends. Actually, with some of your pretty abominable behaviour – such as your hostility toward your wife and your business associates, which you have already spoken about – I'm not sure that I would want to be friendly with you at all, if I met you under social circumstances. I think I would find you bright and interesting and might well want to discuss certain issues with you – but I doubt if I would find you very friendly! If you worked on and got rid of that hostility of yours – yes, perhaps then I would. But right now, with the hostility you show toward others and even with the tone of voice you are now displaying toward me, about my supposed coolness – no, I don't think I would feel very friendly toward you.

'Besides, the purpose of group REBT is not to display friendship, love or warmth from the therapist to the group members, nor even from the group members to each other. If such warmth arises, as it sometimes does, fine. But love and warmth are not exactly group therapy and they are in fact often the reverse. One of the main things that people think they need – and I believe you are well in this class right now – is the undying and near-perfect approval of others. Well, they don't – they only *think* they do. Not that love and approval aren't nice; they definitely are! But *nice* doesn't mean *necessary*! If you want approval and you get it from others, great! That adds to your life. But if you think you *need*, you absolutely *must* have it you are really in trouble. You feel marvellous, of course, when you do get it and very upset and angry – as you and the group members seem to be showing right now – when you don't.

'One of the fundamental propositions of REBT is that people do not *need* what they *want*. Almost all their desires and preferences, however great, are legitimate; and almost all their *needs* and *necessities* lead to trouble. For if you want something very much and don't get it, you are merely keenly disappointed and sorry. But if you think you absolutely need it and don't get it you are destroyed: depressed, anxious, self-hating. So in REBT, we deliberately don't give therapeutic love, for that might encourage you to become a bigger baby than you already are! Unconditional acceptance, full respect for you as an individual, no matter how badly you may perform, is what we do try to give in REBT and also what we try to help individuals to give themselves and to all other humans.

'I am trying to help you – and all the other group members – to unconditionally, fully accept and respect *yourself*. And if I succeed, in spite of or even because of my 'coolness', I will encourage you to accept yourself *whether or not* I approve of you and *whether or not* you act very competently during your life. If I can help you see things that way, you'll really have it made! And the question of whether or not I approve of you or like you will be important, perhaps, but hardly vital.'

If John wanted to talk more about this, I would welcome his doing so. I would try to show him that his anger at me comes not from his desire for me to be a better therapist and not from his feeling sorry and frustrated that I am not – but from his demanding and commanding that I *must* be the kind of good therapist that he wants and that it is *terrible* and I am a *rotten person* if I am not.

At the same time, I would try to draw the other members of the group into his discussion and would attempt to show all of them (1) that I might well be right about my leadership of the group because I have been following, quite deliberately, an REBT pattern of group therapy that usually brings about excellent results with most group members; (2) that I might be wrong about my leadership because I really am an uncaring person and have been missing the boat in several important respects; (3) that even if I am wrong and uncaring, they do not have to put themselves down and make themselves panicked and depressed about my shortcomings as a group leader; and (4) that even if I am wrong and inept they do not have to anger themselves at me for having these failings but can instead regretfully decide that I am not the kind of leader they want and look elsewhere for another type of therapy or another type of REBT leader.

I might possibly, in the course of my talking to the members of the group, deliberately feign anger at and strongly criticize one of them for 'wrongly' being opposed to me. Then I would suddenly stop my verbal attack, especially if the person I picked on became upset and started to attack me back, and show that I had feigned anger as an emotive exercise, to draw out the attacked person's (and the other group members') reactions. We would then explore some of these reactions in detail, see whether various members had felt very hurt or angry at my tirade, show them exactly what they had been telling themselves to create these disturbed feelings, and indicate what they could do to dispute and challenge their irrational beliefs and to rid themselves of these feelings.

I would also try to give some or all of the group members a homework assignment – perhaps one in which they deliberately courted the companionship of a cold, distant, uncaring person, let themselves feel anxious, depressed, self-pitying, or angry when in this person's presence and then work on these disturbed feelings and try to change them into more healthy negative feelings of sorrow, disappointment frustration, and annoyance.

In the above way, I would try to show the group what the REBT version of group therapy is and how it differs from some other forms of treatment. I would try to show them that as REBT firmly posits, A (activating experiences) do not directly lead to or cause C (disturbed emotional consequences). The more direct and important cause or contribution to C is B (people's belief systems about what is happening to them at A).

I would illustrate to them, moreover, in general, and from the events and feelings occurring to them in the group, that their beliefs, at B, almost invariably are of two kinds when they feel disturbed at *C*. First, they have a set of rational Beliefs (*rB*s), which consists of preferences or desires. For example: 'I don't like the leader's behavior! I wish he didn't act that way! What a pain in the neck!' These *rB*s tend to lead them to feel healthy consequences (*hC*s), such as feelings of sorrow, regret, disappointment and annoyance. Second, they have a set of irrational beliefs (*iB*s), which consists of commands or demands. For example: 'The leader *must* not behave the way that he does! How *awful!* I *can't stand* his behaving in that manner! What a horrible leader and a *terrible person* he is!' These *iB*s tend to lead them to feel unhealthy consequences (*uC*s), such as hurt, self-downing, hostility, or self-pity.

I would then show the group members what I had neglected to show them previously: Their irrational, self-defeating beliefs are only hypotheses and not facts, and they can actively and vigorously dispute these hypotheses at point *D*. *D*, or disputing of irrational beliefs, is the scientific method of asking themselves such questions as 'Where is the evidence that the leader must not behave the way he does? Prove that it is awful if he acts badly or inefficiently. In what way can't I stand his behaving poorly, against my and the group's interest? Where is it written that he, because he acts badly, is a terrible person?'

Asking these questions, they would then arrive at *E*, a new effective philosophy. *E* is a realistic acceptance of the way the world (or at least, the group members' world) is. If they would correctly answer their own disputational questions at *D*, they would usually arrive at *E*, along these lines: 'Yes, the leader of this group has probably behaved in an ineffectual, incorrect manner as fallible humans often behave; consequently, he will sometimes continue to act that badly and to lead the group poorly in the future. Too bad! Although I'll never like being inconvenienced by him and his actions, I definitely can stand them and can continue to live and to be relatively happy despite his incompetent performances!'

Notice that the REBT assumptions – like those of most other psychotherapies, but perhaps a little more honestly and openly – are that no matter what goes on in the group (or in the lives of the members when they are outside the group) and no matter how poorly and foolishly the leader acts in the course of the group process, the members still *upset themselves* not by taking something seriously or making it important but by taking it too seriously and making it all important or *sacred*. Virtually everything, therefore, that happens inside or outside the group can be used as a focal point to show any individual member or all the members that they are irrationally creating their own feelings of anxiety, depression, hostility, worthlessness, apathy and self-pity and that they can choose to think, feel and behave much more effectively, in accordance with their own personal goals and values.

Once this idea of people's *self*-conditioning and the *self*-choosing of the way they react to 'obnoxious' stimuli is accepted by group members, they can then be helped to go back to *A*, their activating experiences, and either see them differently (with less prejudice) or try to change them. In this present instance, once I help John and the others see that, however badly I behaved, they do not have to upset themselves about my performance, they will be in a position to see more accurately whether I really did behave that poorly. If I had not acted badly, then they could look into their own hearts and change their own feelings about my 'bad' leadership. And if I had, they could determinedly and undisturbedly try to show me the error of my ways and to get me to change. Or, finally, they could decide that staying in the group was hardly worth their while and could individually or collectively quit.

REBT, then, attempts to help the group members identify their own disturbed thoughts, emotions, and behaviors and to change them and then to consider changing the situation they are in. It does not merely focus on one of these two goals but on both of them. It stresses the constructivist view that people are largely self-disturbers and have the ability to creatively undisturb themselves and also solve their practical life problems.

Critical Incident 3: Mass Group Denial

One of the head nurses from a large hospital in your community has contacted you. She informs you that a group of ten student nurses for whom she is responsible has expressed concern over personal difficulties in dealing with terminally ill patients and their families. She asks you to help. You agree to meet with the nurses as a group over a period of time.

This is session 4. Until now, the group has been dealing with a variety of issues that are not directly related to the primary purpose for coming together. Topics range from how they chose nursing as a career, complaints about the training schedule, insensitivity of some senior nurses, the rewarding experiences they had in the maternity wing, and the like. You observe that today Jean has been rather silent and that when she does speak it is usually to agree with something one of the others has said. This is not her usual way of behaving; typically, she has been an initiator and very active contributor in group discussions. Suddenly, without warning, she blurts out that she does not think the group is truly aware of what nursing is really about and that what they have been dealing with is very safe and neat stuff. The other side, the real side, has a lot of sadness. Her voice is quivering, and she is shaking as she continues to relate to the group the incident she had faced today. A ten-year-old boy to whom she had been assigned, and for whom she had developed a great fondness, died from leukemia shortly before the meeting. Part of her responsibility is to report the youth's death and to be with the attending physician when he or she informs the child's parents. The group fell silent. This is the first time any of them had directly approached the topic of death.

As you observe the silence, your eyes search out each member. You can see that Jean's outpouring apparently has the effect of immobilizing the group. You are about to intervene with a comment about what you have just been observing, when Diane says that the doctor of one of her patients has informed her that the patient has been responding very positively to new treatment. With that, Tom says that he is glad he is having this experience because it helps him realize that he wants to specialize in pediatrics. Julie nods her head as though she were in agreement with Tom. It is not long before the group's discussion seems to be moving away from Jean's disclosure. It is obvious to you that Jean's statement presents an issue that poses a threat to them. You know it is an important topic that needs to be dealt with, but it is clear that the group is avoiding it.

Albert Ellis's response

I would assume, on the basis of Rational Emotive Behavior Therapy (REBT) theory and group therapy in general, that the members of this group are unwilling to deal with the serious issue raised by Jean, but that it probably would be better for them to face it and thereby help themselves and each other come to some kind of resolution about it. The main REBT assumption I would have is that people shy away from discussions of death, their own and others', largely because they have low frustration tolerance. Individuals do not want to accept (1) the fact that, to be afforded the boon of living, we also have to die; and (2) that death is sad and deplorable but not 'horrible', 'awful', or 'depressing'.

Humans naturally and easily tend to believe that death is *awful* because (1) we are born with a tendency to whine about and refuse to accept some of the grimmest realities of our lives; and (2) we are reinforced in these irrational beliefs and reactions by cultural phenomena, such as the teachings of our family, church, mass media, teachers and the like.

The assumption of REBT, on the contrary, is that humans are almost all capable of accepting what they do not like: of facing the harshness and hassles of their existence and gracefully lumping them. We are 'existentially anxious' in the face of dying and death, in the sense that we are virtually all seriously *concerned* about these phenomena and want to do our best to ward them off as long as we can. We have self-preservation drives, partly of a biological nature and partly taught, that motivate us to take death quite seriously and to take precautions against its early occurrence. But our 'anxiety' about it is only existential in the sense that we virtually all feel it. It is not self-preserving, as is deep concern, and it can largely be reduced. 'Anxiety', in REBT terms, is *over*concern or *needless* concern: namely the idea that any unusual hassle or death *should* not, *must* not exist; that it is *awful* when it does; that people *cannot stand* the thought of it; and that the world is a *horrible place* when it inevitably presents obstacles and difficulties of this sort to people.

Although REBT does not therefore try to interfere with concern, cautiousness, or vigilance, it does try to separate these feelings and actions from those of anxiety, obsessiveness with life and safety, and panic. In the group in question, my assumption would be that the members are largely panicked about the thought of (1) dying themselves and (2) the death of their loved ones or their patients. They therefore submerge or squelch this state of panic by refusing to look at the problems that Jean is presenting, and they go back to the same kinds of relatively trivial issues being discussed before Jean 'uncomfortably' raised the topic of death. Although they are quite entitled to do this and to avoid thinking about death if that is what they really want to do, a healthier reaction would be for them to face this issue, deal with Jean's concerns and their own problems regarding it and then 'drop' it largely *because* they have dealt with it and not because they have swept it under the rug.

In an instance like this, where some would say that the group members have 'unconsciously' copped out and avoided the issue of dying, the REBT therapist would agree that this is probably true but would not see their 'unconscious' reaction as one that is exceptionally deep-seated or unavailable to consciousness. Instead, REBT would assume (as I would) that they have semiconsciously (or what Freud originally called 'preconsciously') squelched this issue and that they could fairly easily look at it again and bring it to their consciousness. So, I would make an attempt to get them to do this: to bring the issue of death to their consciousness again and deal with it experientially and philosophically, until they overcome their irrational beliefs about it.

I would open up discussion of this problem by saying something like this to the group: 'I find it very interesting that you are pretty much ignoring the problem of death that Jean has raised and that you are going back to discussing what would seem to be less important and less emotion-filled issues. I am wondering whether there is something you consider 'too uncomfortable' about this problem to deal with. Of course, some or all of you may really have faced it squarely in your own life and resolved it. But I wonder whether you, like Jean, have some real problems when one of your patients dies and whether you are not avoiding dealing with these problems.'

I would assume that, having directly raised this issue, some or all group members would admit to having some problems dealing with issues of dying and that some of them would recognize that they had deliberately avoided the topic that Jean raised, going back to discussing less important things. If so, I would then say, 'Why do you think that you have so much trouble in dealing with the issue of death? What are you telling yourself when you think about it – as you momentarily did before when Jean raised the issue – and then sweep it under the rug?' By this kind of questioning, I would expect some of the group members to admit that they were horrified about death, that they did think it must not exist and that they could not bear to discuss it openly. I would expect these members to say it was very unfair that they and their loved ones had to die some day and that the world was a pretty awful place for having this kind of unfairness in it.

As they brought out these ideas, I would actively dispute and challenge them, and I would try to get them to question each other's irrationalities in this respect. I would ask, 'Where is the evidence that death *must* not exist?'; and I would try to get them to see that it is really inevitable and *has* to exist, if it does. I would ask, 'What makes it *awful* or *terrible* if you or one of your loved ones dies?'; and I would try to show them that it is only highly inconvenient, only very sad – but not 'awful', meaning *more than* inconvenient or sad and more unfortunate than it *should* be. I would ask them to prove that they *can't stand, can't bear* the thought of dying or having one of their loved ones die and attempt to demonstrate that, no matter how much they dislike or feel greatly displeased about it, they definitely can stand it and can even experience a great deal of happiness while they still live on after their loved one has died. Finally, I would ask, 'Why is the world a *terrible place* and life hardly *worth living at all* in view of the fact that we all die and cannot avoid this possibility?' I would attempt to help them see that this is not true: The world is a place where bad things exist – but is not itself, or in its entirety, *terrible* – and that as long as they live, they almost certainly *can* enjoy themselves to some considerable degree, even after suffering the loss of loved ones.

I would, in other words, actively try to help almost all the members of the group see that they are not merely concerned or sad about death and dying but that they are distinctly *over*concerned and exceptionally anxious. I would show them exactly which irrational beliefs are giving them this overconcern and show them how to learn the REBT methods of logically and empirically disputing, questioning, challenging and surrendering these beliefs. I would hope, in the process of my dialogue with the group members (and I would expect to be actively and directively engaging in a Socratic-type dialogue with the group as a whole, or at least with several of them), that I would jolt some of their current ideas about dying and death and help them get on the road of a more rational, self-helping philosophy of death. In the course of my talking with the group members, I would assume that many of their 'hidden' or 'unexpressed' concerns would surface (especially as they backed up each other with irrational ideas) and that some of these would begin, at least, to be worked through.

To get back to Jean's problem and to show the members of the group that their fear of death was not the only issue involved, I would at some point take the conversation back to Jean by saying, 'You seem very sad about the death of the ten-year-old boy who was your patient. I can well understand that since I am sure that you became rather attached to him during the past several weeks and that you also feel exceptionally sorry about the death of any ten-year-old boy, especially from a disease like leukemia. But I would like you to get in touch with your sadness for a short while and tell me what it really feels like, and particularly tell me if it is only sadness or sorrow about the boy.'

Jean, in getting in touch with her actual feelings, would probably reveal other feelings, such as depression, guilt and anger. If this were so, I would say something like, 'Well, I can easily see how you would feel depressed. Most people, having gone through what you have just gone through, would feel about the same. But, perhaps very peculiarly, I would say that they were self-defeating and that you are too, when feeling depressed. I would contend that you – and they – are healthily sad or sorrowful, but that you are unhealthily depressed. Do you know why I would say this?'

The group up to this point has apparently not been taught REBT principles, so Jean is not likely to know why I consider sorrow and sadness healthy but depression unhealthy. If she acknowledged confusion, I would say, 'Your sadness springs from your relief that it is most unfortunate, very bad that this ten-year-old boy has died of leukemia; that it is unfortunate for him, his parents and you. And that is correct; we could rightly and empirically say that it is unfortunate. The boy wanted to live, his parents wanted him to live, and you certainly wanted him to live. And you are all not getting what you wanted and are getting just about the opposite. It is therefore most unfortunate, sad or regretful that this frustrating set of conditions exists; and you and his parents would definitely be foolish if you concluded that it was good or even unimportant. But depression – yours or theirs – comes from an extra, irrational idea that this unfortunate, sorry state of affairs *should not, must not* exist, that it is *awful* that it does exist and that human life is pretty *horrible* and *useless* when such unfortunate events exist. Isn't that what you're really telling yourself – that the death of the boy *should* not have occurred and that it is *awful* that it did?'

Assuming that Jean admitted that she was telling herself something like this, I would show her that it is not the activating experience (*A*) of the boy's death that is creating her emotional consequence (*C*) of depression; rather, it is her irrational beliefs (*B*) *about* this experience that are making her depressed. And I would show her how she could change these beliefs to rational or coping beliefs, such as 'I wish that boy had not died, but he inevitably did. Too bad! But I can definitely *stand* his cruel death even though I'll never like it nor similar deaths of young children' and 'The world is a place in which bad things like this will always to some extent exist, but it is not *totally* bad; it still has a lot of good, enjoyable things in it. And as long as I still live, I can definitely lead a good, enjoyable existence.'

I would try to get the other group members to join in with me, as we all tried to talk Jean out of, not her feelings of sorrow and sadness, but those of depression. Also, if she were guilty or angry, I would show her how she was needlessly creating these feelings – and how the happenings of her life, or what she had done or not done about them, were not the real issue. In getting the group members to help me show Jean that she was healthily sad and unhealthily depressed, guilty or angry about the boy's death, I would be helping them face the problem that they have so far avoided – dealing with death. I would presumably also help some of them with their own expressed or unexpressed feelings of depression, guilt or anger about death.

As this was going on, or after much of it had been completed, I would go back to the group's problem of ignoring the issue of death. I would try to show them that such defensive behavior covers up their underlying anxieties and that if they faced these anxieties by finding their philosophic source and changing their philosophies so as not to make themselves minimally anxious, they could deal much better with their emotional and practical problems.

In several ways then, I would take the current group situation, make a dramatic issue of it and almost force the group members to expose, confront and start to change their disturbed feelings. I would also give them some desensitizing homework assignments such as recording all their thoughts about death, visiting a morgue, or discussing death openly with a friend or with relatives of dying or dead patients. I might also give them the emotive exercise of rational emotive imagery. I would ask them to think about a close friend or relative's death, let themselves feel disturbed (depressed or anxious) about this intensely imagined fantasy; change their feeling to one of keen disappointment, sorrow or regret but not depression or anxiety; see what went on in their heads to effect this change in feeling; and then practice doing this same exercise for, say, 30 consecutive days until they could automatically think about death and *only* or *mainly* feel sorry and regretful but not severely upset.

In various cognitive, emotive and behavioral ways, therefore, I would work with this group on facing the problem of their own and others' death and of feeling appropriately about this. REBT group therapy is one of the few forms of therapy that specifically tries to show group members the difference between healthy negative emotions of sorrow, regret, frustration and annoyance and the unhealthy negative emotions of depression, anxiety, despair, hostility and worthlessness. The group sessions and experiences would be employed largely as an educational device to dramatically help the members think about, feel about and work on their disturbed reactions to death and dying.

Critical Incident 4: A Group Member Chooses to Leave

This group is composed of four men and four women. Initially, members of this group had come to you individually because they felt unhappy with their lot in life. They felt fate had dealt them a poor hand. They presented themselves to you in ways that expressed a low sense of personal worth. Recognizing that they all seemed to have symptoms of low self-esteem, you invited them to join together in a group to deal with what appeared to be a common area of concern. Briefly, the members are described as follows:

Deborah is 22 years old. She is single, holds an associate degree from the local community college, and is employed as a legal secretary.

Peggy is 23 years old. She has been married for 6 years and has three children ranging in ages from two to six years old. She listed her occupation as homemaker.

Jean, short and heavy in stature, is 34 years old and married. She had dropped out of school, after tenth grade. She drives a school bus.

Andrea is 28 years old and recently divorced. She had interrupted her college education eight years ago in order to help her then-husband pursue his doctorate degree. She presently feels at a loss as to where to pick up her life.

Jim is 25 years old. He is single and was recently discharged from the army. He works as an automobile salesman until he can decide what he wants to do with his life.

Bob is 35 years old and married. He was referred to you by his family physician, who was concerned with the disclosures Bob had made about feeling 'trapped and not going anywhere'.

Ron is 32 years old. Recently divorced, he feels his marriage was a disaster. He feels worthless because most everything in his life seems to go the same way as his marriage.

John is 30 years old and is in his second marriage. He was unable to bring his wife with him when he first visited you. He explained that he feels lost in his marriage and is afraid it is going to end as the first one had.

This is session 5. The first three meetings saw the group move through the initial stages of development, which included orientation, resistance, conflict (questions about trust) and a struggle for power and confrontation. Toward the end of session 4, there seemed to be signs of group cohesiveness and a readiness for self-disclosure. Peggy, for example, expressed her disillusionment with her present roles of mother and wife. She said she was unhappy with herself and felt powerless to do anything about it. The group seemed ready to listen to her and willing to offer its thoughts on how she might be able to work out her problem. Andrea disclosed some deep-seated feelings of resentment toward her ex-husband, especially over the way he ignored the sacrifice she made on his behalf. In a similar way, the group appeared receptive to Andrea and demonstrated a willingness to offer assistance to work through her difficulty. This activity had the effect of encouraging other group members, including Bob and Ron, to risk disclosure as well.

Much of what had begun in session 4 carried over into this session. Early in the meeting, Ron begins by stating how much he values the group's willingness to hear him out and that he has given much consideration to their suggestions. He no sooner completes his remarks when John, taking advantage of the very brief silence, announces to the group that he is making this his last session. He says he plans not to return after tonight's meeting. You quickly note the effect his words have upon the group members and that they appear quite stunned.

Albert Ellis's response

I would assume that most of the members feel stunned by their sense of being rejected or deserted by John's withdrawal from the group, for two reasons: (1) These group members are all humans, and virtually all humans are exceptionally prone to feelings of inadequacy and self-downing; and (2) these particular individuals have been placed in this group because they all seem to have 'symptoms of low self-esteem'.

They are probably putting themselves down for not having been more effective in the course of the group process, thereby not helping John enough to keep him as a group member. They are perhaps angry at John for not giving them more of a chance and perhaps also angry at the group leader for not getting things more organized sooner so that John would not quit the group. Because John is also human, and perhaps a typical member of this self-flagellating group of individuals, I would assume that his quitting has something to do with his own feelings of inadequacy and hopelessness. Just as he feels lost in his second marriage and concluded that it is going to end as the first one had, he also feels lost in this group process and has concluded that he is going nowhere in it and is wasting his time by staying.

I might first check out my assumptions by asking John his reasons for leaving the group. If he had 'legitimate' reasons, I would mainly acknowledge these, tell him that the group will probably continue without him, and invite him to rejoin if and when he feels inclined to do so. Even more important, however, because I know that the group members appear 'stunned', I would probably work first with them and their emotional problems. I would assume that 'stunned' mainly means panicked and self-flagellating; I would spend time checking to see if there is evidence behind my assumption.

If it proves that the members are indeed panicked and self-downing, I would take it that this is *not* directly caused by John's proposed desertion of the group but by their overinvolved, personalized and irrational reaction to that desertion. In accordance with Rational Emotive Behavior Therapy (REBT) theory, I would assume that the activating experience (*A*) of the group members, John's desertion, contributes to but by no means 'causes' *C*, their emotional consequences of shock, horror and worthlessness. Rather, *B* (their irrational beliefs) about *A* are mainly 'causative' of *C*.

I would more precisely tell myself, 'The group members are probably assuming that they have done something wrong to merit John's desertion; that they *should* not, *must* not have done this wrong thing; that it is awful that they did; and that they are *pretty rotten* persons for having done it. These neurotic evaluations or conclusions are driving them to a state of panic.' I would find methods to get them to see this and to give up their absolutistic *musts* and consequent self-damnation in order for them to accept themselves with their wrongdoings, assuming that these have actually occurred.

I would also assume that, if the group members are indeed angry toward John or the group leader, they are foolishly *making themselves* irate about these people's 'inequities' and that they can be taught, through the use of REBT, not to enrage themselves about this or about virtually anything else. I would be determined to show them what they are needlessly doing in this respect and how to make themselves less angry and, instead, only sorry and annoyed about John's or the leader's behavior.

I would ask myself where my interventions were likely to do the most good and what specifically these interventions could be. I would, probably choose the group itself, rather than John, as the focal point of these interventions. I would do this for several reasons: (1) The purpose of REBT is to help as many people as possible in the most efficient manner, and helping seven group members seems more important to me than only or mainly helping John; (2) in focusing on the group members rather than on John, he might feel relatively unthreatened and therefore listen better to the REBT problem-solving process and be as much or even more helped than some of the other members; (3) John may well have made up his mind to quit already, and trying to help him at this stage might prove useless; and (4) if time permitted, the first focus on helping the other group members might be shifted back to John so that he might be focused on, too.

Although the group members might be both angry and self-downing about John's proposed desertion, I would probably choose to focus on the latter rather than the former emotional difficulty. For one thing, it seems more important because it is related to the basic problems of virtually all group members. For another, it is less dramatic (though perhaps deeper) and less likely to get the group members off on a melodramatic tangent, which would stir up their feelings, all right, but quite possibly sidetrack them from understanding what is going on in their heads and hearts and from doing anything definite about it.

Shuttling back between dealing with, first, the emotional disturbance of panic and, second, that of anger is not considered de rigueur in REBT. Because we have a kind of quadratic equation with two unknowns, anger and panic, understanding and resolving either of these disturbances are likely to be impeded by dealing simultaneously with both. I would therefore concentrate on only one of these emotions first and would probably choose self-downing behavior as a place to start.

This group has apparently been given no behavioral homework assignments as yet (because who knows what muddled theory of group therapy its present leader is following!), so I would think in terms of in vivo desensitization assignments, both within the group itself and with outside assignments between sessions. On this particular occasion, I would begin this desensitization process by trying to incorporate some of it in this very session in which I am about to intervene.

I would start by addressing the group members along the following lines: 'You seem positively stunned by John's announcement that he is about to leave the group. Am I right about this? How, exactly, do you feel about the fact that this is going to be his last session?' I would then get more details of their feelings, including, probably, rage, depression, hopelessness, inadequacy and panic. If so, I would first zero in on those involving self-recrimination and self-downing: 'It looks like several of you are blaming yourselves for not having managed to build an effective group and therefore not helping John enough. Now, we could argue this point: No matter what kind of a group you build and how effective it generally is, John might not accept help or might not allow himself to benefit from it. But let's suppose the worst: You really haven't worked hard enough to weld yourself into an efficient and helpful group, and John is rightfully quitting because he has got little help from you. If so, why *must* you have been more efficient? Where is the evidence that it is *awful* that you haven't been? In what way can't you stand being so inept? How does your poor group behavior prove that you are basically rotten people?'

In other words, I would show these group members that they were needlessly upsetting themselves about John's desertion of the group and indicate how they irrationally – at point *B* (belief system) – *mustur*bated, awfulized, and put themselves down as humans for their (assumedly) poor and nontherapeutic behavior. I would try to convince them that no matter how legitimately they were assessing their *deeds* and *performances*, they were illegitimately rating themselves for these poor performances. And I would teach them, through individual and collective dialogue, to actively challenge and dispute each other's faulty thinking. I would attempt to get all of them – or at least as many as will dare to change their fundamental philosophies of life – to give up ego- and self-evaluation and to keep their identity or the power to choose more of what they want and less of what they do not want. Otherwise stated, I would attempt to help them enjoy rather than 'prove' themselves.

In attempting this (almost Herculean!) task, I would specify emotive and behavioral exercises for the group members. For an emotive exercise, for example, I might deliberately have John vent his spleen on them and tell them how much he despised them for not being very helpful to him or to themselves. As the group members made themselves enraged or ashamed in the face of his tirade, I would try to help them change their feelings of rage to annoyance and from shame to disappointment and help them see that they could probably only do this by radically changing their cognitions. Thus, if one of them first felt enraged at *John* and later only frustrated by John's *behavior*, he or she would probably be internally saying, 'It really is too bad that John doesn't appreciate the help we've been trying to give him and that he is copping out by quitting the group before he gives us more of a chance to reach him. But that's his prerogative; and there is no reason why he *has* to give us a full hearing.' And if another member first felt ashamed at John's tirade and then only disappointed by it he or she might later think, 'Maybe John is right and I did not do everything I could to understand and help him. That's poor behavior on my part and I'd better do something about it. But I am entitled to my errors, fallible human that I am, and there is no necessity for me to be less fallible and to help John.' Seeing and practicing these new cognitions, after they had temporarily changed their unhealthy feelings (rage and shame) to healthy ones (frustration and disappointment), would then help these group members to feel less enraged and less shameful when new difficulties arose in their lives.

In terms of behavioral assignments, if Andrea (let us say) was very angry at John for not speaking up sooner and letting the group know how he felt about its ineffectiveness, I (with the collaboration of the group) might suggest the assignment of her deliberately keeping in close touch with her ex-husband, at whom she might also be angry, and working on her feelings until she only disliked his behavior and refused to condemn him totally for his behavior. And if Ron was notably self-downing because he felt that he and the group had not helped John sufficiently, I and the group might suggest the homework assignment of disclosing to his friends some particularly foolish acts he had recently done and working on not putting himself down in case they laughed at and denigrated him for these activities,

After dealing with group members individually and collectively, and after trying to see that they really understood that John was not upsetting them and that they had the choice of reacting in healthy or unhealthy ways to his leaving the group, I would try to spend some time helping John with his problem of wanting to quit the group. Assuming, again, that he did not have very good reasons for doing so and that he was falsely concluding that he could not possibly be helped by the group, I would first try to show him that this was a dubious assumption. He certainly might not be helped because of his own and the group's inadequacies, but there was no evidence that getting help was impossible and that under no conditions would he be able to receive it or use it.

In the process of doing so, I would try to show John that – something like the reaction of the other members of the group – he was putting himself down and concluding that, because he had failed in the past, he would *always* and *only* fail; that he was essentially a *rotten person*; and that, as such, he really deserved to keep failing and had no possibility of succeeding at therapy or almost anything else in the future. I would actively dispute (point D) these irrational beliefs (at point B) and would try to show him how to dispute them himself, outside of the therapy. As in the case of the other group members, I would try to devise (with John's help) some emotive and behavioral exercises that would also motivate and encourage him to make a basic philosophic change in his attitudes toward himself.

Thus, I might use rational emotive imagery, in the course of which John would imagine himself seriously failing at some important task and being rejected by others for failing. After he imagined this, and probably felt severely depressed, and after he was in solid touch with these feelings, I would get him to change them to feelings of keen sorrow and regret but not depression. When he had achieved this, he would practice, perhaps every day for 30 or more days, this process of rational emotive imagery to reinforce these more healthy feelings whenever he thought about failing or actually did fail at some project that he considered important.

If time permitted (or in subsequent group sessions), I would work with group members (and with John, if he decided to stay in the group) on their feelings of anger at John, at the group leader, and at the others. REBT clearly distinguishes between people's healthy feeling of being highly annoyed and irritated at the displeasing acts of others and their unhealthy total condemnation of these others as humans. It helps clients make this kind of distinction and feel and express intense displeasure or annoyance without being globally intolerant of the people who exhibit annoying *qualities*.

Would I, in the course of leading this session, neglect some important elements of the group process? Yes, I probably would, for I am not interested – except from a research or general psychological point of view – in group process half so much as I am interested in helping group members. Humans normally live in groups and are healthily and unhealthily affected by group processes. My job, as a psychotherapist, is to help them live more happily; incidental to this goal is understanding what is going on in the group process. More important, I want to understand the group members and how to intervene to teach these members to overcome their emotional disturbances.

Critical Incident 5: A Deep Disclosure Near Session Termination

The group is heterogeneous in composition. During the preinterview sessions, the presenting areas of concern were somewhat similar. The group members appear to be having difficulty dealing with the significant others in their lives. Their relationships seem to be shallow and have very little meaning. The reason they sought you out was to find some way of bringing significance and value back into their personal lives. They all seem tired of bobbing like corks aimlessly on the sea of life.

The membership of the group is composed of five women and three men, ranging in ages from 28 to 45 years old. Briefly, they are described as follows:

Sally is 28 years old, single, and holds a bachelor's degree in biology. She is a laboratory technician and is engaged to be married.

Francine is 34 years old divorced, and has custody of her two children. She is employed as a cocktail waitress.

Janet is 39 years old, married and childless. She is employed as an elementary school teacher.

Sarah is 43 years old. Her husband is a pediatrician, and they have three children; two of them are in college. Sarah has returned to college to get her master's degree in psychology.

Sandra is 45 years old. Her four children have completed college and are on their own. She appears uncertain about the direction her life is going to take. Her husband has three more years before he retires on a very substantial income at age 65.

Samuel is 29 years old. He is married but is living separately from his wife. He is a successful sales representative for an international brokerage house.

Jonathan is 32 years old. He owns a very successful insurance agency in town. He has completed four years of college at the local university.

Franklin is 28 years old. He married his high school sweetheart 11 years ago. He has three profitable gas stations throughout the area and is president of the Chamber of Commerce.

During the first six sessions, which lasted for an hour each, much time was spent exploring each other's values, motives for joining the group, and the like. Before any of the members joined the group, you had told them that there were five or six other persons who seemed to be expressing similar concerns, and if they wanted, they could volunteer to join the group. The expressed goal, or purpose, was to share and perhaps work out what appeared to be barriers to enjoying more effective and meaningful personal lives. All members appeared quite agreeable to cooperate and join. Their general attitude was that they would like to do 'anything' to get themselves out of the holes they felt they had dug for themselves and thus bring them closer to the people they felt they have a deep love for.

Through sessions 1–6, the group had been relatively open. The members tended toward establishing acquaintanceships (orientation) during the first three meetings. Francine seemed ready and willing to move into personal disclosures. This proved threatening to the majority of the members. You observed their uneasiness in their rapid movement away from Francine to topics that seemed away from and outside the group. Jonathan, for example, preferred to talk about the difficult time he has had building up his insurance business – the amount of hours spent on identifying new clients, advertising and public relations. Franklin discussed the difficulty he has contending with the major oil corporation (his supplier) in order to sustain his business. Samuel expressed more personal feelings early in session 4 when he disclosed his discomfort and sense of personal failure for not making a 'proper go' of his marriage. His confusion is further pronounced because none of the members has appeared to have heard him.

Sarah seems to have demonstrated an ability to keep her involvement at an intellectual level and maintain her wits about her. Her disclosures have been very carefully articulated throughout the first six sessions. She has stated on numerous occasions that she believes she and her husband have an 'understanding'. She has her life to live and whatever she chooses to do is all right with him, as long as it does not interfere with or disrupt the medical practice he has so diligently developed.

It is now the seventh session (week) and Sandra, who has remained rather silent over the past six weeks, has been fidgeting and looking extremely restless throughout the first 45 minutes. You are about to make movements to bring the group from an effectively oriented process to prepare them for the session's termination. Sandra has been a very quiet and inactive member of the group. You have attended to this form of nonverbal involvement on her part and felt it would be just a matter of time before she would choose the appropriate moment for herself to actively (vocally) participate. Of course, tonight's session was not very different from previous sessions in which the group had moved rapidly from socializing to confronting. Members appeared to be establishing some overall cohesiveness when suddenly, without any warning, Sandra burst forth. Her exclamation is mixed with blame, bitterness, anger and hostility for her lot in life. On the face of it, it appears she is directing all of her feelings toward the group. She claims no one seems to care about her anymore. They all just seem to be 'takers' who never give anything back. She is tired of giving herself for nothing and not being appreciated. After all, she has her own life to live too. She speaks directly to Jonathan when she says that all he seems to care about is his business and it appears that no one else in his life seems to matter. As she continues to ventilate, her disclosure subsides into deep sobs, and tears roll down her cheeks. She is visibly shaken by all that she had just experienced and said, and she is trembling. As your eyes scan the members, you (the leader) recognize how immobilized the group has become. They have sunk into complete silence. All of them turn their eyes from Sandra and are looking at the floor, fidgeting with their fingers, at a loss for what to do or say.

Albert Ellis's response

This critical incident is quite predictable in groups that are non-directively misled in the manner that this one has been up to now. The therapist who has not only not been trained in typical psychoanalytic, experiential or client-centered therapy but also has unfortunately gone along with this non-directive method, does not seem to have the foggiest idea about how people often block themselves from enjoying a more effective and meaningful personal life. The therapist also does not appear to have any notion of what an effective group leader can do to help the members unblock themselves in this respect. Consequently, he or she is too *helpful* and so is desperately hoping against hope that the group members will somehow muddle through and magically help themselves. As normally happens under these dismal conditions, these members have nicely wasted virtually all their time in the group and have been beautifully diverted from helping themselves in almost any way. Almost all of them are probably now the worse for needless wear and tear and more confused about their goals in life and how to achieve them than they were when they began this form of 'therapy'.

Sandra, being older than the rest, and perhaps recognizing that her precious time is being wasted away in this kind of group process, complains bitterly, in her own natural ineffective way, about what has been going on in the group. Rather than blame the group leader (who she thinks might possibly attack her back), she blames the group in general. This may well represent her usual tendency to blame external people and events instead of squarely shouldering the responsibility for her own thoughts, emotions and actions; or it may represent the fact that she accurately sees that she has been done in to some extent by this inefficient group process. Of course, Sandra has passively and silently consented to this situation for the last several sessions, and now she knows no better way to vent her feelings about this inefficient group process than to whine and scream. Usually, she does this internally, but in this case she feels that enough is enough and atypically lets her inward anger out.

Sandra, moreover, seems to be even more self-hating than hostile to others, and she foolishly believes that she *has to be* approved, loved and helped by others – particularly by those for whom she has some feelings and who *should* care for her. She (like most 'adults') has always been a baby and is fairly determined to be one for the rest of her life – if she can possibly get away with it. She rather envies the 'takers' – such as Jonathan – who at least seem to care for themselves and go after (or at least worry about) what *they* want; but she also at times hates them for not recognizing *her* weaknesses and for not making sure that *she* gets taken care of.

As Sandra lets herself go – with feelings of anger, self-loathing and abysmal self-pity – she recognizes that she is doing the 'wrong' thing because no other group member has 'broken down' like this. So she does what most people do at this turn of affairs: She takes her primary symptoms (anger and self-pity) and creates a set of severe secondary symptoms about them. Her fundamental irrational beliefs are (1) 'I *must* do well and be approved by others! And isn't it *awful* if I am not!'; (2) 'You *must* treat me considerately and fairly! And isn't it *terrible* if you do not!'; (3) 'Conditions must be easy and give me exactly what I want quickly, without any hassles! And isn't it *horrible* when they are not!' After creating her primary emotional symptoms of self-downing, anger and self-pity with these foolish absolutistic ideas, she then uses the same basic irrationalities to create her secondary symptoms.

Thus, when she sees that she has an angry outburst instead of rationally telling herself, 'I wish I wouldn't be so angry and break down in this uncalled for manner; how unfortunate!' she irrationally tells herself, 'I *must* not break down in this uncalled for manner; how *awful*! What a perfect idiot I am!' She then feels depressed and self-downing about her anger (rather than accepting *herself* with *it*), and she exacerbates her state of emotional dysfunctioning.

If the group leader were efficient he or she would not have permitted this kind of situation to go this far in the first place. Once it occurred, however, the therapist can recognize that this kind of passive 'therapy' will often lead to outbursts of this sort and help exacerbate people's problems. The therapist could then, at least, *do* something about showing Sandra, and the group as a whole, what her main problems are, how she (and not the group process itself) is creating them, and what she can do about overcoming them.

Taking over the leadership of this group, I would immediately say to myself, 'What a therapist-caused mess! However, it does have some good points about it because at least I can use this situation to show Sandra and the other group members what they are doing to upset themselves and how they can more assertively, in the future, refuse to go this far with an inefficient leader and try to get themselves some real help. Too bad that I am, as it were, given an already half-drowned person to try to resuscitate. But it is quite a challenge for me to use this near disaster to illustrate some of the main points of human disturbance and perhaps to dramatize them to Sandra and the other group members.'

In other words, in counseling in a bad situation like this one, I would first use Rational Emotive Behavior Therapy (REBT) principles on myself, to make sure that I did not anger or otherwise unnecessarily upset myself about this needless disaster. If I did feel angry at the inefficient group leader, I would quickly do the A-B-C-D-E construct of REBT on myself: 'At point *A*,' I would say to myself, 'let us assume that this leader has behaved inadequately. At point *C* (emotional and behavioral consequence), I feel angry. What am I telling myself, at *B* (my belief system), to make myself angry? Obviously: 'This therapist should not have acted so incompetently! Any leader like that deserves to be drawn and quartered!' But on to *D* (disputing of irrational beliefs): Why *should* not, *must* not he or she behave so incompetently – when that's the way they are! Tough!' And why does he or she deserve to be drawn and quartered for incompetence? Answer: 'There is no reason – he or she is only a confused, fallible human who acted incompetently in this situation, not a totally bad human who deserves to suffer for incompetence. Too bad – but not awful!'

I would show myself that Sandra's outbursts tend to come from her own A-B-C-D-E construct – not from *A*, the activating experiences in the group, that happened to her. I would surmise that she has one or more profound, absolutistic *shoulds*, *oughts*, or *musts* by which she creates her problems – that she (like most humans) is a strong *must*urbator. And I would guess from her highly disturbed emotional reactions what her *musts* were. I would also look for her 'awfulizing', her 'I-can't-stand-it-itis', and her global labeling of herself and others as rotten people (instead of as people who behave rottenly in this instance). I would ask myself whether she had both primary symptoms (anger and self-downing) and secondary symptoms (self-downing about her own anger) and would guess that she probably had both.

I would then start determining what cognitive, emotive and behavioral interventions and homework assignments I would use to help Sandra and the group see how they were disturbing themselves and how they could refuse to do so in the future.

I would recognize the group elements in this situation – but mainly see them as being at point *A* (activating experiences or adversity) in the A-B-Cs of REBT. Sandra, even on her own, probably has a basic philosophy of perfectionism and intolerance of others' imperfections, which will often get her into emotional difficulties. When she is in any kind of a group – even a 'therapy' group – she tends to use this philosophy about how she behaves in the group and how the group members behave toward her. Thus, she tends to think that *especially* when she is in front of other people she *must* act as well as they do and impress them with her goodness or competence; and she tends to think that they (especially the group leader) *must* care for her and rescue her, seeing how helpless she is! So the irrational beliefs and the dysfunctional emotions and behaviors that I would work on in Sandra's case may be even more prevalent and tend to be shown more intensely in the group situation. But following REBT theory, I would not delude myself that the group *makes* Sandra disturbed or *causes* her outbursts. The group and the group situation contributes significantly to her emotional problems, but they really do not cause them.

As a group consultant or therapist I would keep in mind that I am primarily an educator - because, whatever I do with one member, such as Sandra, will be seen and heard by other members. In a group educational setting, then, perhaps I could help several members by talking directly and incisively to one of them. I would also want Sandra to understand (1) herself and her own emotional problems and how to cope with them and (2) how other people continually disturb themselves and how she can accept them with their disturbances and perhaps help them overcome their malfunctioning. I would really like all group members to talk each other out of their irrational beliefs - and thereby automatically and 'unconsciously' talk themselves out of their own. So if time permitted, I would try to get Sandra to work with the other members in a REBT manner, along similar lines to those I used in working with her.

I would first say to Sandra, 'I'm glad you spoke up like that! I think that this group has been run quite badly so far. I think that your outburst shows that you tend to recognize this, too. You are showing your hostility to the group members and especially to Jonathan. But I wonder if you are really quite angry against the group leader for allowing the group to wallow around like this, in a muddled and virtually unled fashion for so many sessions? Do you think that you are angry about that?'

Assuming that Sandra replied that, yes, she was angry about the group process and the ineptness of the group leader, I would then continue: 'Well, let's assume that you and I are right about this: The group leader has been sadly remiss and has helped screw up things and waste your and the group's time. Now, you and I may be wrong about this because maybe the leader really acted well and your very outburst and what it may lead to therapeutically may prove this. But let's assume that the leader has been quite wrong - stupid, incompetent, unhelpful. In REBT, we call that A - your activating experience or adversity. And at point C, the consequence you feel in your gut, you experience real anger. Now you may think that the group leader makes you angry by his (or her) incompetence. But this is quite false! Actually, you *choose* to anger yourself about this; and you do so at B - your belief system *about* the leader's incompetence. Now what are you telling yourself at B, about what has been happening to you at A, that makes you feel so angry at C?'

For the next few minutes, I would continue this dialogue with Sandra, trying to convince her (and the other members who are presumably listening to the two of us) that no one has ever upset or angered her in all her life – but that she, instead, angers herself about things like people's incompetence. And, as briefly as possible, I would also try to get her to dispute (at point D) her irrational beliefs that create her anger, thereby to surrender these beliefs. If she did not understand what she was telling herself to anger herself and what she could do to make herself unangry, I would also try to get other group members to supply these answers, rather than supplying them myself, so that they, too, would see how to dispute, at point D, their own irrational beliefs and to give them up.

After speaking with Sandra, I would ask Jonathan, 'How do you feel about Sandra's attacking you?' Assuming that he said that he felt hurt, depressed, angry, or otherwise upset, I would try to show him that he largely created these feelings and that Sandra, no matter how badly she might attack him verbally, could not make him feel disturbed. I would say to him, 'Let's assume that Sandra is wrong about your caring only about your insurance business and that no one else in your life seems to matter. Let's assume that she has accused you unfairly and unjustly. Her accusation merely constitutes an activating experience or adversity point A – and cannot in itself upset you unless you tell yourself some irrational demand about it. Now, what did you tell yourself, at B, your beliefs about what Sandra did at A, to make yourself angry or hurt at C, your emotional consequence?'

Again, I would help Jonathan, as well as the rest of the members, to see that he upset himself about Sandra's accusation and that she could not make him feel great pain (except physically, of course, in case she actually assaulted him) unless he told himself some strong evaluative sentence *about* what she did.

I would then ask all the members, 'Why did you all let this wasteful group process proceed as it did? Why did you not speak up earlier and try to help the group proceed in a manner that would have been more useful to you? What were you telling yourself about the way things were occurring?' I would help them see that they were probably afraid to interrupt the inefficient group process and risk confrontation with the leader and that they were telling themselves that they could not stand her or his criticism or disapproval if they did so. I would show them how to challenge this irrational belief. I would also show them that some of them probably had an abysmally low frustration tolerance to allow things to go on this way and that they had to take the easy way out because they had irrational ideas such as, 'If I speak up about what really bothers me, that will be very hard. In fact it will be *too* hard! I *can't stand* facing hard things like this! I must have immediate comfort and ease and must avoid all real unpleasantness, even though it might help me in the long run.'

I would show the group, in other words, that some members went along for the leader's ride because of their own irrational fears of disapproval and their natural tendencies to take the easy and less effectual way out of their difficulties. I would help them see, and to help each other see, the precise self-defeating beliefs they told themselves in order to create their evasive and heads-in-the-sand feelings and behaviors; I would indicate how they could question, challenge, dispute and change these beliefs. I would give them emotive and behavioral homework assignments to help them revise their basic irrational philosophies.

Thus, I might encourage Sandra to take the homework assignment of asserting herself promptly in any group situation she happened to be in during the next week or two, no matter how uncomfortable she felt in the process. If she carried out this assignment she could reinforce herself with something she found rewarding; if she failed to carry it out she would penalize herself by engaging in some distasteful activity (such as cleaning her house or burning a $20 bill). Similarly, depending on how the other group members reacted and disturbed themselves, each of them would preferably agree to do a homework assignment that would help them act and work against their self-defeating ideas and feelings.

Group REBT includes a good many emotive-evocative exercises, which may be experienced during the group sessions or outside the group. Because Sandra and most of the other members of this particular group seem to feel ashamed of expressing themselves and acting in a 'foolish' or 'humiliating' manner, they might perform one of the REBT shame-attacking or risk-taking exercises. In the group itself they might all be asked to do something that they consider risky, such as saying something negative to another group member, confronting the group leader, or acting in some 'ridiculous' manner. For outside homework, they might be asked to do something 'shameful' during the week, such as telling a stranger that they just got out of the mental hospital, walking a banana on the street, or yelling out the time in a department store. They would then be asked why they considered this task risky or shameful, how they felt about doing it, and how they could get themselves to do it without feeling ashamed, embarrassed, humiliated or self-downing.

The preceding interventions are suggestive of those that I would make in this group or in one of my own regular REBT groups. The main goal is to show all group members that they do not just get seriously upset but instead mainly *upset themselves*. They do so by strongly believing in absolutistic and unrealistic *shoulds*, *oughts* and *musts*. To change their irrational beliefs and the dysfunctional emotions and behaviors that derive from them, they had better persistently and actively (not to mention robustly!) force themselves to think, feel and behave quite differently. As an REBT group leader, I vigorously question, challenge, teach, direct, intervene, and – in a very real sense of this term – *lead*.

Critical Incident 6: A Group Member Maintains Distance

This is a group of four women and three men. During your pregroup interview sessions, you discovered that all members had expressed a personal concern over their inability to be assertive. This prompted you to offer them an opportunity to deal with the issue in a group setting. The members are briefly described as follows:

> Francie is 35 years old and married. Her husband drives trailer trucks for long-distance hauling. She has two teenage daughters. When she first met with you, she explained that she had the primary responsibility of raising her children. She is having difficulty dealing with her parenting role and wants more active support from her husband.
>
> Kathy is 28 years old and employed as a librarian. She lives at home with her parents, both of whom are in their seventies. She is the youngest of five siblings. She would like to live a life of her own but feels obligated to take care of her parents. This situation has also caused her much consternation in other areas of her personal and professional life.
>
> Michele is 42 years old and has been married for 22 years. She has disclosed her dissatisfaction with spending the rest of her life as a homemaker, but she has been under considerable pressure from her husband and children to remain at home.
>
> Jackie is 30 years old, lives apart from her husband, and has custody of their six-year-old son. Jackie is employed as an executive secretary for a large corporation. The job demands that she be decisive and work independently. She is experiencing a great deal of anxiety because her new boss has not acknowledged her abilities or defined her responsibilities, yet she fears confronting him. It seems this symptom is also appearing in other phases of her life, particularly with her husband.
>
> Troy is 36 years old, single and presently employed as a senior high school science teacher. He has tried, on a number of occasions, to obtain an administrative position and not succeeded. He says he seems and feels very inept at expressing himself, especially in areas where he must compete or take a stand on what he believes.
>
> Jim is 28 years old, and has recently married. He sought you out because he feels he has always been taken advantage of; this is especially true with significant others in his life. He is very upset with himself for not being able to say no when others ask him to do things for them.
>
> Joe is 33 years old and has been married for six years. A foreman at a local brewer, he has expressed discontent with himself and his job. He says he does not know whether he is 'fish or fowl'. His subordinates demand one thing of him and his superordinates another. He feels as though he must serve two masters.

This is session 7, and there has been a great deal of disclosure on the part of all members except Joe. In previous sessions, whenever the others would share their concern about being unable to speak out on their rights or their own mind, Joe would insist that he had no such problems. Now, it is the middle of the session, and the group has been grappling with the difficulty of holding different opinions and taking a personal stand on important issues. Joe again states that this is not the case for him. He no sooner completes his statement when the entire group attacks him and accuses him of not being honest. Jackie leads the attack by stating that people such as him scare her and that if she could she would not have anything to do with that kind of person. Jim follows by offering that he has taken some big risks in saying some of the things about himself; it is people like Joe who takes advantage of such information and makes it hard for Jim to be his own person. The inter-action gains intensity, and the more the others accuse Joe, the more he states that he has no problems. This in turn only serves to increase their attack. Throughout this exchange, Joe has given no clues about how this whole series of events has affected him.

Albert Ellis's response

I would assume, as usual in situations of this sort, that the group members are not merely healthfully confronting Joe (and trying to get him to admit to some of his major problems and to do something about them) but that they are also angry at him, they feel that he *has to* disclose himself to them and admit that he is holding back displaying his feelings, and he should do his best to change his ways. I would tell myself that they are quite probably correct about Joe's holding back and about his sabotaging himself in the process of doing so but that they are wrong about making themselves seriously upset about what he is doing or not doing.

I would also tell myself that, in accordance with Rational Emotive Behavior Therapy (REBT) theory, their hostile and confrontative manner toward Joe will in all probability encourage him to be angry at them, to become more defensive, and to avoid, rather than to seek, looking more intently at his own problems. I would therefore first choose to talk with the group members about their anger and would try to get them to reduce it. I would keep in mind that helping them undo their anger might help Joe see more clearly some of his own problems. One advantage of group therapy is that people often understand others' problems more clearly than their own and, in getting them to do so and to work to help these others, they can frequently be persuaded to work, consciously or unconsciously, on their own emotional difficulties.

I would therefore first say to the group, or to one of the hostile members of the group, 'I can see that you are quite upset about what you consider to be

Joe's holding back and his refusal to acknowledge some of his deep-seated problems. And let's assume, for the moment, that you are right about him. Jackie, let's assume that Joe acts in a 'scary' manner and that people like him scare you and put you off, so you want nothing to do with them. Even if this is so, you are still condemning Joe for his holding back and for his scariness. Now, why *must* he not hold back and be unscary? And in what way does he become a louse or a rotten person if he continues to act the way that he does?'

I would try to show Jackie that, whatever Joe's deficiencies may be, she is commanding and demanding that he not have them and, by her unrealistic and irrational demands, she is foolishly upsetting herself, making herself exceptionally irate at him. I would first try to get her to give up her demands, while keeping her strong desire that Joe not act the way he is acting, and then try to help her work with Joe to get him to change some of his ways.

I would also try to show her that Joe's behavior may be bad or self-defeating and that it may be against the group's best interests, but it is not really 'scary'. She makes it scary by needlessly frightening herself about it – by contending, in her own head, that she cannot stand his acting that way and that she cannot allow herself to be comfortable and unscared if he continues to act that way.

I would work with Jackie, with the help of the other members of the group – whom I would induce to join in and to question and dispute Jackie's irrational beliefs about Joe's being 'scary' – to give up frightening herself about his behavior and to stop blocking her own openness and honesty just because he chose to be closed. At the same time, I might get Jim into the center of the stage and show him that he, too, is taking Joe too seriously, is making it harder for himself to be his own person, and then assuming that Joe is making it hard for him to act openly. I might particularly try to help Jackie see that Jim is upsetting himself needlessly about Joe and help Jim see that Jackie is gratuitously upsetting herself about Joe. I would assume, while talking with both of them (and the other group members), that Joe really had a serious problem of defensively keeping himself closed; and I would show Jackie, Jim and the group members that they viewed this problem in an overdramatic light and *made themselves* upset about it.

I would also try to show them that, if they really *wanted* (and not *needed*) Joe to be more open, they would hardly persuade him to act better by beating him over the head, complaining viciously about the way he is acting – thereby encouraging him to be even more defensive. If they are more open themselves, despite Joe's remaining closed, and if they mainly ignore his shut-off qualities for the moment, he may well take after their good modeling and make himself more open and honest.

In other words, I would show Jackie, Jim and the other group members that although their goals and desires (to have Joe be more open and to feel safe in opening up themselves) are highly desirable, their method of achieving these goals is not very effective or productive. They are really asking Joe to open up *first*, and then they will presumably begin to do so themselves. But they can make themselves open – as they actually had been doing up to now – whether or not Joe acts openly.

I would show the group members who complained about Joe that in some ways they are probably right, that he may well be defensive and may be doing himself little good by holding back, and that he may also be harming the group process. But I would also show them that he has a right to be wrong – as have all humans – and that, although his behavior may be 'bad' or 'harmful', *he* is not a *bad person*. I would try to show them that unless they accept this kind of philosophy about Joe and his errors they are unlikely to accept themselves when they do badly. I would try to get them, as well as Joe, to see that all humans are fallible. Most of us have a very difficult time opening ourselves to others and admitting that we have serious problems, but if we stop putting themselves down for *having* such problems (and stop denigrating others for having similar problems or for denying such problems), we will be able to face ourselves much more openly and success-fully.

In the process of talking with members of the group, I might tell them something of myself and some of the difficulties I have had, to show them that I too am fallible and have screwed up during my lifetime. I might give them a specific self-disclosure exercise such as thinking of something secret they have not revealed to anyone in their entire lives and then revealing this secret to the group right now. I would show them that whatever they revealed there is nothing to feel ashamed of or to put themselves down for, even though their act may well have been immoral or reprehensible. And I would show them how not to feel ashamed or embarrassed, now that they have revealed this secret to the group. In the course of this exercise, I would especially try to induce Joe to reveal something 'shameful' or 'humiliating' and try to show him that he could do so without condemning himself for having done it or for revealing it.

I might also give all group members some kind of shame-attacking or self-disclosing homework exercise such as revealing some 'shameful' act (including ones they have already revealed in the group) to an important person outside the group who might condemn them for this disclosure. If Joe, in particular, could not do this kind of thing, I would try to induce him to think, during the week, about something that he has not yet revealed to the group about himself that he would hesitate to reveal and then disclose it next week.

In various cognitive, emotive and behavioral ways, such as those just listed, I would try to keep the group centered for a while on this problem of disclosing oneself to others. I might even spend several sessions trying to help members see what they tell themselves to keep themselves closed up, how they can dispute their dysfunctional beliefs that make them secretive and defensive, and how they can actively push themselves to become more open with members of the group and with significant people outside the group.

CHAPTER 4

Rational Emotive Behavior Therapy and Its Application to Women's Groups

KRISTENE A. DOYLE

This chapter was written to demonstrate the application of Rational Emotive Behavior Therapy (REBT) specifically to women's groups. Although an argument could be made that similar issues arise regardless of the type of group, there are specific issues that REBT addresses which take into account various social and political factors affecting women. The role of leader and co-leader, common myths of women's groups, common irrational beliefs that are addressed in women's groups, and the 'work' to be done will be explored in this chapter. The chapter is based upon experience at the Albert Ellis Institute co-leading a mixed gender group with Dr Albert Ellis, the founder of REBT, and currently co-leading the women's group with Dr Janet Wolfe, whose experience leading women's groups spans thirty years. When appropriate, comparisons will be made between women's groups and co-ed groups to highlight the differences.

The women's group held at the Albert Ellis Institute in New York City meets once a week for approximately two hours. The group ranges in age, professional background, not to mention the reasons for entering such a group. We prefer to limit the group to between six and eight individuals to ensure that an appropriate amount of time is dedicated to each woman. Furthermore, it seems that cohesion of group members is more likely with a size of six to eight. It has been our experience that a group of less than six or more than eight breaks up continuity from week to week due to absences of members (J.L. Wolfe, personal communication, April 2000).

Approaching a women's group from an REBT perspective allows for a wider age range of members. This is because of the common irrational beliefs, namely, self-downing, that women embrace and endorse, regardless of their age. These common irrational beliefs of women will be discussed later in this chapter. One might conclude that a 26-year-old female would not be able to understand the difficulties of a 50-year-old newly divorced woman.

91

However, it becomes clear rather quickly that both women may have the tendency to 'compare and despair', making their age difference irrelevant. Furthermore, having women of different age ranges in the group serves to broaden the perspective of the group. It is not uncommon for an older woman with more experience in a particular area to point out some distortions and irrational beliefs of another member who may be lacking such experience. The converse is true as well. Younger women can bring to the group a 'fresh' perspective for others who may be 'stuck' in their ways of thinking and/or behaving.

A striking observation is that irrespective of the professional background of each woman, there are common links among them, most probably due to social and political factors that women face. Historically, women have been socialized to nurture and care for others and refrain from being assertive. This becomes evident almost immediately in a women's group. Therefore, the *type* of job one does is less important than the *experience* it brings for each woman. What is seen often in the women's group is a lack of assertiveness, rating oneself rather than the behavior, and comparing oneself to others and subsequent self-downing. The diversity in employment that members bring to group does not work against their goals or the goals of the group but rather serves to strengthen the cohesion of the group. This is because the women see that there are common experiences among them and can draw support from one another as a result. A useful technique for leaders of REBT women's groups is to have two members role-play different rational ways of coping with difficulties at work. This may include a member who has deficient assertiveness skills practice with another member ways to more assertively communicate with a boss or significant other. Members can then provide feedback in a supportive, yet constructive manner.

An REBT women's group has several inclusion and exclusion criteria that warrant attention. We generally do not prefer women with a diagnosis of Borderline Personality Disorder to enter the group, mainly because cohesion is disrupted. Women who are not willing to do weekly homework assignments, a very important component of the group, are also excluded. The use of homework assignments is an integral part of progress in REBT and Cognitive Behavior Therapy, and resistance to it should not be taken lightly. It could be argued that the majority of the work is done outside of the group, and if a prospective member is unwilling to comply with this, inclusion in the group is seriously questioned.

Inclusion into an REBT women's group is dependent on several factors. A general understanding of the CBT framework is necessary for inclusion because the questions that are posed by the therapists, the disputes that are made, and the homework that is assigned are all based upon a CBT/REBT framework. Additionally, women wanting to join the group are required to have specific goals they would like to work towards achieving. A Three Month Goal Sheet (Wolfe, 2000) (see Appendix 4.1) is used frequently with new members when they join the group. This goal sheet serves several purposes, including helping to focus clients on thoughts, feelings, behaviors and sensations they would like both to increase and decrease, as well as track progress made or obstacles preventing progress. This goal sheet is completed by group members within the first week of the group, and then is reviewed in group and revised where necessary. Approximately one month later, the sheet is revisited to monitor progress and discuss obstacles. Three months later goals are again discussed, adding new ones as progress is made. Regular use of the three-month goal sheet appears to be unique to the women's group.

Inclusion in an REBT women's group also requires a willingness to discuss gender issues and how they relate to the specific problems in each woman's life (Wolfe, 2000). Finally, completing weekly homework assignments is a necessary criterion for the group. Having a co-leader is often valuable in such instances. As group members are discussing the events of their week and any particular problems they are currently experiencing, the co-leader, in addition to contributing clinically, also contributes administratively by keeping notes and assigning relevant homework. Availability of a co-leader also ensures continuity of the group process, in cases when the leader is absent due to illness, vacation or professional lectures or workshops. If there were just one leader facilitating the group, cancellation would be necessary in the aforementioned instances. Although the co-leader often assigns relevant homework, there are times, however, that each member will be required to assign homework to themselves. We have found that when members are included in designing their homework assignment, they are more likely to complete it. A creative way of building cohesion within a women's group is to have members assign other members their homework. By doing so, the women demonstrate that they care about each other, they are listening to one another, and that they are willing to challenge one another. Dr Ellis has pointed out that often, cognitive work is done within a group therapy setting, and the homework assigned is often behavioral (A.E. Ellis, personal communication, 1999). In the women's group at AEI, equal time is dedicated to both cognitive and behavioral aspects. Depending on the nature of the problem, the assignment will often include both a cognitive and a behavioral piece. For example, practicing a rational coping statement of unconditional self-acceptance, while at the same time forcing oneself to attend a party that would normally be dismissed, may be a homework assignment for a woman who has *conditional* self-acceptance and social anxiety. An especially attractive feature of REBT women's groups is the use of challenging other members when they do not complete an assignment. The members can use REBT on one another to identify and dispute the irrational beliefs that prevented them from completing the homework. Members can become exceptionally forceful when they are doing their homework and others are not. In response, light, playful competition may emerge among members to complete assignments.

Finally, women wishing to enter an REBT women's group should be willing to commit for anywhere from six months to a year. This is because more work can be done within this time period. There are instances when less time is needed to complete goals; however, it has been our experience that a minimum of six months is necessary.

According to Wolfe (1985), key ingredients for an REBT women's group include consciousness raising, goal setting, therapist role modeling, partici-pant role modeling, assertiveness training, positive self-messages, self-pleasuring assignments, encouragement of female friendships and a focus on environmental resources and societal change. In addition, I would add a focus on self-care as a primary ingredient. Adequate nutrition, exercise and sleep are areas that are emphasized repeatedly during group. Especially noteworthy is what appears to be a relationship between a member's number of irrational beliefs during the week and her inability to combat them, and her lack of proper nutrition, rest and exercise. It is not uncommon for a member to come into a group session and 'fall apart' recounting her week to the other members. Upon probing, it becomes clear that she has not had an adequate amount of sleep and has had little to no protein in her diet. As a first measure, the importance of a well-balanced diet and adequate sleep are discussed and made a priority homework assignment for the upcoming week. If followed, she will often return to therapy the following week appearing transformed. Therefore, therapists working with women individu-ally and in groups may benefit from making self-care a priority of the clinical work to be done. This is especially true for women who have been socialized to believe that 'everyone else's needs are more important than my own', and 'I am not worthy of adequate self-care.'

Common Myths of REBT Women's Groups

The women's group is just a forum for bashing males

The number of times I have heard men (and some women) ask what else goes on in the group besides castrating men is salient and speaks to a greater societal issue that women in numbers are a threat. In fact, there is no male bashing in the women's group, in concordance with the philosophy of unconditional other-acceptance (UOA). When a situation arises with a group member that involves a male (which is often the case), the attention is diverted from 'other-downing' and focusing on the male, to the experience of the woman and how that experience is partly the result of messages she has received growing up and her perpetuation of these self-defeating messages. Thus, the focus is put on building each woman's self-worth within a healthy framework, *rather than* destroying a man's worth. REBT women's group leaders are wise to keep this in mind to avoid indirectly or directly rating others' worth based on their behaviors, something REBT espouses over and over again. It is important when working with women in a group to model appropriate ways of separating worth from behavior, be it that of a man or a woman. It is the philosophy of REBT women's group leaders that more is to be gained by working on expanding one's self-worth beyond the approval and acceptance of men, to areas of competency in friendships, employment, other relationships, and unique characteristics of each woman.

Women that enter a women's group have a host of problems that most women do not experience

This is a common misunderstanding of women entering a women's group. In fact, what has emerged from co-leading the women's group at AEI for two and a half years is that most of the women, despite their background, have similar core irrational beliefs, or have held similar beliefs at one time or another. Furthermore, what is even more striking is that despite the successes of each of the women in the group, much of the time they engage in self-downing when a negative comment is made to them by either a man or a woman. All of the positive characteristics and traits each woman holds are almost guaranteed to be dismissed by one negative (or sometimes neutral) comment. This phenomenon is not typically seen in other groups, and appears to be a unique quality of women's groups and women in particular. In addition, it is exceptionally useful when members are able to point out to each other their strengths that they are voluntarily filtering out, and often you will find that members laugh at themselves when they see that they too engage in such illogical self-ratings and self-downing. The support that emerges in such times can be most therapcutic. The women's group could be likened to a pendulum that swings back and forth, from one member to another. When one member is having an especially bad week, others will step up to the plate and help that member conquer irrational beliefs, help remind them of their strengths, and brainstorm ways in which they can overcome their weaknesses. Much of this can be done simply because the women identify with one another and their experiences.

Women's groups are just about a bunch of whiners and neurotics getting together and complaining about how unfair life is

Much of what occurs within an REBT women's group is accepting the unfairness of life and finding ways to systematically get the most out of it with the least emotional disturbance. Perhaps it is when a member first joins the women's group that time is spent on that individual's experiences and some focus is put on any inequities she has faced. Support is given from other members at this time, serving to build trust in that member and demonstrate understanding. However, one necessary quality of an REBT group leader is skill at balancing empathic support for members and gentle pushing towards acceptance of immutable realities of life. It would be useless to have group members spend their time each week talking about how someone did them wrong, asking themselves and each other why is life so unfair, and so forth. Rather, spending the majority of the time identifying irrational beliefs *about* the situation (i.e. She SHOULD NOT have spoken to be that way; Life MUST NOT be unfair), and disputing such beliefs, leaving members better able to problem-solve ways to help reach goals is where the focus of work is put. In fact, a healthy amount of humor about one's situation can prove quite useful for women's groups. However, it is up to the leader to demonstrate and see to it that members understand that laughter is being directed towards the situation or irrational beliefs, and not the person. Often laughter helps members see how seriously they are taking events in their lives, and helps them to see the 'lighter' side of their situations.

Women who enter a women's group leave angry and aggressive – ready to fight the world

This myth cannot be further from the truth. In most cases, women who enter the women's group do not have adequate assertiveness skills, either because they never were modeled such skills, or because they have a discomfort for confrontation, or a need to be approved and accepted all of the time. Thus, REBT is used to help women make a philosophical shift from one of passivity to one of assertion. A point that is made by therapists is that being assertive does not necessarily mean that you will get what you want, but it increases the likelihood. It is too easy for others to conclude that a woman is aggressive when she expresses her wants and desires for the first time. Furthermore, because society often reinforces the myth that a woman who expresses her feelings and desires is aggressive and hostile, it is especially important for the therapist to warn clients of this possible reaction in others. Women can then take the opportunity to explore their emotional reactions to the accusation that they are aggressive, and role-play with other group members different ways of responding. The irrational belief 'I can't stand to upset others' could be disputed and replaced with the more rational alternative, 'I do not like it when others are upset about my behaviors, but it is not the end of the world.' For many women who enter a women's group, this is the first time they address areas such as assertiveness.

REBT women's groups aim to teach women that they should want to be alone and satisfy themselves

This is part myth, part truth. By no means do group leaders convince their members that they should be alone; *however*, a point that is emphasized is that while the desire to be with another person is indeed rational, the *need* to be with one is self-defeating. Therefore, the subtle point to be made is that while it may be highly preferable to be with another individual, believing that you need to in order to feel complete is irrational. Leaders will want to dedicate time during the group to work with members to strongly prefer companionship while at the same time enjoying oneself and one's company. For years many women are given the message from parents, teachers, friends and society, that 'you are only a success in life if you are in a successful relationship'. Women then take it upon themselves to reindoctrinate this belief. Therefore, one of the first tasks of group leaders is to demonstrate to members that although they are bombarded with such messages on a daily basis, they too are responsible for buying into them and continuing to self-condition such irrational beliefs. A point should be made that because of such heavy societal messages, members will have to work extra hard to combat them through REBT cognitive and behavioral assignments. Different homework assignments will be discussed further below.

Common Irrational Beliefs Seen in Women

I am worthless without a man (woman)

This is one of the most common irrational beliefs seen in women who enter a women's group. As previously mentioned, society regularly sends out the message that one's self-worth is determined by factors such as whether or not one is in a relationship. Therefore, this irrational belief requires much attention because many women buy into it and repeatedly self-down when they are not in a relationship. In addition, a fear of being alone, which carries with it a host of other irrational beliefs ('I am a loser if I am alone'; 'I am incapable of taking care of myself'; 'Being alone would be horrible and I couldn't stand it'), often results in women staying in or entering relationships that not only are not rewarding, but also quite self-defeating. One of the goals of REBT women's groups is to assist women in focusing on other areas, such as their career, female friendships, and their skills, and to broaden each woman's concept and definition of self-worth beyond a sex-love relationship. The preference to be with a partner is certainly not the target of change, but rather the demand for it and subsequent self-downing that occurs when this goal is not met are targeted for change.

I should be prettier (smarter, wealthier, taller, skinnier, etc.)

As one former women's group member stated poignantly during a session, 'compare and despair'. Although this is somewhat of a generalization, one striking contrast between men and women in REBT groups is a woman's tendency to blame herself when things go wrong, or when things do not turn out the way she hoped they would. Conquering the propensity to compare and self-down is one of the highest priorities of focus in REBT women's groups. Especially therapeutic is to have other members provide feedback and objective perspectives to a member who is experiencing the 'compare and despair' cycle. The term 'cycle' is chosen carefully, for it is not uncommon for a member to have a really bad week of comparing and self-downing and report this to the group and dispute the irrational beliefs associated, and to then have a very good upcoming week. A core common irrational belief women endorse at various points in their lives is the notion that 'If I was _____ , then this would not be happening to me, or I would have received the promotion, etc.' This tendency to assume complete responsibility for negative events and self-down in response to this assumed responsibility is less apparent in men. REBT is used to encourage women to accept themselves regardless of what they view as flaws, and to engage in more healthy comparisons. Comparing aspects of oneself to others can be a very healthy exercise in that it may serve to motivate individuals to work towards their goals. However, a shared phenomenon between men and women is the 'unfair comparison', in which you filter out evidence contradictory to your irrational beliefs, and selectively focus on evidence that supports your beliefs. Typically, this manifests itself in only taking in those experiences with people who are smarter than you, better looking, and wealthier. REBT therapists, regardless of the client's gender, urge them to look on both sides of the continuum and see that there will always be individuals who have more and less than they.

I should have achieved more by now and because I have not, there is something wrong with me

Again, Unconditional Self Acceptance (USA) is the primary goal for clients to strive towards. Often, women will set unbelievably high standards for themselves, bordering on perfection. Despite all that she has achieved, she focuses on what she has not yet accomplished, and self-downs. Women's group leaders take a two-pronged approach to work on this. First, an emphasis is made on accepting oneself as they are in the present and not self-downing, regardless of what has or has not yet been achieved. Secondly, practical problem-solving is done with all group members' involvement to assist the member in reaching her goals. The rationale behind this approach is that emotional disturbance is best worked on first, and practical problems second. Clients typically are better problem-solvers when they are not making themselves disturbed.

I am not strong enough to reach my goals without a sex-love partner

This irrational belief has been seen in numerous women in REBT groups, irrespective of professional background, sexual orientation or age. This particular irrational belief is especially common in women, partly due to societal messages directed towards women. It is not unusual for women to discuss the messages they received from parents, friends and the environment regarding the importance of being with a partner and the implications of failing to do so. A variant of this irrational belief is the demand that many women place upon themselves that they must have a sex-love partner in order to achieve their goals, whether they are professional or personal goals. REBT is used to dispute this need and replace it with a very strong desire to have a partner. In addition, a strong emphasis is directed towards incorporating women friends into the lives of group members, and to break the mainstream notion of deriving support solely from sex-love partners. REBT therapists will want to dedicate some time to developing alternative schemas for those members who endorse the belief that only sex-love relationships are important. Fostering female friendships and widening the circle of social support beyond sex-love relationships is often a focus during the group.

I must have the approval of others

This irrational belief is not necessarily specific to women, although it is often seen among women who attend REBT groups. A preference for approval is distinguished from the demand, and efforts are made by group leaders and members to dispute such a need. Furthermore, derivatives of this demandingness are addressed, including awfulizing, low frustration tolerance, and global ratings of self-worth when members do not have the approval of others.

Common Exercises Used in REBT Women's Groups

Role-play

This exercise is commonly used when a member is working on a particular skill needing improvement, such as assertiveness with a boss or friend. Typically, a member will express discomfort concerning an interaction with someone, wishing that she said something different or responded in a different manner. A member may also present a situation and ask the group to help brainstorm different approaches of handling it. One of the goals for group leaders to keep in mind is to draw upon other members' experiences that are similar to the one being presented. Members can serve as role models for one another, sharing details of comparable problems and the ways in which they resolved it. By doing this, group members' successes are reinforced, their REBT skills are strengthened, and group members' roles as facilitators are fostered. One of the benefits of role-playing a true problem with other group members is that it provides an opportunity to uncover any irrational beliefs that may impede a successful interaction, such as 'My boss SHOULD listen to me and treat me with respect.' In addition, role-plays of this nature allow members to receive feedback on the nature of their non-verbal communication, which is often a key ingredient for successful interactions. Following a role-play, members who observed the interaction talk about what they liked and found to be strengths, as well as areas for improvement. This type of exercise is useful in that it allows for the practice of skills that may be deficient, as well as providing a forum for uncovering subtle irrational beliefs and unhealthy emotions that impede successful behaviors. This is an instance in which the cognitive, emotive and behavioral components of REBT are demonstrated to group members in a systematic nature. Group members are shown via the role-play how their irrational beliefs, such as demandingness and awfulizing contribute to dysfunctional emotions, such as anger and anxiety, resulting in a lack of assertiveness or passive-aggressive interactions. A follow-up to this type of exercise is an REBT homework assignment such as cognitive disputation of the irrational beliefs that are blocking assertiveness, and then a subsequent behavioral piece of acting assertively to another individual.

In-vivo disputation

Group members' irrational beliefs are challenged throughout group sessions as they arise. The rationale behind this is threefold. First, the group is viewed as a microcosm of the outside world, and therefore, irrational beliefs that emerge within the group are to be disputed to encourage generalization of disputation outside of the group. Secondly, by not disputing beliefs as they arise, there is more likelihood that progress and goals will be impeded. Finally, by disputing irrational beliefs as they arise within the group, it allows for (1) therapist modeling of effective disputation, and (2) client practice of disputation. This is especially effective when new members join the group and do not have much experience with this technique. As members gain skill in disputing, a more proactive stance is assumed, as they challenge one another's irrational beliefs.

Honest feedback from group members

It is not uncommon for a woman to come into the group and present what appears to be a very distorted view of herself. This view may be the culmination of years of comparing and despairing, society's constant bombardment with the idea that 'thin is in', and a biological predisposition towards self-downing. REBT women's groups take this opportunity to utilize group members in providing honest feedback to others. The group leader may ask members to go around and give their feedback and views of the particular individual, with an emphasis on her strengths and things she does well. This is not to say that weaknesses are not addressed during this type of exercise; however, too often women in such groups have a pull towards focusing on their weaknesses and disregarding their strengths. It should be noted that when doing such an exercise, Unconditional Other-Acceptance is emphasized and used to gain Unconditional Self-Acceptance. Members are asked to discuss each other's *behaviors*, making a clear distinction from their *self-worth*. Honest feedback of this nature serves several purposes, including helping to challenge and ultimately correct the irrational beliefs of group members, providing members with the opportunity to hear how other, more objective people view them, and building cohesion. Often after such a group exercise, members will thank one another for their feedback and agree to take it into consideration over the course of the week.

General topics for discussion

One of the more interesting exercises that has been incorporated into the women's group is a topic of interest to be discussed by members. Topics can range from how you spend free time, to what you consider important ingredients in a relationship, to passion and hobbies. Often, a group member who is struggling with a particular issue will come into the group and pose the question to other members. Group leaders contribute to this discussion as well. This particular exercise is beneficial for a number of reasons. First, it provides members with a host of interesting perspectives and ideas to think about and integrate into their lives where appropriate. Secondly, it fosters cohesion among group members. When a topic such as 'passion' is discussed, group members share with one another what are often very intimate details about themselves. Members leave the group not only with some fresh ideas, but developing closer relationships with fellow female members.

The Group as a Support System

The women's group members at the Albert Ellis Institute are actively encouraged by the group leaders to use one another as a social support outside of the group, particularly during times of distress or hardship. Contrary to most psychodynamic oriented groups, with the permission of group members, phone numbers, e-mail addresses and work numbers are exchanged and updated as new members join the women's group. Knowing that group members can rely on one another outside of the group helps to build cohesion within the group. In addition, having the outside support of group members is especially advantageous for those women who do not have a strong network of female friends to call upon during times of need. For example, in the women's group held at AEI, one member with a history of unhealthy male relationships and a lack of female friends was going through a particularly rough period. Group members and leaders each volunteered one night where they would check-in with this member and help dispute any irrational beliefs, and lend words of support. This practice was especially helpful in that it demonstrated to this member that healthy relationships with women are both possible and rewarding.

Another advantage of distributing phone numbers to group members is that it allows for the 'work' that is done during the group to be continued outside of the group. For example, a member may be working on improving her health by exercising more frequently during the week, but a lack of friends to go running with often prevents her from doing so. Having heard this, a group member may turn to her and tell her to call during the week and they can go running together. Having phone numbers available may encourage members to take the initiative and build upon their own weaknesses with using other members' strengths.

Common Homework Assignments in REBT Women's Groups

One of the distinguishing characteristics of an REBT women's group is the type of homework assignments given to combat both the individual and cultural messages members endure. *Self-pleasuring* assignments are often given to women who have a difficult time caring for themselves if and when they are not in a sex-love relationship (Wolfe, 1985). Cultural messages such as 'Others' needs should be placed before mine own' and 'I am selfish if I care for myself' are challenged via self-pleasuring exercises. Such exercises include taking a hot bubble bath, getting a massage, buying pretty flowers, or setting the table with fine dinnerware and candles, and treating oneself to a dinner (that is not eaten in front of the television out of Tupperware!). Self-pleasuring exercises are given at various times to all group members, but they are especially therapeutic for those members who endorse the belief 'what is the point of doing all of that if I am alone?' Members are specifically asked to dispute the irrational beliefs that 'going to such measures are useless if I am alone' and 'I am not worthy of having an extravagant meal if I am alone' while engaging in the activity, whatever it may be. By doing so, women are challenging those messages they receive from society and continue to self-condition, both from a cognitive as well as a behavioral stand-point. The goal is that by doing this regularly, changes in irrational beliefs and unhealthy behaviors will occur and generalize.

Positive self-talk assignments are also frequently given to members in an effort to challenge and replace the negative messages that are played over and over again in their minds. A useful exercise for all group members to do during a group session is to go around the room and offer four or five characteristics they like or admire about themselves. It is remarkable how many women have difficulty with this exercise, failing to come up with more than one or two positive characteristics. In such cases, other members may be asked to help a particular member out who is experiencing difficulty. Following this group exercise, those women who had difficulty may be given a homework assignment to engage in positive self-talk throughout the course of the week. This should be done utilizing as many different modalities as possible. For instance, members are asked to write down their positive traits, speak them aloud in front of a mirror, record them on a cassette and listen during the week, and think about them in their minds. The goal of this assign-ment is to break the all-too-comfortable cycle of negative self-talk and reindoctrination of a negative self-image. For those members who have an especially hard time engaging in positive self-talk, or on one level are resistant to giving up such negative talk, it is helpful to have them apply the 'equal time rule' whereby an equivalent amount of time is allotted to thinking about themselves in a negative and positive light.

Empowerment exercises, in the form of information gathering and data collection are also frequently assigned. Many women who are part of women's groups are raised with the message that they are incapable of making decisions on their own, or making purchases such as apartments or houses on their own, or adopting and raising a child on their own, and that a partner (typically male) is a necessary component. To combat this notion, women are asked to be their own 'agents', and collect as much information on the topic as possible, with the goal being the more knowledge they have the more empowered they become. Women will report back to the group on the information they have accrued throughout the course of the week, often with a sense of accomplishment and control. Such exercises also serve to facilitate a unique aspect of REBT women's groups, resource sharing. It is not uncommon for a woman to be discussing a problem, be it a health, financial or legal issue, and be in need of an expert in the particular area. Other members spontaneously offer names, phone numbers or infor-mation on the subject. This is especially useful for circumstances in which several group members are working on similar goals. For example, it is common for members to be addressing their finances, with the goal of consolidating their debt. Other members who have gone through this in the past, or who are working on it presently, may know of a service or office that may be of help.

Conclusion

The application of Rational Emotive Behavior Therapy to women's groups brings with it several unique components. Cognitive, emotive and behavioral techniques are employed with the aim of challenging individual and cultural beliefs and messages that have a defeating effect on women. Therefore, irrational beliefs that result from biology, society and self-conditioning are attacked and replaced with more effective, rational beliefs. A common focus of REBT women's groups is the overriding goal of Unconditional Self-Acceptance and breaking the cycle of self-downing. This is partly accomplished through therapist demonstration of Unconditional Other-Acceptance, cohesion that is built and maintained throughout, and sense of social support that is fostered during group.

Distinct in-session exercises and homework assignments are also integral aspects of REBT women's groups. In particular, self-soothing homework assignments including massages, bubble baths and special one-person dinners are designed to help combat the irrational beliefs 'I am not worthy of doing nice things for myself' and 'I can not enjoy my life without a man'. To fight the overwhelming negative self-talk that women embrace, group members are encouraged to practice positive self-talk during the course of the week. In-vivo role-plays working on the acquisition of skills such as assertiveness are also frequently carried out. Initially, group leaders may model for the group an assertive response to a given situation, yet as the group's cohesion builds and members become more practiced at such skills, they will take the place of group leaders and model for other members.

Finally, REBT women's group members are actively encouraged to serve as supports for one another, especially during times of need. The importance of female companionship is stressed as a means of instilling nurturance, love, and care into their lives, as well as to break away from the notion that a sex-love relationship is the sole means of doing so.

References

Wolfe JL (1985) Women. In AE Ellis, ME Bernard (eds) Clinical Applications of Rational-Emotive Therapy (pp. 101–27). New York: Plenum Press.

Wolfe JL (1995) Rational emotive behavior therapy women's groups: a twenty year retrospective. Journal of Rational-Emotive and Cognitive-Behavior Therapy 13(3): 153–70.

Wolfe JL (2000) 3-Month Goals. In ME Bernard, JL Wolfe (eds) REBT Resource Book for Practitioners (p. III–98). New York: Albert Ellis Institute.

Appendix 4.1

3-MONTH GOALS

Name:_____   Date: _____
                                        (3 months from today)

Behaviors I wish to increase:
_____
_____
_____

Behaviors I wish to decrease:
_____
_____
_____

Feelings I wish to increase:
_____
_____
_____

Feelings I wish to decrease:
_____
_____
_____

Sensations I wish to increase:
_____
_____
_____

Sensations I wish to decrease:
_____
_____
_____

Thoughts I wish to increase:
_____
_____
_____

Thoughts I wish to decrease:
_____
_____
_____

Source: Janet Wolfe (2000) REBT Book for Practitioners. ©2000 Albert Ellis Institute. www.rebt.org

CHAPTER 5

The Florence Nightingale Hospital CBT Group Therapy Programme

WINDY DRYDEN

In this chapter, I will describe a group therapy programme that I direct at the Florence Nightingale Hospital in London for in-patients and day-patients. In addition, I will discuss assessment of patient suitability, the qualities that effective group therapists who work on the programme need to have, a number of management issues and the difficulties that my colleagues and I have encountered while working on such programmes.

The Florence Nightingale is a private psychiatric hospital that offers a variety of group oriented programmes for in-patients, day-patients and residential patients. Patients can be referred to one of the following programmes: The High Dependency Unit (HDU), the Substance Misuse Unit (SMU), the Eating Disorders Unit (EDU) and Cognitive Behaviour Therapy (CBT). Occasionally, a 'mixed regime' is suggested where a patient will attend selected groups from two programmes, but in general, patients follow one programme.

The CBT group therapy programme is informed largely, but not exclusively, by the principles of Rational Emotive Behaviour Therapy, a leading approach within the broader cognitive-behavioural tradition. Ellis (1980) has argued that there are two approaches to REBT, one which follows its core tenets (to be described below) in a rigorous fashion (called specific REBT) and the other which makes liberal use of other CBT techniques (called general REBT) with less emphasis on its particular view of psychological disturbance and its remediation. The CBT programme that is run at the Florence Nightingale Hospital falls between these two stools. Some groups are run along specific REBT lines while others can be said to reflect general REBT or broader-based CBT. The main reason for this mixed approach is that the hospital prefers its programmes to be broad in nature and not to be associated too closely with any specific approach. This is why the programme is known as the Florence Nightingale CBT programme and not the Florence Nightingale REBT programme. However, since the programme is rooted in REBT, I will now proceed to give a brief description of this approach for those who are not familiar with it.

Rational Emotive Behaviour Therapy

As I have already said, Rational Emotive Behavior Therapy (REBT) is a therapeutic approach within the cognitive-behavioural tradition of psychotherapy. It was created in 1955 by Albert Ellis, an American clinical psychologist, who up to that point had moved from practising psychoanalysis to psychoanalytic therapy to eclectic therapy, but was disappointed about the ineffectiveness and inefficiency of these methods. As described in Ellis (1994), Rational Emotive Behaviour theory holds that people disturb themselves by holding rigid and extreme beliefs or ideas about themselves, other people and life conditions. These ideas are often expressed in the form of demands, awfulizing beliefs, low frustration tolerance (LFT) beliefs and depreciation beliefs. The major goal of REBT is to help patients to identify these irrational beliefs (as they are called) and to change them to their flexible and non-extreme alternatives (known as rational beliefs). These rational ideas are often expressed in the form of full preferences, anti-awfulizing beliefs, high frustration tolerance (HFT) beliefs and acceptance beliefs. REBT offers patients a variety of cognitive, imagery, emotive-evocative and behavioural techniques to help them to weaken their conviction in their irrational beliefs and strengthen their conviction in their rational beliefs. When REBT is practised with the goal of belief change it is known as specific REBT.

REBT also holds that people can be helped even when they do not or cannot change their irrational beliefs to their rational alternatives. Thus, patients can be helped to challenge their negatively distorted inferences, to change or stay away from situations in which they disturb themselves or to change their behaviour in these situations. When REBT is practised with these goals in mind rather than belief change as its objective, it is known as general REBT. Ellis (1980) has argued that general REBT is synonymous with cognitive-behaviour therapy.

On the programme to be discussed we vary our approach according to the patients' needs and present capacities and according to how much time they are likely to be on the programme. The more they are able to work at the belief level and the longer they are likely to be on the programme the more likely that we will practise specific REBT with them. Conversely, the less able they are at working at the belief level and the less time they will spend on the programme, the more likely it is that we will practise general REBT. Sometimes it happens that a person's insurance cover is extended and/or they become more able to work at the level of belief change. In such cases, we move from using general REBT to specific REBT and focus more on helping them to identify, challenge and change their irrational beliefs.

The Core Elements of the CBT Group Programme

Before I provide a detailed description of the Florence Nightingale CBT Group Therapy Programme, I will review its core elements.

Structured

The CBT group therapy at the Florence Nightingale Hospital is quite structured in nature. It seeks to provide patients with information about their problems and with a range of skills to assess and deal with these problems and the therapeutic curriculum of this programme is structured accordingly.

Theoretically coherent and internally consistent

It is generally accepted that one of the major features of effective group therapy programmes, such as the one under discussion, is theoretical coherence and internal consistency. As I discussed earlier, the Florence Nightingale CBT Group Therapy Programme is based on REBT/CBT principles and as such it has a reasonable degree of theoretical coherence and internal consistency. When I was given the brief to revise the programme which had been in existence since 1993, but did not have a director at the time of my brief, I was specifically told that the hospital did not want a programme that was too closely linked with any specific approach within the broad cognitive-behavioural tradition. This was due to the flexible nature of Florence Nightingale group therapy programmes and the difficulty of replacing staff on programmes having a very specific orientation.

The effect that this brief has had on the programme is that while much of the programme is based on REBT lines some of the theme-oriented sessions on anxiety, depression and anger and assertion are based on a broader CBT approach. This does, at times, cause some patients confusion, particularly for those who find it difficult to tolerate ambiguity, but it rarely causes significant problems. Following Ellis (1980), my own practice has been to conceptualize the programme as having roots in both specific REBT and general REBT (see above) and to emphasize the degree of fit between these elements rather than the degree of conflict. I am also happy for the programme to be known as a CBT programme rather than an REBT programme which is an important consideration for the hospital. It is a matter of conjecture what effect making the programme more consistent with REBT would have both within the programme and on the wider hospital setting.

Educational emphasis based on the principles of informed consent

A major element of the programme is its educational emphasis. It seeks to give patients explicit and clear information concerning (1) how REBT/CBT conceptualizes their problems and (2) what treatment strategies and techniques can be used to help them to overcome these problems. We use bibliotherapy to facilitate patient learning in both areas and a number of books (e.g. Dryden, 1994; Traverse and Dryden, 1995) are available for purchase at the hospital.

Together with this educational emphasis, we strive to operate according to the ethical principle of informed consent. This means that patients are informed about the therapeutic procedures on offer and asked for their consent to proceed. In this sense, we see the therapeutic relationship between staff and patients as that of informed allies, with both working with one another as allies and both informed about their own role and that of the other (Dryden, 1999).

Skills-oriented

Perhaps the defining feature of the Florence Nightingale CBT Group Therapy Programme is that it is skills-oriented. CBT is based on the principle that the long-term effects of therapy are enhanced by patients actively using cognitive-behavioural skills to deal with future problems. Thus much of our effort on the programme is directed to help patients acquire and internalize these skills. This issue will be discussed more fully below.

Intensive

The therapeutic curriculum that we have devised is intense and quite demanding of patients. Consequently, while some patients attend the entire programme, others attend part of the programme until they are well enough to benefit from all the groups. Patients who have attended the entire programme for at least six weeks have remarked that they have received a thoroughgoing emotional re-education, thus reflecting the intensive nature of the programme. Groups are held throughout the day in the week and plans are presently being made to run a weekend CBT programme.

Flexible

Anybody who has worked on a group therapy programme in a private hospital will soon discover the need to be flexible. Therapists who dig their heels in over points of practice quickly find out that working in this setting is not for them. I once attended a seminar on group therapy programmes in the NHS and the private sector at which one NHS therapist was complaining long and hard about the conditions under which he had to work. 'Every week when I facilitate my group, the chairs are different,' he exclaimed. I retorted thus: 'You think you have problems. Every week when I run my group, the chairs are the same, but the patients are different!' For this is what working in a private hospital is like. Patients come and go with alarming alacrity and in order to offer any kind of quality service, you have to be flexible.

We demonstrate our flexibility in several ways on the CBT Group Therapy Programme. First, we have arranged the programme so that once a patient has been assessed as suitable to join the programme he or she is oriented to the programme and, where appropriate to REBT/CBT, almost immediately (see section below on 'orientation to the programme'). Secondly, we endeavour to meet patients' idiosyncratic 'needs' as far as we can. Thus, if a patient has a sight problem and cannot read the whiteboard and fill in the forms (to be described presently), we will arrange to tape-record sessions (with the agreement of other patients) for later patient review and if we have the staff available we will arrange for someone to see the patient individually during sessions when other patients are doing their written work. Thirdly, we can accommodate partial patient attendance at the outset when consultant psychiatrists indicate that they wish their patients to attend part-time or to attend groups on more than one Florence Nightingale group programme. And, as patients improve, we can plan with the day-care team a suitable programme of partial attendance to help such patients integrate their care with the gradual resumption of their life responsibilities outside hospital. Finally, we are responsive to feedback from both patients and from their consultants and whenever we consider that implementing such feedback is both feasible and will improve the programme we will effect the necessary changes. Thus, the programme is fluid as well as flexible.

Assessment of Patient Suitability

When a patient is referred to the CBT group programme (usually by their consultant psychiatrist) they are assessed for their present suitability for the programme. As will be seen below, the programme is divided into two 'strands' known as cognitive strand 1 (where the emphasis is on helping patients to identify unhelpful thoughts, feelings and behaviours), and cognitive strand 2 (where the emphasis on helping patients to change unhelpful thoughts, feelings and behaviours).

Patients are assessed as suitable for cognitive strand 1 if:

•   they need to develop awareness and insight into their current feelings and behaviours;
•   they are unable to identify triggers and precipitating factors in relation to their current difficulties;

- they present as confused and unable at that time to identify specific issues/problems;
- they require time to adjust to being in a group;
- they are not willing or presently able to work with cognitive self-help forms or complete homework assignments both in and/or outside of group sessions;
- they need time to talk about and explore events (past or present) in detail;
- they have reservations about CBT and are unsure about embarking on it;
- they are currently too emotionally disturbed to focus on issues/problems in a structured way.

The greater the number of these criteria that a patient meets the more likely it is that he or she will be assigned to cognitive strand 1.

Patients are assessed as suitable for cognitive strand 2 if:

- they have a good level of awareness and insight into their current feelings and behaviours;
- they can identify triggers and precipitating factors in relation to their current difficulties;
- they are able to identify specific issues/problems;
- they do not require time to adjust to being in a group;
- they are willing and able to work with cognitive self-help forms or complete homework assignments both in and/or outside of group sessions;
- they do not wish or need time to talk about and explore events (past or present) in detail;
- they are enthusiastic about CBT and are prepared to embark on it;
- they are not too emotionally disturbed to focus on issues/problems in a structured way.

The greater the number of these criteria that a patient meets the more likely it is that he or she will be assigned to cognitive strand 2.

We also have a set of criteria for excluding patients from the programme. Thus we exclude patients who are:

- not willing to talk about their problems in a group setting;
- manic, disturbed or psychotic;
- having difficulty concentrating or are unable to sit in a group for an hour and a half;
- aggressive/violent and will disturb the group process and interfere with the therapy of other group members;
- likely to monopolize the group.

When a patient who has been referred to the CBT Group Therapy Programme is judged to be unsuitable then a report is written to their consultant detailing reasons for the exclusion and giving, where relevant, alternative treatment recommendations. It sometimes happens that the same patient is re-assessed later and accepted on to the programme because their mood has been stabilized and they are deemed able to concentrate sufficiently on the material presented in the groups.

Another important purpose of patient assessment is to enable a CBT formulation of the patient's problems to be made generally available so that consistency in the patient's therapy can be maintained. This is also facilitated by the patient's liaison worker (see the section on 'management issues').

Description of the CBT Group Programme

The CBT group programme at Florence Nightingale comprises several components. Here is a brief description of each component.

Orientation to the programme

When a patient is assessed as suitable for the CBT group, then he (in this case) is inducted into the programme. The nature of the CBT Group Therapy Programme is explained to the patient and the patient is told which strand they will be beginning on. Later they will be given an indication of criteria for moving from strand 1 to strand 2 (see below).

In addition, group rules are outlined (no entry to groups 10 or more minutes after the group has begun; attendance for the duration of the group; no eating, smoking and drinking in groups apart from water; no sub-grouping and physical expression of aggression; and for in-patients, no wearing of night attire, dressing gowns and slippers).

Patients are encouraged to ask questions about the programme and to express any doubts, reservations or anxieties that they have about joining the programme. Both their questions and their reservations are responded to clearly and sensitively and at the end they are given written material which explains each element of the programme in greater detail.

There are major reasons why we give patients a very clear idea of the group programme. First, as discussed above, this reflects the educational nature of REBT/CBT where clear information is given as explicitly as possible, and secondly, it enables patients to give their informed consent to participate in the programme. With patients who are unsure about proceeding, we suggest that they attend the programme for two or three days to enable them to judge first hand whether or not the programme meets their 'needs'. This is in accord with REBT/CBT theory that holds that open-minded experimentation will help patients to test out their doubts and reservations better than therapist or consultant persuasion. Very occasionally, patients decide that they do not wish to attend the CBT Group Therapy Programme, but their consultant psychiatrist insists that they attend. We normally resolve such situations by presenting a clear written statement for the consultant concerned outlining why we think that it is counterproductive for the patient to attend the programme at this time and presenting, if relevant and if politic, a rationale for an alternative treatment. It goes without saying that being non-medically qualified, therapists on the CBT programme do not comment on patients' medication.

Cognitive strand 1: identifying unhelpful thoughts, feelings and behaviours

As shown above the major purpose of strand 1 groups is to help patients identify their unhelpful thoughts, feelings and behaviours and to begin to understand and to specify their psychological problems. These groups are held from 11.00am to 12.30pm four days a week. Two group therapists run two groups per week. The time is divided so that group members who wish to can have an opportunity to talk

The role of the group therapist is to help patients to formulate their problems and to set realistic healthy goals. The group therapist works to help patients to understand feelings and behaviours that are unhealthy and to help them to begin to understand the beliefs that fuel these responses. The group therapist also encourages group members to give one another relevant feedback.

When a new patient joins strand 1 the group therapist helps them to talk about what led to their hospital admission (either as an in-patient or as a day-patient) and encourages them to open up so that they can get used to discussing their problems in a group setting.

Perhaps the major task of strand 1 group therapists is to help them to be specific about their problems so that they can move to strand 2 as and when appropriate. They do this by:

- encouraging group members to stick with specific problems;
- helping group members to focus on one problem at a time;
- orientating patients to the principle of emotional responsibility;
- helping patients to identify their unhealthy emotions and behaviours;
- putting REBT terminology into patients' own words;
- helping patients to identify their activating events;
- helping patients to identify the costs and benefits to change if appropriate.

With most patients the main goal of strand 1 groups is to get them to a stage when they can move to cognitive strand 2. Patients are ready to do this when they can:

- accept the principle of emotional responsibility;
- demonstrate an ability to discuss a specific emotional problem in a group setting and not to drift continuously to the general;
- show the beginnings of a written problems and goals list where problems are specific and goals are achievable, specific and concrete;
- show that they have read step 1 of *Ten Steps to Positive Living* (Dryden, 1994) which is on assuming personal responsibility; and
- agree to attend strand 2 groups regularly and indicate that they are willing to talk at every group.

In addition to four strand 1 morning groups there is, at the end of the week, a group where strand 1 group members meet with one another and a group therapist to reflect on their progress that week, offer one another feedback on their progress and group participation and discuss any homework assignments they have carried out that week.

Introduction to the ABC framework

Once a patient is deemed ready to move to cognitive strand 2, they are given a formal introduction to the ABC framework as shown in Figure 5.1.

This session, which is run by a therapy assistant five days a week, can be run for individual patients or in a small group format. It is divided into the following four parts and group members are encouraged to ask questions throughout the presentation.

Description of the situation in which the problem occurred =

A =   Aspect of the situation about which you were most disturbed =

B =   Beliefs about A

    (i)   Demand =

    (ii)   Awfulizing Belief =

    (iii) Low Frustration Tolerance Belief =

    (iv)   Depreciation Belief =

C =   Consequences of B

    (i)   Emotional =

    (ii)   Behavioural =

Figure 5.1. Introduction to the ABC framework.

1. The ABC model is presented and explained in detail and examples are used to aid patient understanding. Patients are also encouraged to use the framework with their own examples. During this part of the session, the principle of emotional responsibility is emphasized.
2. The eight unhealthy emotions (anxiety, depression, guilt, shame, hurt, unhealthy anger, unhealthy jealousy and unhealthy envy) and eight healthy alternative emotions (concern, sadness, remorse, disappointment, sorrow, healthy anger, healthy jealousy and healthy envy) are presented and the cognitive consequences and action tendencies for each are discussed. Some examples of meta-emotions are also provided.
3. The four main irrational beliefs (demands, awfulizing beliefs, LFT beliefs and depreciation beliefs) and alternative rational beliefs (preferences, anti-awfulizing beliefs, HFT beliefs and acceptance beliefs) are presented with examples.
4. Patients are given a problems and goals sheet on which they write two specific problems (identifying the unhealthy negative emotion and unconstructive behaviour) and respective goals (identifying the healthy emotion and constructive behaviour). They are asked to continue this task for homework.

Cognitive strand 2: changing unhelpful thoughts, feelings and behaviours

Cognitive strand 2 groups are designed to help patients to change the irrational beliefs that underpin their unhealthy emotions and behaviour. They are held every morning five days a week.

'Dealing with Specific Problems' group

In this group, which is held twice a week, patients have an opportunity to deal with specific examples of their problems with the group therapist (usually myself) taking the lead in helping them to use what they have learned in the other groups to deal with these specific problems. A feature of this particular group is that every patient who attends is given time to discuss his or her problems. For this to be achieved, sufficient time is devoted to this group (two and a half hours as compared with one and a half hours devoted to the other groups already described). My goals in running this group are: (a) to give each patient something concrete to take away from the discussion of their chosen item in the form of a homework assignment; (b) to encourage some input from other group members, in the discussion of agenda items – without allowing this to develop into an extended discussion of one patient's problems; (c) to encourage patients to reflect on the relevance of the problems discussed to their own situation; and (d) to act as a gatekeeper, keeping order and sifting useful from unhelpful patient contributions. In doing so, I endeavour to introduce humour when appropriate and to make vivid interventions to hold patients' attention.

'Developing Self-acceptance' group

In this group, which runs for one hour and a half and is held once a week, the focus is on helping patients to understand the concept of unconditional self-acceptance (USA), how it is a healthy alternative to the concept of self-esteem and how they can implement the concept of USA in their own lives. The curriculum for this group includes: the role of low self-esteem in psychopathology, dealing with ego-related unhealthy negative emotions not covered elsewhere on the programme (in the psychological education strand), e.g. shame, guilt, unhealthy jealousy and envy and techniques to develop unconditional self-acceptance (cognitive: disputing techniques, rational portfolio, zigzag techniques, rational-emotive imagery; behavioural: assertion and risk-taking; and emotive: shame-attacking exercises).

'Raising Frustration Tolerance' group

In this group, which is also run for one hour and a half once a week, the focus is on identifying LFT issues as they manifest in patients' problems and helping patients to address issues. A number of topics are covered in this group where LFT is featured (e.g. procrastination, lack of exercise, addictions, some types of unhealthy anger and self- and other-pity). On a practical level, patients are encouraged to identify behaviours they would like to increase and behaviours they would like to decrease. They are helped to identify, challenge and change the LFT beliefs that impede goal attainment and to design and implement relevant behaviour change programmes.

In addition to the four strand 2 morning groups, there is, at the end of the week, a group where strand 2 group members meet with one another and a group therapist to reflect on their progress that week, offer one another feedback on their progress and group participation and discuss any homework assignments they have carried out that week.

Psychological education groups

As noted earlier in this chapter, the Florence Nightingale CBT Group Therapy Programme has a decided educational emphasis. We teach patients the REBT/CBT model of psychological disturbance and instruct them in the skills that they will need in order to assess and overcome their problems. We also hold theme-based groups that have an educational purpose. Thus, we run weekly theme-based groups on 'Dealing with Anxiety', 'Dealing with Depression', 'Dealing with Anger and Assertion', 'Relationship Issues' and 'Healthy Living'. In these groups, the REBT/CBT perspective is taught to patients who are encouraged to use this framework to explore their own problems with anxiety, depression, relationships, anger/assertion and unhealthy living and a variety of different methods are introduced to help patients deal with these troublesome feelings and behaviours in everyday life. It is in these groups that experiential and role-play methods are used to make the group experience more evocative and emotive. For example, in 'Dealing with Anger and Assertion', patients are taught the rules of assertion and encouraged to put them into practice in a role-play scenario where the group leader plays the role of someone smoking in a non-smoking part of a restaurant, the goal being for the patient to assert himself or herself constructively with the group leader/smoker. Patients then give one another feedback on their performance and beliefs interfering with constructive assertion are elicited and challenged.

These groups are held from 2.00pm to 3.30pm and are open to both strand 1 and strand 2 patients.

Other groups

The groups that I have described so far form the backbone of the CBT group therapy programme. However, other groups that are run provide a valuable support to this backbone. These groups, some of which are run in conjunction with other hospital programmes, include:

Relaxation groups and yoga groups

These groups are held for an hour (yoga) or for 30 minutes (relaxation) on five or six days a week and help patients to learn and practise these useful skills.

Aftercare support group

Florence Nightingale Hospital offers all patients on the CBT Group Therapy Programme a free 'aftercare support group' for up to six months after discharge where patients can gain support from one another and discuss with other group members their experiences of using CBT skills on their own.

Qualities of Effective CBT Group Leaders

The approach to CBT that forms the foundation of the programme that I have just described is active-directive, educationally oriented and skills-based. Thus, people who work as group therapists on the programme have to be comfortable with being active and directive in therapy and with teaching skills, concepts and ideas. In addition, they have to have the following qualities:

Able to think quickly

In many of the groups that I have described, patients may ask therapists a variety of questions that require a well-considered, quickly formed answer. Thus, therapists who work on the programme need to be able to think quickly and answer such questions on the spot.

Able to present complex material in an understandable form

In essence, good REBT/CBT group therapists are good communicators. They need to be able to present to patients material that may be quite complex, in ways that can be readily understood. They have to speak at a rate that facilitates patient understanding and write clearly on the whiteboard. They also have to check with patients that the latter really do understand the points being made and are not feigning comprehension.

Able to use good gate-keeping skills

As you will have quickly discerned, REBT/CBT groups are very different from groups run on analytic lines. Therapists who work on the CBT group therapy programme not only have to be good teachers, they also have to be able to control the group process in ways which (a) facilitate patient learning, (b) enable patients to share their experiences with one another so that all stay on track and benefit from the mutual sharing and (c) ensure that patients neither dominate the proceedings nor stay silent. Thus, group therapists need to be able to assert themselves in the group process to direct this group process in ways which maximize the learning process for all without antagonizing any patients. As might be expected, experienced group therapists are more successful at achieving this balance than less experienced group workers. Gate-keeping issues (together with a host of other issues to do with patient care and the successful running of the group programme) are discussed in the regular staff meetings that are held several times a week.

Management Issues

The success of a hospital-based CBT group therapy programme depends on effective management of that programme. No matter how talented the group therapists are or how conscientious the therapy assistants who service the programme may be, if the whole programme is not effectively managed the programme will not be effective. Let me outline the ways in which management issues affect the Florence Nightingale CBT Group Therapy Programme.

Team management

It is very important that all workers on the programme understand and commit to carry out their own particular role with enthusiasm and that everyone understands the roles that other workers have. If anyone is unclear about their own role or the role of others or if anyone is unenthusiastic about their role, then this will have a deleterious effect on team morale and eventually team effectiveness.

To address these issues the team needs to be effectively led. At the Florence Nightingale Hospital, the team has (1) a clinical director who oversees matters to do with the clinical running of the programme and ensures that people know what to do clinically and when to do it; and (2) good administrative management. Weekly team meetings are held to deal with issues that crop up and which both impede and enhance effective team functioning. In particular, changes are periodically made to prevent group therapists from becoming stale. This is done by therapists swapping round the groups that they lead. In addition, some in-house training is held and there is a budget for some external training. Also a monthly 'Journal Club' is run so that therapists have the opportunity to present an article which they deem to be important and/or are enthusiastic about.

Programme administration

In addition to team management the programme needs to be efficiently administered. This is done primarily by the programme co-ordinator whose job it is to ensure that the day-to-day tasks are done efficiently and effectively. She (in this case) ensures that all groups are covered (in case of illness) and that the programme is run without disruption to accommodate staff holidays. In addition, she makes sure that the paperwork that needs to be done is kept up to date and that team meetings and patient progress reviews (see below) have an agenda and that action points that arise from these meetings are implemented by the staff members concerned. She also ensures that assessments are done and liaises with ward and day care personnel. She is ably assisted by therapy assistants who undertake much of the routine but necessary work of the programme.

Finally, the clinical director and programme co-ordinator have daily meetings for the latter to give the former a verbal report on the day's activities and to address any issues that have emerged during the day.

Monitoring of patient progress

It is important that patient progress is regularly monitored so that patients get the most out of their stay on the programme. This is done in a number of ways. First, after a patient has been assessed, he or she is assigned to a patient liaison worker. This role is not a therapeutic one and it would not happen that a patient liaison worker would also be the patient's individual therapist. This worker, who is one of the five group therapists who staff the programme, has the following tasks in this role:

- to meet with the patient briefly every week to agree with him or her a therapeutic focus for the week and to deal with any of the patient's questions about being on the programme;
- to liaise with the patient's consultant if necessary;
- to liaise with ward or day care personnel if necessary.

Secondly, after every group, therapists give one of the therapy assistants verbal feedback en each patient's contribution to the group. This report is then written up by the therapy assistant. Finally, a weekly formal patient progress review is held and a written report on each patient is sent to the patient's consultant psychiatrist.

Team supervision

The group therapists and the therapy assistants receive weekly supervision.

The Difficulties of Working on CBT Group Therapy Programmes

I have worked on several CBT group therapy programmes over the past ten years and in this closing section, I will discuss the difficulties that my colleagues and I have encountered on such programmes. My remarks, therefore, will refer to all my experiences and should not be taken to just refer to my time with the Florence Nightingale CBT Group Therapy Programme.

Patients spending a short period of time on the programme

Perhaps the most frustrating aspect of working on a CBT group therapy programme in the private sector is that a sizeable proportion of patients only spend a limited time on the programme. This may be due to a number of reasons, of which limited private insurance cover is perhaps the most common. For whatever reason, this means that we are quite limited in what we can achieve with such patients. On the Florence Nightingale CBT Group Therapy Programme, patients need to spend at least six weeks with us to learn sufficient skills to benefit from their stay. This period needs to be longer with more disturbed patients. What is particularly frustrating for us is that we often do not know at the outset how long patients will be with us and also patients do not know this. This is because consultant psychiatrists often have to apply to insurance companies for treatment extensions for their patients and such extensions may not always be granted.

The consequence of this situation is that many patients leave the programme only having learned a few skills which are usually not sufficient for their long-term care. This is not so bad if a patient bas been referred to a CBT therapist for ongoing individual therapy, but if patients are referred to a non-CBT individual therapist or if they have no individual therapy, we have to accept the grim reality that we cannot do as much for these patients as we would like. This is frustrating!

Patients who have concurrent non-CBT therapy

Some consultants are particularly fond of a mixed therapeutic regime and may refer a patient to the CBT group therapy programme and to a psychoanalytic therapist for individual therapy, for example. In some cases, this mixed regime works quite well and patients can use what each approach to therapy has to offer, but more often patients get quite confused by being in two different types of therapy. On these occasions, we bring this situation to the attention of the patient's consultant psychiatrist and suggest that the patient's therapy regime is made internally consistent. Problems can persist when this suggestion is not taken up and in such cases we do the best we can under difficult circumstances.

Difficulties with consultant psychiatrists

My own experience in working with consultant psychiatrists in the private sector has generally been good. When a consultant has made an inappropriate referral to the CBT programme and I have provided a reasoned argument, either verbally or in writing, why the referral was inappropriate then, normally, the consultant has accepted this. On occasion, the consultant has insisted that the patient come on to the programme and in such situations it has been useful to ask another consultant or the therapy services manager to intervene with the consultant concerned.

Sometimes, consultants ask for special dispensation for their patients. For example, problems used to arise when consultants scheduled appointments with their patients and expected patients to be able to leave or join groups accordingly. This was incredibly disruptive until we introduced the rule that stated that patients could not join groups after ten minutes had elapsed and if they had a later appointment during group time and informed consultants of this rule that had hospital backing. Nevertheless, as I said, a small number of consultants ask for special dispensation for their patients and don't take kindly when this is denied. This can put a strain on junior therapists who have to assert themselves with the consultant concerned. However, with the backing of the therapy services manager, these situations can usually be resolved.

In one hospital where I worked, a consultant psychiatrist who had a special interest in CBT had set up the CBT group therapy programme and was closely associated with it. This certainly helped when problems with other consultants occurred because the CBT consultant could sort this out fairly quickly with his colleague.

One of the difficulties that I have personally experienced in this regard is due to the limited time I can devote to working in the hospital setting. This means that I have limited contact with consultant psychiatrists who are generally incredibly busy professionals who are as hard to contact by telephone as I am. When a problem occurs, I do eventually speak with the consultant concerned, but there is so much more I could do to facilitate consultant–CBT staff relationships if I were working full-time in the hospital setting.

Difficulties with non-CBT therapists

The final difficulty that I wish to discuss concerns relationships between therapists working on the CBT programme and therapists working on other group therapy programmes. From my experience, these difficulties arise particularly when regular meetings between CBT and non-CBT therapists are not held. They also arise when certain misconceptions regarding CBT held by non-CBT therapists are allowed to go unchallenged.

When staff from all therapy programmes are willing to discuss the strengths and weaknesses of their particular programme and to acknowledge the strengths of other programmes and where a good team spirit among all staff exists, then difficulties with non-CBT therapists are kept to a minimum. On the other hand, where a competitive, envy-based environment bas been allowed to develop between staff on different programmes, then these difficulties persist unchecked and can breed festering resentment among all concerned with predictable negative consequences. Fortunately, in my experience, this latter situation has rarely occurred.

In this chapter, I have described the Florence Nightingale CBT Group Therapy Programme and discussed a number of factors that both enhance and impede the effective running of this and other similar programmes. It is my hope that this chapter will spark a debate that will result in the increased effectiveness of such programmes nationally.

References

Dryden W (1994) Ten Steps to Positive Living. London: Sheldon.

Dryden W (1999) Rational Emotive Behaviour Therapy: A Personal Approach. Bicester: Winslow Press.

Ellis A (1980) Rational-emotive therapy and cognitive behavior therapy: similarities and differences. Cognitive Therapy and Research 4: 325–40.

Ellis A (1994) Reason and Emotion in Psychotherapy. Revised and updated edition. New York: Birch Lane Press.

Traverse J, Dryden W (1995) Rational Emotive Behaviour Therapy: A Client's Guide. London: Whurr.

CHAPTER 6

Teaching the Principles of Unconditional Self-Acceptance in a Structured, Group Setting

WINDY DRYDEN

In this chapter I will describe an eight-week psycho-educational group that I run in which I teach group members the principles of unconditional self-acceptance. These principles stem from the theory of Rational Emotive Behaviour Therapy (REBT).

In the chapter, I will: (1) briefly review the concept of ego disturbance in relation to REBT theory; (2) present the principles of unconditional self-acceptance; (3) outline the steps of a self-acceptance group and some of the exercises that I use at each step and discuss briefly the context in which I run these groups.

REBT and Ego Disturbance

Rational Emotive Behaviour Therapy is an approach to counselling and psychotherapy which can be best placed within the cognitive-behavioural psychotherapeutic tradition. One of its basic premises is that psychological disturbance stems primarily from the irrational beliefs that we hold about ourselves, others and the world. However, REBT theory holds that the way we feel, think and act are intertwined so that when considering their clients' feelings of depression, for example, Rational Emotive Behaviour therapists will consider not only the beliefs that underpin the clients' depression, but also the behaviour which may serve to perpetuate their depressogenic beliefs.

REBT therapists can, in my view, best be seen as psychological educators in that they will teach their clients the basic REBT view of disturbance and once the latter have indicated that they wish to work in this way will teach clients how to identify, challenge and change the irrational beliefs which underpin their psychological problems. For a much fuller consideration of the theory and practice of REBT see Dryden (1995a, 1995b).

Since this chapter concerns a structured, group approach to teaching clients unconditional self-acceptance I will first outline the REBT concept of ego disturbance before presenting the REBT concept of unconditional self-acceptance.

Ego disturbance

REBT theory distinguishes between two major types of psychological disturbance: ego disturbance and discomfort disturbance (Dryden, 1994). Ego disturbance stems from irrational beliefs related to a person's 'self', while discomfort disturbance stems from irrational beliefs related to that individual's personal domain unrelated to his 'self', but centrally related to his sense of comfort.

Ego disturbance results when a person makes a demand on himself, others, or the world and when that demand is not met the person puts himself down in some way. The following themes are usually involved in ego disturbance:

- failing to achieve an important target or goal;
- acting incompetently (in public or private);
- not living up to one's standards;
- breaking one's ethical code;
- being criticized;
- being ridiculed;
- not being accepted, approved, appreciated or loved by significant others.

Ego-related irrational beliefs are found in a variety of emotional disturbances. Please note, however, that I am not saying that these ego irrational beliefs completely account for the emotions listed below. Rather, I am saying that these beliefs are often found when clients report these emotional experiences. In the following examples, you will note that each of these irrational beliefs contains two elements. First, there is a demanding belief which often takes the form of a 'must', 'absolute should', 'have to' or 'got to'; secondly, there is a self-downing belief which takes the form of a global negative evaluation of one's total 'self'. REBT theory states that self-downing beliefs are derived from the musturbatory beliefs.

Depression

'Because I have failed the test, as I absolutely should not have done, I am a failure.'
'Since my partner has rejected me, as he absolutely should not have done, this proves that I am no good.'

Anxiety

'If I fail at my upcoming test, which I must not do, I will be a failure.'
'If he rejects me as I think he will soon, but which he must not do, I will be no good.'

Guilt

'I have hurt the feelings of my parents, which I absolutely should not have done, and therefore am a bad person.'
'I failed to help a good friend of mine. The fact that I did not do what I absolutely should have done proves that I am a rotten person.'

Shame

'I have acted foolishly in front of my peers, which I absolutely should not have done, and this makes me an inadequate person.'
'I have been having sexual feelings towards my sister, which I absolutely should not have, and the fact that I have these feelings makes me a shameful person.'

Hurt

'My ex-boyfriend is going out with my best friend, which absolutely should not happen. Since it is happening, this proves that I am unlovable.'

Anger

'You absolutely should not have criticized me in the way that you did. Your criticism reminds me that I am a failure.'

Jealousy

'If my husband looks at another woman, which he must not do, it means that he finds her more attractive, which must not happen and proves that I am worthless.'

Envy

'My friend is making better progress than I am in our respective careers. I must have what he has and because I don't this makes me less worthy than I would be if I had what he has.'

Unconditional Self-Acceptance

Ego disturbance occurs when a person makes a global negative evaluation of her total self, which in turn is based on the existence of a musturbatory belief. REBT theory states that the healthy alternative to ego disturbance is based on a set of beliefs centred on the concept of unconditional self-acceptance. In this section I will outline the ten principles that underpin this concept.

Human beings cannot legitimately be given a single global rating

In the previous section I gave several examples of the ways in which people put themselves down (e.g. 'I am a failure', 'I am a bad person'). Each of these involves the person giving himself or herself a single global rating. Indeed, the concept of self-esteem frequently advocated by the majority of counsellors and psychotherapists is based on this same principle. Low self-esteem involves the assignment of a single, negative, global rating to a person, and high self-esteem involves the assignment of a single, positive, global rating to the person.

REBT theory argues that it is not possible to give a person a single global rating, be it negative or positive. This is best shown if we define clearly the terms 'self' and 'esteem'. First, let's take the term 'self'. Paul Hauck has provided a very simple, but profound definition of the self. He says that the self is 'every conceivable thing about you that can be rated' (1991: 33). This means that all your thoughts, images, feelings, behaviours and bodily parts are part of your 'self' and all these different aspects that belong to you from the beginning of your life to the moment just before your death have to be included in your 'self'. Now let's consider the term 'esteem'. This term is derived from the verb to estimate which means to give something a rating, judgement or estimation. The question then arises: can we give the 'self' a single legitimate rating, estimation or judgement which completely accounts for its complexity? The answer is clearly 'no'. As Hauck (1991) notes, it is possible to rate different aspects of one's 'self', but a person is far too complex to warrant a single, legitimate, global rating.

Even if it were possible to give a person a single global rating – a task which would involve a team of objective judges and a computer so powerful that it could analyse the millions upon millions of data produced by that person – as soon as that global judgement was made, it would become immediately redundant since that person would continue to produce more data. In other words, a person is an ongoing, ever-changing process and defies the ascription of a single, static, global judgement.

To summarize, it is not possible, in any legitimate sense, to give one's self a single global rating since you are too complex to merit such an evaluation; and you are an ongoing ever-changing process who defies being statically rated by yourself or by others.

By contrast, the concept of unconditional self-acceptance does not involve any such rating or evaluation. However, and this is a crucial point, unconditional self-acceptance does allow you to rate different aspects of yourself. Indeed, it encourages this type of evaluation, since doing so allows you to focus on your negative aspects and do something to improve them without self-blame. Conversely, if you focus on your negative aspects from the standpoint of self-esteem, then you are less likely to change them because you are sidetracked by giving your 'self' a global negative rating for having these aspects. It is difficult to change anything about yourself while you are beating yourself over the head for having those aspects in the first place.

Human beings are essentially fallible

REBT theory holds that if human beings have an essence it is probably that we are essentially fallible. As Maxie Maultsby (1984) has put it, humans have an incurable error-making tendency. I would add that we frequently make more serious mistakes than we are prepared to accept and that we often keep repeating the same errors. Why do we do this? As Paul Hauck (1991) has put it, we keep repeating our errors out of stupidity, ignorance or because we are psychologically disturbed. Albert Ellis (1994) has noted that humans find it very easy to disturb themselves and difficult to undisturb themselves. Self-acceptance, then, means acknowledging that our essence is fallibility and that we are not perfectible.

All humans are equal in humanity, but unequal in their different aspects

This principle follows on from the two listed above. If the essence of humanity is fallibility then all humans are equal in their humanity, and since human beings cannot be rated it follows that no human is worthier than any other. This principle reveals Rational Emotive Behaviour Therapy as one of the most, if not the most, humanistic of all psychotherapies. However, this principle of parity does not deny that there is a great deal of variation among human beings with respect to their different aspects. Thus, Adolf Hitler may be equal in humanity to Mother Theresa, but in terms of their compassion to human beings, the latter far outscores the former.

The rational use of the concept of human worth

From the principles discussed thus far, you will see that the concept of human worth is problematic since it rests on the assignment of a single global rating (worth) to a process (the 'self') which defies such a simple rating. However, a number of clients want to retain the idea of human worth even though it has inherent problems. The main problem with the concept is that people normally make their worth contingent on variables that change (e.g. 'I am worthwhile if I do well in my exams', which implies that if I do not do well then I am not worthwhile). Even if a person fulfils the conditions of worth at any given moment, she is still vulnerable to emotional disturbance if those conditions are not continually met.

The only way that a person can apply the concept of human worth in a rational manner is to make her worth contingent on one of two constants. First, she can say that she is worthwhile because she is human. Secondly, she can say that she is worthwhile as long as she is alive. This can even be applied by people who believe in an afterlife ('I am worthwhile as long as I am alive in this life or any future life that I may have'). The difficulty with this concept, as Ellis (1972) has shown, is that someone can just as easily say: 'I am worth-less because I am alive' or 'I am worthless because I am human'. For this reason, most REBT therapists discourage their clients from using the concept of human worth.

Unconditional self-acceptance avoids errors of overgeneralization

When people apply the concept of conditional self-esteem they constantly make errors of overgeneralization, or what might be called part–whole errors. In the part–whole error, a person infers that he has failed to, achieve a certain goal (which represents a part of the person), evaluates this failure negatively and then concludes that he (the whole of the person) is a failure. In other words, he rates the whole of himself on the basis of his rating of a part of himself. Applying the concept of unconditional self-acceptance to this example, the person would still infer that he has failed to achieve his goal and would still evaluate this failure negatively. However, his conclusion – that his failure proves that he is a fallible human being – would be perfectly logical.

Unconditional self-acceptance is based on a flexible, preferential philosophy

Earlier in this chapter I pointed out that self-downing beliefs are derived from rigid, musturbatory beliefs, as in Albert Ellis's memorable phrase: 'Shouldhood leads to shithood. You're never a shit without a should.' What follows from this is that unconditional self-acceptance beliefs are derived from flexible, preferential beliefs. For example, if you believe that you are inadequate because you acted in a socially inappropriate manner then this self-downing belief stems from the rigid belief: 'I must not behave inappro-priately in a social context.' A self-accepting alternative belief would involve you accepting yourself as a fallible human being who is not inadequate. This belief in turn would stem from the flexible belief: 'I would prefer not to act in a socially inappropriate manner, but there's no reason why I absolutely must not do so.'

Self-acceptance promotes constructive action, not resignation

If we can accept ourselves as fallible human beings with all that this means, paradoxically we have a much better chance of minimizing our errors and psychological problems than if we condemn ourselves for having them in the first place. Such acceptance, then, does not imply resignation, as many people think. Rather, it promotes our constructive efforts to learn from our errors and minimize our tendency to disturb ourselves. Self-acceptance does this because, as shown above, it is based on a flexible philosophy of desire, in this case a desire to live as happily as possible. This desire motivates us to take constructive action. Conversely, resignation is based on the idea that there is nothing we can do to improve aspects of ourselves so there is no point in trying. This, then, is the antithesis of self-acceptance.

Unconditional self-acceptance is a habit that can be acquired (but never perfectly, nor for all time)

Behaviour therapists often construe self-defeating behaviour as bad habits that can be broken, and many clients resonate with the idea that self-downing is a bad habit that can be broken. If you want to use the idea of self-downing and unconditional self-acceptance as habits you can do so, but with the following caveats. Be careful to stress that the 'habit' of self-downing can be broken, but never perfectly and not in a once and for all manner. Similarly, stress that unconditional self-acceptance can be acquired, but again never perfectly nor for all time. Emphasize that it is the very nature of fallible human beings to go back to 'self-downing' under stress even though your client may have worked very hard to break this habit. In doing so you are helping your client to accept herself for her lack of self-acceptance!

Internalizing the philosophy of unconditional self-acceptance is difficult and involves hard work

Understanding the concept of unconditional self-acceptance is not that diffi-cult. Internalizing a philosophy of unconditional self-acceptance so that it makes a positive difference to the way we think, feel and act most certainly is difficult. Here, it is useful to help clients view the acquisition of self-accep-tance as similar to the acquisition of any new skill that has to be learned against the background of a well-ingrained habit that has been overlearned (such as golf or tennis). Acquiring self-acceptance will involve your clients in a lot of hard work; work that has to be done even though clients will experi-ence feelings and tendencies to act, that are consistent with their more thoroughly ingrained philosophy of self-downing. This means that clients will have to tolerate a period of 'feeling all wrong' as they strive to internalize a philosophy that makes perfect sense, but is not yet believed. Such conviction comes from repeatedly challenging self-downing beliefs and acting in a way that is consistent with self-accepting beliefs.

Self-acceptance requires force and energy

The hard work mentioned above can be done in two ways. It can be done with force and energy where, for example, clients challenge their self-downing beliefs with a great deal of force and throw themselves into acting in ways that are consistent with their newly acquired self-accepting beliefs. Or it can be done in a weak, 'namby-pamby' fashion. Since people tend to hold their self-downing beliefs quite rigidly, the latter way of trying to acquire a philosophy of self-acceptance will just not work. It is important to help clients understand the importance of meeting strength with strength or fighting fire with fire. Given this, the more clients use force and energy as they strive to accept themselves, the better their results will be.

Running Self-Acceptance Groups

I will begin this section by providing a brief outline of the basic assumption that underpins self-acceptance groups. Then I will describe the context in which I run these groups before providing a session-by-session account of a typical self-acceptance group.

Basic assumption

The self-acceptance groups that I run are based on the idea that the philosophy of self-acceptance can be taught, in a structured, educational manner and can be understood by group members in a short period of time. Although internalizing this philosophy is a long and arduous endeavour which takes far longer than the eight-week period over which the group is run, it is possible in this short period to help group members to take the first steps in integrating this philosophy into their belief system.

The context

The context in which a therapy group is run has a decided impact on how it is established, and how much impact it has on the well-being of its members. As one colleague complained, 'How can you run a group when every week the chairs are different?' To which I replied, 'Where I work the chairs are the same every week, but the group membership is different!' I work one morning a week in a private hospital setting where two types of group are offered: open groups where people come and go, and every week the size and membership of the group is different; and closed groups where the same group of clients meets every week for a time-limited period. The self-acceptance groups to be described here are, in my experience, best run as a closed group. If they were run as an open group, I would have to introduce the same ideas every week and group cohesion would be lost. A closed group means that clients are introduced to the same ideas and the same techniques at the same time, which means that they can help one another in a way that they couldn't if the group were open.

One issue that does need to be addressed if you work in a private hospital is the timing of clients' appointments with their consultant psychiatrists. Unless you inform consultants of the times of your self-acceptance group and elicit their agreement that they will not schedule appointments during this time, then the group will be disrupted by clients coming back from or going out to see their consultants.

Forming the group

Before you form the group, you need to make decisions about the size of the group, how often it is to meet and how long each session will be. In a private hospital there is the additional constraint that many clients, once they have become 'day patients', do not attend for long periods of time, unless they can afford the high fees or their insurance cover permits long-term attendance. Consequently, my practice is to run a self-acceptance group weekly for one and a half hours over an eight-week period. I have found that a group of between seven and nine clients works best (allowing for one dropout per group).

Since my attendance at the hospital is limited to one morning a week, I do not have the time to interview all the people who wish to join the group. I leave the selection of group members to one of the full-time workers at the hospital who know the nature of the group and the types of client who will benefit most from it. These are people whose problems are mainly ego-related and who have had previous exposure to REBT or cognitive therapy and agree with the idea that dysfunctional beliefs are at the core of psycho-logical disturbance. In addition, group members need to commit to weekly attendance over the life of the group and be prepared to put into practice what they learn from the group, which means the regular completion of homework assignments.

A session-by-session outline of a self-acceptance group

Session 1

Introductions

The members of the group and I introduce ourselves to one another.

Clarifying the preconditions for attendance

Here, I stress that the group is for people whose problems are to do with negative attitudes towards the self and that weekly attendance is expected from all. I also explain the usual rule of confidentiality for group members and elicit members' willingness to comply with this rule.

Who wants high self-esteem?

I normally begin a self-acceptance group by asking members who among them would like to have high self-esteem (or feel better about themselves). Virtually everyone raises their hands. I then ask each member to indicate what would raise their self-esteem. The kind of answers I get are:

- 'Doing well at work.'
- 'Being a better mother.'
- 'Being loved.'
- 'Living up to my principles.'
- 'Doing voluntary work.'

Teaching the principles of unconditional self-acceptance

Before I deal with the responses to the question, 'What would raise your self-esteem?' I spend most of the first session teaching the ten principles of unconditional self-acceptance outlined in the first half of this chapter. After teaching each point I pause for questions and observations from group members.

Another look at self-esteem

After I have finished teaching the ten principles of self-esteem, I ask the group members to reconsider their answers to my question, 'What would raise your self-esteem?' I help them to see that their responses do not serve to raise their self-esteem, but are desirable things to have or achieve in their own right. I show them that self-esteem is contingent upon doing well at work, being loved, and so on and if they were to do poorly at work later or lose the love of a significant person, for example, their self-esteem would plummet. Helping group members to understand that the concept of self-esteem is the cause of their problems and not the solution is very liberating for most.

Homework

Virtually all the members in my self-acceptance groups have been exposed to REBT or cognitive-behaviour therapy and therefore are familiar with the important role that homework assignments have in the therapeutic process.

Since it is beyond the scope of this chapter to deal with cases where group members do not do their homework assignments or modify them in some way, I refer the interested reader to Dryden (1995b).

The first homework assignment I suggest that group members carry out before the second group session is to read Chapters 1 and 3 of Paul Hauck's (1991) book on self-acceptance entitled *Hold Your Head Up High*. Chapter 1 outlines the problems that occur when people do not accept themselves and Chapter 3 presents the principles of self-acceptance. These chapters serve as a reminder of the material covered in the first session. I suggest that while reading the material group members make a note of points that they disagree with or are unsure of for discussion the following week.

Session 2

Reviewing homework

It is an important principle of REBT that if you set a homework assignment then you review it the following session. So at the beginning of this session (and all subsequent sessions) it is important to review what the group members did for homework. In doing so, I correct any misconceptions that group members display in their reading of the chapters in Hauck's book.

Goal-setting

At this point, the group members are ready to consider what they can achieve from the group and what they can't. I point out that my role is to teach them both the principles of self-acceptance and some techniques to help them to begin to internalize this philosophy. What I can do is to help them begin the journey towards self-acceptance. In eight weeks, I cannot help them to complete this journey. Given this, I ask them to set suitable goals for the group. 'What,' I ask, 'will you have achieved by the end of the eight weeks that would show you that you have begun the long and arduous journey towards self-acceptance?' I encourage members to divide into smaller groups and to make their goals as realistic and specific as possible. I then ask one group member to make a written note of everybody's goals, which I then photocopy and distribute at the end of the session so that everybody has a copy of the goals of each member.

Dealing with a specific example of the target problem

I ask group members to choose a specific example of a situation in which they considered themselves to be worthless, inadequate, bad, etc. I then ask each member in turn to talk about the experience briefly to the rest of the group. After the person has finished relating the experience, I use the ABC framework of REBT to help assess it, where A stands for the activating event,

B for her musturbatory and self-downing beliefs and C for her major disturbed negative emotion and/or self-defeating behaviour.

Homework

For homework, I ask each group member to use the ABC framework to analyse another example of 'low self-esteem'.

Session 3

Reviewing homework

At the beginning of the session, I check each person's ABC assessment and offer corrective feedback where relevant.

Teaching disputing of ego irrational beliefs

A central task of group members in a self-acceptance group is to learn how to dispute their musturbatory and self-downing irrational beliefs. Thus, I devote the bulk of this session to teaching this core skill. As DiGiuseppe (1991) has shown, disputing involves group members asking themselves three different types of question of their irrational ego beliefs: (a) are they consistent with reality?; (b) are they logical?; (c) do they yield healthy results? As I showed in the first half of this chapter, the answer to these questions is 'no' when they are applied to self-downing beliefs (see Dryden, 1994, for a full discussion of why musturbatory beliefs are also inconsistent with reality, illogical and yield unhealthy results for the individual concerned).

Disputing also involves helping group members to construct preferential and self-accepting beliefs as healthy alternatives to their irrational ego beliefs. So I spend a good deal of the third session helping group members to construct rational ego beliefs.

Homework: identifying and disputing irrational ego beliefs in specific situations

Armed with their new skill of disputing irrational ego beliefs and constructing alternative rational ego beliefs, group members are now ready to put this new skill into practice in their everyday lives before the next session. This forms the basis for the homework assignment for that week.

Session 4

Reviewing homework

I begin by reviewing the previous week's homework assignment and offering corrective feedback as before.

Teaching the rational portfolio method

As mentioned above, disputing irrational beliefs is a core client skill in Rational Emotive Behaviour Therapy in general and in self-acceptance groups in particular. As I have recently shown (Dryden, 1995c), the purpose of disputing in the present context is to help group members understand why their irrational ego beliefs are irrational and why their alternative rational ego beliefs are rational. Once group members have understood this point, they need additional help to enable them to integrate this understanding into their belief system so that it influences for the better the way they think and feel about themselves and the way they act in the world. Helping them to develop a rational portfolio of arguments in favour of their rational ego beliefs and against their irrational ego beliefs is the cognitive technique that I use to initiate this integration process.

Having introduced the idea of the rational portfolio, I suggest that group members spend about 20 minutes in the session developing their own portfolio of arguments. Then I ask them to work in two small groups, reviewing one another's arguments and suggesting additional arguments. During this time I act as consultant, listening to the small group discussion, offering feedback on the arguments developed and being available as a troubleshooter if either of the groups gets stuck.

Homework

For homework I suggest that group members review and add to the arguments they have developed for their rational portfolio. I also suggest that they make a particular note of any arguments about which they have objections, reservations or doubts, or that they do not find persuasive.

Session 5

Reviewing homework

I begin by reviewing the previous week's homework, paying particular attention to arguments about which group members have objections, doubts or reservations or do not find persuasive. I initiate a group discussion on these arguments and intervene to correct misconceptions or to provide additional explanations to help dispel these doubts etc. and to make their rational arguments more persuasive.

Teaching the zigzag technique

As noted above, it is common for people to respond to their own rational arguments developed in favour of a self-accepting philosophy with what might be called irrational rebuttals, i.e. arguments which cast doubt on the concept of self-acceptance and which in fact advocate a return to the philosophy of self-downing. The zigzag technique formalizes this debate between the irrational and rational 'parts' of the person and gives the person practice at defending her rational ego belief against her own irrational attack. This technique helps group members to integrate their rational ego beliefs into their belief system.

In the zigzag technique, the group member begins by writing down a rational ego belief and rating her degree of conviction in this belief on a 0–100 rating scale. Then she responds to this belief with an irrational argument, which she then rebuts. The group member continues in this vein until she has responded to all of her attacks and can think of no more. She then re-rates her degree of conviction in her rational ego belief, which is usually increased if the person used the technique properly.

Once I have taught the group members the rudiments of this technique I ask them to carry out the technique on their own in the session. I stress the importance of keeping to the point, since it is easy for the person to get sidetracked when using this technique. As group members do this task I go from person to person ensuring that they are doing it correctly and, in particular, keep the focus of the debate on their target rational ego belief (see Dryden, 1995c for an extended discussion of the zigzag technique).

Teaching tape-recorded disputing

Tape-recorded disputing is similar to the zigzag method in that group members put the dialogue between their rational and irrational ego beliefs on tape. In addition to emphasizing once again that it is important to keep to the point while using this method, it is useful to stress that group members respond to their irrational attacks with force and energy. It should be explained that since people often hold their irrational ego beliefs very strongly, weak rational responses will have little lasting effect on irrational attacks. It is useful to give the group members some examples so that they can discriminate between weak and forceful disputing (see Dryden, 1995c for an extended discussion of tape-recorded disputing).

Homework

Tape-recorded disputing is a good homework assignment to set at this point, but it is important to establish first that group members all have access to tape recorders. If not, suitable arrangements should be made for them to gain such access. In addition, I usually suggest that group members read and note any objections to Chapter 4 of Paul Hauck's 1991 book, which considers the importance of behavioural methods in the development of self-acceptance. This will be the focus of the next two group sessions.

Session 6

Reviewing homework

In checking group members' tapes, it is important to pay particular attention to their ability to stay focused on the target beliefs and to the tone they used during disputing, and suitable feedback should be given on these two points. As with other reading material, particular emphasis should be given to group members' reservations about the place of behavioural methods in developing self-acceptance.

Providing a rationale for the conjoint use of cognitive and behavioural methods in real-life settings

REBT theory states that behavioural methods have a central role to play in the therapeutic change process. Unless group members act on their rational ego beliefs, the benefits they will derive from the group will ultimately be minimal. However, the power of behavioural techniques is best harnessed when they are used conjointly with cognitive methods designed to give group members the opportunity to practise their rational ego beliefs in a real-life setting.

Negotiating behavioural-cognitive tasks

After you have provided group members with a rationale for the conjoint use of behavioural and cognitive techniques, it is important to encourage them by setting one or two behavioural-cognitive tasks which they can implement as homework assignments before the next group session. These tasks should preferably be related to group members' goals.

Teaching rational emotive imagery

Rational emotive imagery (REI) is an evocative technique designed to give group members practice in strengthening their rational ego beliefs in the face of negative activating events (As). In self-acceptance groups I suggest the use of REI as preparation for the implementation of the behavioural-cognitive techniques discussed above. Once group members have set a behavioural-cognitive technique, I ask them to imagine a worst-case scenario which constitutes the A in an ABC episode and have them identify and get in touch with an ego-related, disturbed negative emotion (e.g. hurt). Then, while they are still imagining the same negative A, I ask them to change their emotion to a self-accepting, healthy negative emotion. As I have noted elsewhere (Dryden, 1995c), group members achieve this by changing their irrational ego beliefs to rational ego beliefs (see Dryden, 1995c for a fuller discussion of REI).

Homework

For homework, I suggest that group members practise REI three times a day for a few days before implementing their behavioural-cognitive tasks.

Session 7

Reviewing homework

In checking group members' use of REI, you need to make sure that they did, in fact, change their irrational ego beliefs to their rational alternatives rather than change the negative activating event to something more positive. In reviewing their behavioural-cognitive tasks, you need to ensure that they actually faced the situation that they wanted to confront or acted in the manner planned, and that they practised thinking rationally while doing so.

Agreeing other behavioural-cognitive tasks

If members were successful in implementing their behavioural-cognitive assignment it is important to capitalize on this success by negotiating two additional behavioural tasks. Encourage group members to choose tasks that are challenging, but not overwhelming for them. However, if any group member struggled with their initial behavioural-cognitive task, you will have to be less adventurous in the next such assignment you negotiate with that person.

Explaining and agreeing shame-attacking exercises

Shame-attacking exercises involve group members acting in a so-called 'shameful' manner and accepting themselves as they do so. They should attract attention to themselves without alarming others, breaking the law or getting themselves into trouble at work. Examples of good shame-attacking exercises are as follows:

- wearing different-coloured shoes;
- asking to see a three-piece suite in a sweet shop;
- singing off-key in public;
- asking for directions to a road one is already in.

I suggest that group members do at least one shame-attacking exercise before the final group session.

Homework

The last set of homework assignments is as described above. In addition, I ask group members to come to the last session prepared to talk about what they have achieved from the group and to give feedback about their experience of being in the group.

Session 8

Reviewing homework

For the last time, I check on group members' homework assignments and give corrective feedback as usual. Group members are usually keen to learn about one another's shame-attacking exercises and this generates a sense of fun which, in my opinion, is quite suitable to the ending of a group of this educational nature.

The self-acceptance quiz

In the spirit of fun and to assess what group members have learned, I ask them to complete in writing a short written quiz (see Figure 6.1).

Why not do the quiz yourself to see what you have learned from this chapter?

SELF-ACCEPTANCE OUIZ

Give reasons for each answer

1   Having the love of a significant other makes you a more worthwhile person.
True or false?

2   If someone you admire is better than you at an important activity, he or she is a better person than you.
True or false?

3   If you fail at something really important, you are not a failure, but a fallible human being.
True or false?

4   You can give a human being a single global rating which completely accounts for them.
True or false?

5   Someone who rapes a small child is wicked through and through.
True or false?

6   Mother Theresa has more worth than Adolf Hitler.
True or false?

Figure 6.1. Self-acceptance quiz.

Evaluating progress and eliciting feedback on the group

I then ask group members to relate what progress they have made towards self-acceptance and whether or not they have achieved their goals. I also ask them to give feedback on the group experience, my way of running it and how it might be improved. Since all group members are involved in other groups in the hospital and many are also in individual psychotherapy, it has not been possible for me to carry out formal research into the effectiveness of self-acceptance groups.

Helping group members to maintain and extend their gains

The final task that I ask group members to do is to develop a list of ways of maintaining and extending the gains that they have made from participating in the group (see Dryden, 1995b, 1995c for a fuller discussion of these two points). I stress that they have taken the first few steps along the road to self-acceptance and that how far they go along this road will largely be dependent on the amount of work that they are prepared to do on themselves using the methods that I have taught them during the group. On this point, I wish them well and we say our goodbyes.

References

DiGiuseppe R (1991) Comprehensive cognitive disputing in RET. In ME Bernard (ed.) Using Rational-Emotive Therapy Effectively. New York: Plenum Press.

Dryden W (1994) Invitation to Rational-Emotive Psychology. London: Whurr.

Dryden W (1995a) Preparing for Client Change in Rational Emotive Behaviour Therapy. London: Whurr.

Dryden W (1995b) Facilitating Client Change in Rational Emotive Behaviour Therapy. London: Whurr.

Dryden W (1995c) Brief Rational Emotive Behaviour Therapy. Chichester: Wiley.

Ellis A (1972) Psychotherapy and the Value of a Human Being. New York: Institute for Rational-Emotive Therapy.

Ellis A (1994) Reason and Emotion in Psychotherapy: A Comprehensive Method of Treating Human Disturbances, revised and updated edn. New York: Birch Lane Press.

Hauck P (1991) Hold Your Head Up High. London: Sheldon Press.

Maultsby MC Jr (1984) Rational Behavior Therapy. Englewood Cliffs, NJ: Prentice-Hall.

CHAPTER 7

Rational Emotive Behavior Therapy Intensives

ALBERT ELLIS

Therapeutic lectures, classes, and sermons have been given for many centuries by Confucius, Epictetus, Mary Baker Eddy, Emile Coué, Dale Carnegie, Normal Vincent Peale and other teachers and preachers. After the experiential movement got going in the 1960s, Werner Erhard and a number of his imitators started in the 1970s to combine emotive-evocative exercises with impassioned lectures and to give weekend Intensives. These include lectures, experiential exercises, and emotional sharing and are usually given to groups of 50 to 200 people.

I (AE) had a series of planning sessions with several of our therapists at the Albert Ellis Institute in New York in 1983 and we devised a 9-hour Rational Emotive Behavior Therapy Intensive. I, Ray DiGiuseppe, Diana Richman, Janet Wolfe and a number of Fellows and Associate Fellows of the Institute have been giving these Intensives every year in New York and other major cities and have found them to be quite effective. In fact, a study that we did of self-ratings of participants before they took the Intensive and two months after they took it showed significant improvement in their healthy Beliefs (Ellis, Sichel, Leaf and Maas, 1989). Personal communications by participants who were new to REBT and also by those who had some REBT sessions before taking the Intensive also bear out this finding.

The REBT Intensive commonly used by the Institute usually has six major sections, each of which takes about $1^1/_4$ hours: (1) 'The ABCs of REBT and Disputing of Irrational Beliefs', (2) 'Perfectionism and Unconditional Self-Acceptance', (3) 'Dealing with Anger and Rage', (4) 'Dealing with the Dire Need for Approval and Love Slobbism', (5) 'Dealing with Low Frustration Tolerance' and (6) 'Goal-Setting and Homework'.

Each section starts with a strong, evocative lecture on the REBT approach to understanding and handling a major aspect of emotional disturbance, followed by experiential exercises that all the participants are encouraged to perform. Then there is a 15-minute period for the sharing of thoughts and feelings about the lecture and about participation in the exercises. By the end of the 9-hour Intensive almost all the participants have been drawn into the exercises and the sharing of their feelings. Many of them report dramatic personal experiences in the course of the Intensive, as well as later changes in their lives.

The Intensive has a number of cognitive advantages for the participants, including learning the general principles of REBT; learning to take responsibility for many of their emotional and personally and personality problems; modeling themselves after other Intensive participants who begin opening themselves up; seeing their own problems, of which they were previously unaware; and seeing how many other people are suffering from similar problems.

A good deal of cognitive restructuring is included in every Intensive. Each lecture shows that Irrational Beliefs (IBs) are quite different from Rational Beliefs (RBs) and lead to unhealthy feelings and behaviors. Several of the sections show participants how to dispute and change their IBs and how to reach Effective New Philosophies (Es). Methods of reframing and of REBT cost-benefit analysis are explained and illustrated. When the participants give unrealistic and illogical answers during some of the exercises, the leaders of the Intensive briefly and sometimes humorously respond to them and show them and the rest of the participants what more practical solutions would be. Participants are encouraged to ask questions and briefly raise personal problems; and these are answered by the leader in terms of REBT philosophies. Some illustrative disputing of the dysfunctional Beliefs of several participants is done. Several people are shown how to specifically question their own IBs, to come up with alternative RBs, and to take for homework assignments the steady and vigorous repetition of their newly arrived at Effective Philosophies.

Emotively, the Intensive participants receive forceful presentations of REBT and engage in some of its dramatic-evocative exercises, such as its famous shame-attacking exercise. They are encouraged to take verbal and activity risks, participate in the singing of rational humorous songs, and urged to be adventure-seeking and pleasure-seeking.

Behaviorally, participants are given active-directive instructions, are encouraged to take on goal-seeking and homework assignments, and are given practice in carrying out REBT thinking, encountering and skill training. The Albert Ellis Institute in New York also offers a series of follow-up talks and workshops on various aspects of REBT that are open to any Intensive participants who want to take part in them. If some individuals realize, in the course of the Intensive, that they have ongoing personality problems, the Institute also offers regular sessions of individual and group therapy that they can arrange to take. As usual, the Institute also distributes a good many pamphlets, books, audio- and video-cassettes, and other self-help materials that Intensive participants can use for continuing homework assignments.

As is also true of individuals who have effective REBT Marathon experiences, those who benefit from REBT Intensives may experience a cognitive and emotional 'high' for a few weeks following their participation but may easily fall back later to their former lower levels of functioning. This has been found in participants of all kinds of marathons and intensives. Therefore, follow-up procedures and materials had better be available for participants who are willing to use important aspects of REBT on a continuing basis.

It has been found that participants who benefit from various kinds of Intensives, including that especially designed for REBT, often feel a cognitive and emotional 'high' immediately after and sometimes for several weeks following their participation. They quickly 'get' some of the main goals of REBT and start putting them into practice – thus improving their lives considerably. However, this improvement may be short-lived and they may soon stop applying some of the principles they learned during the Intensive and fall back to their former lower levels of functioning.

This is probably because some of the best elements of Rational Emotive Behavior Therapy can be quickly seen, agreed with, and applied by some people in a few sessions of therapy, or by reading REBT materials, or in a nine-hour Intensive. This is especially true if people are highly motivated to change. But gaining sensible insights and enthusiastic feelings will not alone permanently modify dysfunctional behavior. As REBT has indicated from its inception, changing habitual disturbances indeed requires cognitive and affective insights; but it also requires persistent behavioral practice (Ellis, 1958, 1962, 1994). So the quick and dramatic improvements that participants sometimes display after taking a REBT Intensive have to be followed up with hard work that solidifies them. Just as people have low frustration tolerance (LFT) that interferes with their persisting at beneficial exercises, dieting, and other programs of improving their health; so do they often energetically start but fail to continue to work at their mental health programs. So their enthusiastic gains from a nine-hour Intensive may give them a valiant propulsion to helping themselves – but hardly provide them with a finished project.

At the Albert Ellis Institute, we therefore include homework assignments as an important part of our Intensive, and we find that many participants help themselves with these assignments. But we also provide other REBT procedures for those participants who choose to choose from. Thus, our psychological clinic has a score of therapists who are available for regular individual and group therapy. It schedules many talks, seminars and workshops. It provides my regular Friday Night *Problems of Daily Living* Workshop, where live demonstrations of REBT with volunteer clients are given, along with active audience participation. As many as 200 people may attend this regular Friday presentation and a dozen or so more actively join in the discussion. Many members of the audience attend it 20 or 30 times (see Chapter 8).

The Albert Ellis Institute also publishes a large number of books, pamphlets and audiovisual material on REBT and CBT. Its professional staff gives many outside talks, workshops, courses, radio and TV presentations on REBT and its clinical and research findings.

These supplementary programs and materials of the Institute provide Intensive participants with regular follow-up possibilities of learning REBT theory and practice. We find that the Intensives are good in their own right but that, when simultaneously engaged with other REBT activities, many participants not only benefit quickly but more importantly, with some degree of permanence. This tends to show that the more persistently people work and practice REBT, the better results they reap. The REBT Intensives are a special kind of group therapy that makes an important addition to widen its armamentarium of therapeutic techniques.

Manual for Leaders of the REBT Intensives

All leaders of the Intensives are given a special training course, which starts with their actually being regular participants themselves in several Intensives. Then they are given a manual with a detailed outline of instructions for the Intensive. As they lead some Intensives, they are evaluated by members of the groups that they lead and by special observers assigned by the Albert Ellis Institute. Each Intensive leader is also a seasoned Graduate Fellow of the Institute.

Here are some major excerpts from the Training Manual for leaders. Some parts of this Manual are omitted, in order to discourage untrained leaders from giving Intensives.

INSTRUCTIONS FOR PARTICIPANTS IN THE REBT INTENSIVE

1. Welcome as a participant in this REBT Intensive! If you adventurously and actively throw yourself into it and plumb its experiential qualities to the full, you will most probably have a highly enjoyable – and most busy – day!
2. Be sure to come early! The Intensive will begin promptly at 9:00 a.m., and special instructions and arrangements will be made at the beginning. So make sure that you are actually checked in by 8:45 a.m. No later!
3. The Intensive will be a large group experience and will not break up into small groups. This kind of large group encounter is quite different from other participations you may have had and has some unique experiential qualities. Try to savor it to the full and get the most out of it.
4. When you are in the main room, do not sit next to someone you know but sit next to a stranger. You will be in this main room for, at most, one and a quarter hours at a time and will be able to go to the bathroom or go out to smoke regularly. Try, when you are seated in the main room, to stay there and NOT run to the bathrooms. If you cannot wait for a full hour and a quarter, try to get an aisle seat. Running to the bathroom or for water while the Intensive is in progress in the large room is not awful but it is damned inconvenient and disruptive for the rest of the participants. Try to avoid it!
5. Once again, throw yourself into it and have a happy Intensive!

9:00 a.m. THE ABCs of REBT and DISPUTING IRRATIONAL BELIEFS

GOALS (G) AND PURPOSES: TO STAY ALIVE AND BE HAPPY. DEFINITION OF THE TERM 'RATIONAL' AS USED IN REBT

1. Rational Beliefs tend to aid Human survival and happiness.
2. Rational means efficiently aiding survival and happiness.
3. Nonabsolutistic and nondogmatic. Probabilistic.
4. Describes and is in accord with Social reality.
5. Leading to healthy feelings.
6. Including effective, functional action.
7. Preferences, desires and wishes rather than absolutistic demands and commands.

ABCs of EMOTIONAL HEALTH AND DISTURBANCE

A (Activating Event or Adversity) contributes to and may significantly affect C but does not wholly CAUSE C (emotional and behavioral consequences or concomitants). Blocks goals (G).

B (Belief System) more directly and importantly contributes to or 'causes' C. A *times* B equals C.

Because you can usually choose or control B, you are mainly (though not entirely)

responsible for believing B and for the emotional consequences you thereby create.

C consists of rational Beliefs (rBs) and irrational Beliefs (iBs).

MOST COMMON AND IMPORTANT IRRATIONAL BELIEFS (iBs) THAT LEAD TO DISTURBED CONSEQUENCES

1 Musts, shoulds, oughts, absolutistic demands (Examples: 'I must do well!' 'I have to be loved!' 'You should treat me fairly!') Main iBs derived from musts:

2. Awfulizing, horribilizing, terribilizing (Examples: 'It is awful when I fail as I must NOT!' 'Because you must love me, it is horrible when you don't!' 'Since justice MUST exist, it is terrible when it doesn't!')

3. I-can't-stand-it-itis. (Example: 'Because I must get a good job, I can't stand it when I am turned down!')

4. Self-downing (Example: 'Since I failed at school, which I ought not have done, I am a stupid, rotten person!')

5. Other-downing (Example: 'Because you treat me poorly, as you must not, you are a thorough louse who deserves to be punished!')

6. Life-downing (Example: 'Because life is too hard, as it must not be, the world is a horrible place and it is hardly worth living in it!')

7. Allness: (Example: 'Because I have miserably failed, as I must not, I'll always fail and never succeed at this important task!')

TECHNIQUES FOR DISPUTING IRRATIONAL BELIEFS (iBs)

1 Cherchez le should, cherchez le must! Look for the should, look for the must! Don't give up!

2. Why should I or others do well?

3. Where is the evidence that I have to be approved or loved?

4. Prove that the world must be fair.

5. In what way do I have to be as good as others?

6. Where is it written that because I failed this time, I'll always fail?

7. In what manner can't I *stand* serious problems and hassles?

8. Show me how it is terrible and awful if things go wrong.

9. Is it true that I can't cope with adversity?

10. Why *can't* I change my ways and get over my misery?
11. Will the world come to an end if I fail to keep this job?
12. What's the worst thing that will happen if the person I love completely rejects me?
13. Are people really against me as I think they are?
14. Was it actually my fault that I got rejected?
15. Is this bad thing that happened actually that bad?
16. Can no good come of my failing in this instance?
17. If I see myself as worthless does that prove that I really am no good for anything?
18. How does my rotten performance make me a totally rotten or inadequate person?
19. How do I know that my predicting that they won't like me is correct?
20. Why must I be totally right about the things I do? Why can't I sometimes be wrong and still get pretty good results?

EXERCISE FOR ABCs OF REBT

Here is a list of rational Beliefs (rBs) and irrational Beliefs (iBs). I am going to read you this list, one at a time and have you shout out **yes, rational** or **no, irrational** to each item on the list. For example, if I say, 'I thoroughly dislike bigotry and narrow-mindedness!', you would yell out, **yes, rational**. And if I read, 'I thoroughly hate all people who are bigoted and narrow-minded,' you would shout, **no, irrational**. Again, if I say, 'Having a good job is very important to me,' you would yell out **yes, rational**. But if I say, 'Having a good job is sacred to me, and I cannot be happy at all if I don't have one,' you would shout, **no, irrational**. Ready, now? After each statement that I read, you shout **yes, rational** or **no, irrational**. Okay – let's go!

I find it highly obnoxious when I fail at important tasks.	**Yes, rational**
Making money is the most important thing to me.	**Yes, rational**
Hitler was a completely rotten person!	**No, irrational**
Because I work hard, I absolutely deserve to succeed.	**No, irrational**
Because my parents made sacrifices for me, I owe them love.	**No, irrational**
You have no right to treat me unfairly!	**No, irrational**
I enjoy proving that I can do better than others.	**Yes, rational**
I loathe dancing and do my best to avoid it.	**Yes, rational**
When people act unfairly they ought to be severely damned and punished.	**No, irrational**

I need to be loved by people I find important.	**No, irrational**
I very much want to be competent and outstanding in tasks that I find important.	**Yes, rational**
I think that love is the most important thing in the world.	**Yes, rational**
People who act abominably make me angry.	**No, irrational**
I must fully understand where I got my irrational Beliefs in order to change them.	**No, irrational**
When I perform badly or weakly I would like others to help me.	**Yes, rational**
When I do good deeds, like helping others who are in trouble, I am a good person.	**No, irrational**

EXERCISE FOR DISPUTING IRRATIONAL BELIEFS

I am now going to read you, one at a time, a number of irrational Beliefs and I want you to figure out how to Dispute them. After I read aloud each irrational Belief, raise your hand to show me that you have a method of Disputing it. (At this point read the following irrational Beliefs, one at a time, and ask people with raised hands to Dispute each one. Comment on and add to the Disputations. Make sure that you or a member of the audience answers each of these iBs correctly):

1. I am now 39 years of age and have not had a lasting relationship yet, and I am therefore sure that I never will have one.
2. Because I am a nice person other people should always treat me nicely and fairly.
3. If the person I truly love and have loved more than anyone else in the world thoroughly rejects me, that is awful and I can't stand it!
4. People who keep seriously harming others are no good and should be thoroughly damned and severely punished.
5. If I fail this very important test I will never finish school and get my degree. Therefore, I have to pass it.
6. Giving up smoking for the rest of my life would be so painful that I couldn't stand doing so and therefore I might as well continue to smoke.
7. The world has so many exceptionally bad things in it - such as mugging, bigotry, murder, and terrorism - that there's no way in which I can really be a happy person and I might just as well kill myself.
8. I can certainly stand not being approved or loved by most people much of the time, but if no one in the world really cared for me and I had to be without intimate and deep relationships for the rest of my life I couldn't possibly bear this and lead any kind of a happy life.

9. Now that I am alive I can't stand the thought of being dead and not being able to live and enjoy myself in any way after I have died.
10. I can tolerate my doing stupid and bad things but if I really acted very immorally and hurt some people very much, I could never accept myself and would feel guilty and damnable for the rest of my days.
11. If someone I really care for and have done my best to treat nicely rejects me that means that there is something very wrong with me and that I'll never be able to win anyone I truly love.
12. If I get cancer it would be so bad that I think of it continually and can't stop imagining that I may have it and worrying about it.

EXERCISE FOR DISPUTING IRRATIONAL BELIEFS

Close your eyes. Imagine yourself in one of the worst situations you can think of – such as failing at an important job, being rejected by someone for whom you really care, having a serious disease or injury, or giving a very poor public presentation and being laughed at by the audience. Let yourself feel very upset about this – anxious, depressed, guilty, or self-downing. Really let yourself feel miserable. Now take another look at the bad situation which you are imagining yourself in and see it much differently. See that it is really not that serious. Change your expectations about it. Look at it somewhat humorously.

Open your eyes. How do you now feel? How are you seeing things differently? What can you do to cope with this situation if it actually arises again? How can you take a more positive attitude toward it?

SHARING: How do you feel about this lecture and these exercises on the ABCs of REBT and on disputing and changing irrational beliefs? What ideas and emotions did this material evoke in you? What did you learn about disputing? How would you use this knowledge to help yourself to dispute your own irrational Beliefs in the future?

10:30 a.m. PERFECTIONISM AND SELF-ACCEPTANCE

Definition of perfectionism

1. Attempting to achieve the impossible.
2. Always succeeding, never making serious errors.
3. Refusal to accept social reality.

4. Grandiosity about how you *should* behave.
5. Belief that errors are horrible and catastrophic.
6. Must get OTHERS to act perfectly well.

Results of perfectionism

1. Self-defeating.
2. Too much sadness, sorrow, regret, frustration.
3. Anxiety, depression, hostility.
4. No lasting happiness.
5. Interference with success, achievement, efficiency.
6. Addiction to overeating, smoking, etc.

Cognitive techniques for combating perfectionism

1. Question your grandiosity. Can you or others be perfect?
2. Accept your fallibility – and that of others.
3. See that the world doesn't come to an end when you and others are imperfect.
4. See that perfectionism doesn't equal happiness.
5. See that perfect behavior really doesn't exist.
6. Focus on process of tasks, not just outcome of tasks.

Emotive techniques for combating perfectionism

1. Shame-attacking exercises.
2. Risk-taking exercises.
3. Rational-emotive imagery.
4. Develop sense of humor.
5. Use forceful anti-perfectionistic coping self-statements.

Self-acceptance: Why humans cannot be legitimately rated

1. No standard by which to rate them as a whole.
2. Traits can only be rated according to a chosen purpose.
3. The purpose of self-rating is really nobility or grandiosity.
4. It is an overgeneralization. A table 'isn't better' than another table but HAS 'better' characteristics.
5. I am not a psychologist. You aren't a failure.
6. We falsely accept our parents' 'You are a good boy or a good girl". They don't really MEAN this.

Advantages of rating traits

1. Helps you perform and achieve better.
2. Helps you change poor traits.
3. Helps you relate better.

Behavioral methods for aiding self-acceptance

1. Force yourself to do some things imperfectly.
2. Focus on the task, not just the outcome.
3. Take risks.
4. Give yourself a limited amount of time for some projects.
5. Give yourself time limits for certain individual acts.

EXERCISE: DEALING WITH IMAGINARY SHAME AND SELF-DOWNING

Close your eyes. Imagine yourself caught in an act that you would be ashamed to be seen doing. Imagine, for example, that you are lying in bed in your own room masturbating and that you are sure that you are alone and unobserved, but you suddenly see that a TV camera is trained on you, recording your every move, and that the full picture of you lying naked in bed and vigorously masturbating is being transmitted to a dozen of your friends and other people who are in the next room and who are laughing uproariously about what you are doing.

Let yourself feel exceptionally ashamed, self-downing, depressed, or whatever you feel about being caught in this presumably shameful and laughable position.

Now, after you have felt ashamed and embarrassed for a while, work on your thoughts and your feelings so that you are able to cope with this situation very well and are no longer upset about it.

Open your eyes. Did you feel ashamed when you imagined yourself caught in this act or some other 'shameful' act and being laughed at by others? If not, how did you feel? Were you able to get over your feelings of shame and to cope with the situation very well? If so, how did you manage to do this?

EXERCISE: SHAME ATTACKING

We are now all going to do one of the famous shame-attacking exercises of REBT – right now, right here. Close your eyes and think for a minute or two of something you can actually do, right here in this room, that you would consider shameful, ridiculous, foolish, embarrassing, or humiliating. Don't consider anything that would harm you (such as standing on your finger) or harm anyone else (such as slapping someone). Don't do anything that would get you into trouble (such as walk out of this building naked or tell your boss what a shit he or she is). But try to imagine something you personally consider shameful, vividly imagine your doing this so-called shameful act. It could, for example, be something practical, like telling someone here, or the authorities here, that you don't like something about them or about this Intensive. Or it could be something quite silly, such as singing at the top of your lungs, or telling this group how crazy you are, or deliberately farting in public. (Give participants a minute or two to imagine doing a 'shameful' act.)

Open your eyes. All right, now that you have imagined yourself doing this presumably shameful, foolish or silly act. I want some of you to volunteer to come up here in front and actually do it; and while you do it, do your best not to feel ashamed or embarrassed. Let yourself go and do this so-called 'shameful' thing but work on your feelings so that you accept yourself while doing it, and while others may be laughing at you; and make yourself feel quite unashamed rather than feel ashamed to do it and to reveal it.

It will really help you and you'll get a lot out of it if you come up and do this act that you consider shameful or ridiculous. You will truly help combat your perfectionism and aid your self-acceptance.

Now those of you who would like to get the most out of this exercise will line up right here, in the center aisle. Which of you will dare to line up to do a shame-attacking exercise? Who will take the risk of doing something unusual, something foolish – and of working on your feeling so that you will NOT feel ashamed? Who will be first? Now who will be next? Who will join this line up here?

(When the volunteers line up get them, one at a time, to do their shame-attacking exercise, then each can be asked: 'How did you feel about doing this exercise? Did you feel ashamed while doing it? Do you still feel ashamed? What did you do to work on giving up your shame? How do you feel now?')

SHARING: How do you feel about this lecture and these exercises on perfectionism and self-acceptance? What ideas and emotions did they evoke in you? What did you learn about you and your perfectionistic tendencies? What did you learn about accepting yourself unconditionally? How could you use this knowledge to help yourself dispute your perfectionistic beliefs and to *un*conditionally accept yourself now and in the future?

12:15 p.m. NEED FOR APPROVAL AND LOVE SLOBBISM

Definition of need for approval

1. Not desiring or preferring, but absolutely needing or commanding significant others to love you.
2. Feeling that something is radically wrong with you if they don't.
3. Acting like love slob and practically killing yourself to win others' approval.
4. Feeling depressed, and usually like a worm, if you don't get others' approval.

Irrationality of having a dire need for approval

1. Sets up a perfectionistic, unattainable goal.
2. Many people have no ability to love or approve you.
3. Many people will only love you if you have special traits that you can't possibly have (tallness, blue eyes).
4. Even if you win approval, you will have to keep winning it.
5. People will tend to disrespect and despise you if you are needy for their approval.
6. Leads to anxiety, depression, despair, wormhood.
7. Leads to inaction, withdrawal, alienation from people.

Cognitive techniques for overcoming dire need for approval and love

1. No law of the universe says that someone I care for must approve of me (although that would be lovely!).
2. I can get love for many people and do not need it from only one.
3. If the worst happens and no person I care for cares for me, I can still find other enjoyments.
4. If the person for whom I care does not care for me, it will be most frustrating and inconvenient but not awful!
5. Many people who are not loved (and do not love) lead quite happy lives.
6. If someone I love rejects me, it may show that I have some poor, unlovable traits but not that I am a rotten, unlovable person.
7. Even if I were totally unlovable, I would not be a bad, undeserving person.
8. Being unloved and alone has certain advantages: I can spend more time and energy on other things I like.
9. If I am unloved I can make some good things happen: I can devote time to winning someone else; I can engage in other enjoyable pursuits; I can

accept the challenge of being happy without being loved; I can work at fully accepting myself even though I am not loved.

Emotive techniques for overcoming the dire need for approval and love

1. Focus on self-acceptance, no matter how poorly you behave or how much others may reject you.
2. Focus on devising and engaging in many pleasurable pursuits which have little or nothing to do with love and approval.
3. Use rational emotive imagery: Imagine some of the worst rejections that could happen to you and make yourself feel only disappointed, sorry, regretful, and frustrated, and not self-downing, depressed, or angry.
4. Very forcefully say to yourself rational self-statements, such as:
   - 'I don't have to be loved, though I would definitely like to be!'
   - 'If I am rejected by someone I care for that does not prove that I am an unlovable person!'
   - 'I can enjoy myself even when I am not approved or loved by significant people!"
   - 'People who do not care for me have a right to their tastes and prejudices!'
5. Have very forceful dialogues with yourself, in which your rational arguments win out over your irrational arguments when you feel you are not loved and approved and when you feel depressed or self-downing about this.
6. Work on being rationally jealous if your beloved favors someone else – feeling sorry and regretful about this – but not on being irrationally jealous – and not putting yourself down and hating your beloved for favoring someone else.

Behavioral techniques for overcoming the dire need for approval and love

1. Take the risks of trying to win the approval of people whom you think may well not care for you and show yourself that it is only unfortunate and not horrible if you fail.
2. Do shame-attacking exercises that you think others will laugh at you for doing and show yourself that you never need these others' approval.
3. When you are in a love relationship force yourself not to be too sacrificing for your partner.
4. At times, deliberately engage in pleasurable pursuits that have nothing to do with your being approved or loved and that may even take you away from love relationships for a while.

EXERCISE NO. 1: RATIONAL EMOTIVE IMAGERY

Picture to yourself, or fantasize, as vividly and intensely as you can, some severe rejection from someone whom you very much want to accept you and perhaps love you. Intensely see that this person doesn't want to have anything serious to do with you and would very much like to ignore you.

As you strongly imagine this kind of severe rejection by someone for whom you care, let yourself feel distinctly disturbed – for example, anxious, depressed, ashamed, self-downing or hostile. Get in touch with this disturbed feeling and let yourself fully experience it for a brief period. Don't avoid it – on the contrary, face it and feel it!

When you have actually felt this disturbed emotion for a while, push yourself – yes, push yourself – to change this feeling in your gut, so that instead you only feel keenly disappointed, regretful, or frustrated and not anxious, depressed, ashamed, or hostile. Really work at changing your feeling from the unhealthy or self-defeating one of anxiety or depression or self-downing to a healthy one of sorrow or disappointment.

Now that you have changed your feeling to new healthy feelings, look at what you have done in your head to make yourself change it. If you observe yourself clearly, you have in some manner changed your Belief System (or Bull Shit!) at point B, and have thereby changed your emotional Consequence or Concomitant, at point C – so that you now feel regretful or frustrated rather than anxious, depressed, or hostile.

Which of you now wants to tell us what feeling you had when you imagined yourself being seriously rejected by someone for whom you care, and how you changed your disturbed feeling to an appropriate feeling of sorrow, regret or frustration?

(Give several members of the Intensive an opportunity to raise their hands and tell the whole audience what they felt and how they changed their feelings. If they go wrong, point out where they went wrong. If they are correct, congratulate them on doing the exercise properly, and emphasize how every member of the Intensive can do it in a similar way and help themselves by rational emotive imagery to imagine the worst that can happen and still change their feelings from unhealthy or self-defeating to appropriate ones.)

EXERCISE NO. 2:

Imagine yourself, once again, being rejected; and imagine that you are telling yourself rational Beliefs (rBs) and self-statements that are helping you cope well with this rejection. Make sure that you persist in this imaging and self-statements until you are able to cope satisfactorily with serious rejection. Which of you now wants to tell us what you imagined, what your rational self-statements were, and how you pictured yourself coping with serious rejection?

EXERCISE NO. 3:

Imagine yourself a voluntary prisoner of love. You have selected this comfortable room, with a wonderful king-size bed, and a companion who supposedly cares for you and will do anything you want. But you now see that your companion is often boring, doesn't really care for you that much, insists that you do many burdensome things to please him or her, and won't let you escape. The room is sealed, the door is barred, and there is no way for you to let yourself out and to enjoy the rest of life and to relate to other partners or friends. How do you feel about being trapped like this?

What can you do to get yourself out of this prisoner of love predicament? Figure out what you can do to break your own dire needs for your companion and how you can get out of his or her clutches and restrictions. Raise your hand when you have figured out how to get yourself out of this predicament. (Let those with raised hands respond and comment on their responses.)

SHARING: How do you feel about this lecture and these exercises? What ideas and emotions did they evoke in you? What did you learn about your Need for Approval and about your Love Slobbism? How could you use this knowledge to help yourself to Dispute your irrational Beliefs about needing others' approval and to change your actions and phobias about rejection?

1:30 p.m. LOW FRUSTRATION TOLERANCE

What is low frustration tolerance or discomfort anxiety or discomfort depression?

- Demanding immediate gratification instead of long-range pleasure.
- Ignoring long-range harm that follows from immediate gratification.
- Demanding that discomfort and inconvenience should not and must not exist.

- Insisting on gain without pain ('I should be able to benefit from therapy without work and effort!')
- Being horrified rather than displeased by discomfort ('It would be awful if I went to a dance and met no one!')
- I-can't-stand-it-itis ('I can't stand breaking up another relationship; so I'll stay away from dating.')
- 'Thinking of oneself as so fragile that others have to treat one with kid gloves ('Because he knows I worry so much, he absolutely should not stay out late!'

Harm of low frustration tolerance and discomfort anxiety

- Procrastinating and making yourself inefficient.
- Avoiding pleasures that have hassles attached to them (e.g. dating or socializing).
- Addictions that are self-defeating (e.g. overeating, alcoholism, smoking).
- Thrill-seeking that leads to self-destruction (e.g. gambling, taking cocaine, carousing all night).
- Picking easy goals rather than those that would be more interesting and enjoyable (staying with a dull job instead of looking for a more interesting one).
- Never finishing projects that would be interesting and useful (taking courses and not finishing them; exercising for only a short period of time).
- Impatiently refusing to stay with slow-moving but highly useful projects (e.g. going on a crash diet instead of a prolonged program of eating well).
- Making oneself feel bored because one concentrates on life's hassles and inconveniences.
- Leaving good jobs or relationships because they include some hassles and inconveniences.
- Going for 'exciting' love and sex partners when these people are not good for you in the long run.

COGNITIVE TECHNIQUES FOR OVERCOMING LFT

Rational coping statements and philosophies

- 'I do not need immediate gratification, even though it would be great to get it!'
- 'I can let myself feel uncomfortable in order to later arrange for comfort and pleasure.'
- 'I **can** let myself feel anxious and depressed. These are only inconveniences. If I experience them and accept them, I can then work on getting rid of them.'

- 'This extra food or alcohol will make me feel good right now at this moment; but it will harm me considerably later!'
- 'I don't have to stop smoking or overeating, but I had damned well better!'
- 'Life consists of many hassles; but I can still greatly enjoy myself if I don't focus on them and exaggerate them!'
- 'Nothing in life is awful and horrible – only inconvenient!'
- 'The very worst things that can happen to me are still only severe inconveniences, and I can still enjoy myself when I keep experiencing them.'
- 'I can stand practically all the things that I don't like; and I am determined to stand them to get more joy out of life in the long run.'
- 'Let me work very hard at changing the obnoxious things in my life that I can change; at accepting the bad things I cannot change; and at having the wisdom to know the difference between the two.'
- Make a list of the real disadvantages of indulging yourself in immediate gratifications that in the long run will harm you. Go over these several times a day for a period of time until you really solidly accept them.
- Make a list of the real advantages of disciplining yourself and going through uncomfortable situations (such as stopping smoking or continuing to diet steadily). Go over these several times a day for a period of time until you really solidly accept them.

EMOTIVE TECHNIQUES FOR OVERCOMING LFT

- Rational emotive imagery: Imagining some very uncomfortable but useful activity; letting yourself feel angry or depressed about doing it; and changing your feeling to one of disappointment and regret and determination to do it for long-range gains.
- Imagine yourself doing difficult and disciplined tasks (such as finishing a term paper or dieting) and getting so involved in these tasks that you actually begin to enjoy the challenge of doing them and enjoy some of the activity of doing them.
- Very forcefully tell yourself rational self-statements or coping statements, such as:
  - 'Being self-disciplined is hard, but never too hard!'
  - 'A hassle is never a horror!'
  - 'Working at changing myself should be hard – because that's the way it usually is!'
  - 'I can really **enjoy** many of the self-disciplined things that I force myself to do!'
- Have forceful dialogues with yourself and record them, to see how well and how vigorously you are talking yourself out of your irrational Beliefs,

such as 'I shouldn't have to give up the pleasure of smoking even though I am destroying myself by indulging in it!'
- Let a friend of yours uphold some of your self-defeating ideas that lead to low frustration tolerance; and then vigorously talk that friend out of these ideas.

BEHAVIORAL TECHNIQUES FOR OVERCOMING LFT

- Deliberately make yourself stay in an uncomfortable situation (such as a job you dislike) until you overcome your feelings of horrible frustration, anger and depression. Then, and then only, let yourself get out of this situation.
- Reinforce yourself with something you enjoy (like eating some special food, reading or listening to music) only after you have forced yourself to discipline yourself in some way (such as by exercising steadily or dieting).
- Break down unpleasant tasks you want to accomplish into pieces, so that you can do them half hour at a time. Steadily do that small part of the task every single day; and use reinforcements and penalties if you don't.
- Write yourself a script in which you play the role of a person who has high frustration tolerance; and who does not procrastinate seriously; who refuses to give in to addictions; who is quite disciplined. Actually play this role, in real life, for a solid week, to show yourself that you can do so and that you are able to be more disciplined.
- Use time management techniques, such as first things first, organize your tasks properly, get proper information on how to do them before you start, arrange for people to do them with you, etc.
- Associate with more disciplined people more of the time. Form groups to work on difficult goals that you have in common – such as, get a few people together who want to stop smoking, and plan to help each other do so.
- Do many onerous task immediately, without any debate, and with no excuses.
- Don't allow yourself to do easy and enjoyable tasks until *after* you have done difficult and more important ones.

EXERCISE NO. 1:

(Give the whole group an exercise on the ABCDEs of procrastination.)

Now all of you think about something on which you often procrastinate, even though you know it is foolish of you to do so - something like getting up in the morning on time, doing a term paper, writing out business reports, exercising or cleaning the house. Okay: Make sure that you all have procrastination in mind. In other words, using the ABCs of REBT, start with a C of procrastination. Now that you are thinking of yourself procrastinating, tell us what A, the Activating Event, is. What are you mainly and importantly procrastinating about? What is our A, your Activating Event? (Let them raise their hands and get several A's.)

Fine. Now let's look for your rational Beliefs about the thing you are procrastinating about. Rational Beliefs are preferences, wishes, desires – such as 'I wish that I would do this exercise, and it is unfortunate if I don't do it.' Or 'I don't like writing this paper, but I'd better do it and get it over with.' Or 'What a pain in the ass it is to wash the dishes, but it would be preferable if I got them out of the way.'

When you find this rational Belief and get in touch with it, you will tend to feel sorry and disappointed about the task you are procrastinating on; but you still will have a tendency to do it – for you will feel even *more* sorry and disappointed about *not* doing it and getting it out of the way. What are some of your rational Beliefs in regard to procrastination? (Let them raise their hands and give several RBs.)

Now look for your irrational Beliefs that actually lead you to important procrastination. These irrational Beliefs are musts, shoulds, oughts, commands and demands. Such as: 'This exercise is so hard to do that I should not have to do it and it's awful that I do have to get around to it!' Or 'I hate writing this paper and therefore I must not have to do it even though it's a very important paper! I can't stand doing it right now!' Or 'It's such a pain in the ass washing the dishes that I ought not have to do them! What a rotten world this is when I have to keep doing such horrible tasks every day!' 'What are some of the irrational Beliefs that you are now finding that lead you to procrastinate?' (Let them raise their hands and give several irrational Beliefs.)

You're doing fine! Now let's do some disputing of these irrational Beliefs. What questions and challenges, what disputes, would you ask yourself to rip up your irrational Beliefs that are leading to procrastination? You might ask, for example, 'Why should I not have to do it?' Or 'Even though I hate writing, where is it written that I must not have to do this important paper that I want to finish?' Or 'Where is the evidence that I ought not to have to wash the dishes just because it's a pain in the ass to wash them?' What are some of the disputes that you can use to give up your irrational Beliefs that are leading you to procrastinate? (Let them raise their hands and give several disputations.)

Finally, think now about some of the new effective rational beliefs that you could wind up with after you dispute your irrational Beliefs that are leading you to procrastinate. You could answer your disputes with these effective rational beliefs: 'There is no reason why I should not have to do this hard exercise. And there are several good reasons why I had better do it!' Or 'It is not written anywhere that I must not have to do this important paper that I want to finish. So, because it would be good to do it, I had better get going on it!' Or 'There is no evidence that I ought not to have to wash the dishes just because it's a pain in the ass to wash them. I don't have to do them, but I'd damn well better do so and get them out of the way!' Now, what are some of the effective rational beliefs that some of you have just come up with? Let's hear some of them. (Let them raise their hands and give several effective rational beliefs.)

Fine! You have now seen how to do the ABCDEs in regard to any procrastination problems that you may have, and you may also use them, and keep using them, for any other kind of problem of lack of discipline, discomfort, anxiety, or low frustration tolerance which you keep bringing on yourself.

EXERCISE NO. 2:

Bend down in your chair and make yourself assume a bowed-down burden-some posture, as if all the woes and burdens of the world were on your back and shoulders. Think about all your troubles and problems, all the stresses and strains of your life, and make yourself feel very, very burdened by them.

Now, sit up straight or leap up from your chair and shake your burdens of your shoulders and back. Shout out, 'Away with you!' 'I've had enough of this needless pain!' 'I don't have to bear this!' Make yourself feel really free of your burdens – or at least able to cope with them and still lead a good and happy life in spite of them. See yourself as a very strong, upright, and stalwart individual who can accept troubles and problems and not feel overly burdened by them. OK: Get up and lift those burdens off your back and shoulders! Shout them away! See that life can be good with them and without them. Get up and shout!

SHARING: How do you feel about this lecture and these exercises on low frustration tolerance? What did you learn in this part of the REBT Intensive?

How can you tackle your problems of procrastination and low frustration tolerance in the future? How can you live and be happy in spite of the many hassles of the world?

3:00 p.m. OVERCOMING ANGER

Kinds of anger

- Hostility, Rage, Fury, Downing others
- Impatience
- Aggression, Revenge, Violence, War, Genocide, Racial intolerance, Terrorism

Accept self-responsibility for anger

- *I* made me angry, not *he*, or *she* or *they* made me angry.
- *They* acted badly or unfairly; but *I* still chose to be angry.
- *I* made myself mad at her stupidity; not *her stupidity* made me mad.
- I can *easily* make myself angry after the way they behaved; but not I *should* be angry after the way they behaved.

Irrational Beliefs (iBs) leading to anger

1. You should not act that way toward me!
2. How awful for you to treat me so badly!
3. I can't stand the way you behave!
4. You are a terrible person for treating me that way! You deserve to be punished for doing so!
5. The world is a horrible place for not giving me what I want and for treating me unfairly.

Advantages of anger

- Assertion, determination
- Emotional release, good feeling, exciting, energizing
- Interference with anxiety and depression
- Self-preservation; can lead to change; preserves freedom

Disadvantages of anger

- De-energizing, unproductive
- Sidetracks efforts to change

- Foments more anger and opposition in others
- Preoccupation with revenge and vindictiveness
- Compulsivity and lack of control
- Obsession with enemies
- Jehovahistic and absolutistic
- Psychosomatic reactions: high blood pressure, ulcers, Type A personality
- Violence, wars, genocide, nuclear holocaust

Advantages of ridding yourself of anger and not merely expressing it

- Lack of inefficiency
- Real freedom from obsessions and compulsiveness
- Freedom to act against injustice and frustration
- Minimizes violence and wars
- Leads to good physical health, good feeling, pleasures of constructive nature

Cognitive techniques for dealing with anger

- Why must others treat you well and fairly? – They never have to.
- Why can't you stand unfairness? – Of course you can.
- In what way is injustice awful? – It is only unpleasant and inconvenient.
- How do people's rotten acts make them terrible people? – They don't; they are only people who do bad acts.
- Where is it written that the world must treat me the way I want it to do? – Only in my nutty head!

Rational self-statements or coping statements:

- There is no reason why people must treat me kindly and 40 million reasons why they often won't!
- A hassle is not a horror!
- I can stand what I don't like!
- I never need what I want!
- People can only hurt me physically, but not emotionally – unless I let them do so.
- People's acts may stink but they are never stinkers!
- No human is subhuman!
- People have the right to treat me badly, though I hope that they rarely exert it!
- When people treat me unfairly they are usually thinking only of themselves and not personally of me.

Emotive techniques for overcoming anger

- Rational emotive imagery: Imagine great injustice and make yourself feel appropriately disappointed and displeased, not inappropriately angry and furious.
- When someone does you in, think about the good and pleasant experiences you have also had with this person.
- Forcefully tell yourself rational self-statements, such as:
  - So the world is unfair – tough.
  - I *can* take injustice – and stubbornly refuse to be unjust to myself by making myself enraged about it.
  - When I deal badly with others I am not a *rotten person* – nor is any one damnable when he or she deals badly with me!
  - Sing rational humorous songs that make anger seem silly.

Behavioral techniques for overcoming anger

- Assert yourself when you are displeased with others' behavior, and long before you enrage yourself at them for this behavior.
- Deliberately stay in bad situations (keep working, for example, with an unfair boss) and show yourself that you don't have to leave them until you make yourself unangry.
- At times, do things that you are pretty sure will help make people angry at you – and practice taking their anger well and not being angry back at them.
- Stay in situations where you normally would feel hurt and self-pitying; and work against the hurt and self-pity feelings that often lead you to make yourself angry.

ANGER EXERCISE NO. 1:

Please listen to these instructions before you do anything. I'm going to ask you to think of someone (or it could be a group of people) that you hate most. Think of this person (or persons) really treating you very badly and unfairly; and let yourself feel quite angry about this – let your angry feelings erupt to their fullest intensity. Now that you are thinking of this person and imagining how badly he or she is treating you, push yourself – yes, push yourself – to change your deep feeling of anger, which is unhealthy, into the much healthier feeling of disappointment, annoyance, or (if you want to call it that) make yourself feel angry only at this person's act, and not feel that the person is bad or damnable. So first make sure that you really feel angry and upset at this person; and then push yourself to feel *only* disappointed and annoyed at his or her behavior.

Now look carefully at what you have done to feel less angry. You probably used the REBT you learned today to change your belief system in some manner to produce more healthy and more self-helping feelings. Take a really close look at what you were telling yourself to feel disappointed or annoyed. Perhaps you told yourself, 'This person has a right to act obnoxiously, even though I certainly don't have to like it.' Or perhaps you told yourself, 'He or she has inconvenienced me greatly by this unfair behavior, but my world won't come to an end because of that inconvenience. I can stand it!' Or perhaps you told yourself, 'Too bad if she or he didn't give me what I want, but I don't need it desperately, so I don t have to be destroyed by what he or she did.'

Now, who wants to tell us what we were angry at and how you were angry and how you changed your unhealthy feeling of anger or hate to a healthy feeling of disappointment, sorrow or annoyance?

(While members of the Intensive are commenting on what they did, the leader can add his or her own comments, correcting their responses, augmenting them, giving new ideas against anger, etc.)

Now we would like you to repeat what you first did to feel the anger and then deliberately change it once more to a healthy feeling, such as annoyance or disappointment. We call this procedure rational emotive imagery and it is good to repeat it many times – in fact, to repeat it every day for at least thirty days, until you really get into the habit of feeling sorry and annoyed but not angry and enraged at people and things that treat you badly. Once more, then, make yourself truly angry at someone that you really hate. Allow yourself to really get into this anger; and now that you feel it fully, push yourself to change your feeling of anger to one of disappointment or irritation at the person's act but not of damnation of the person himself or herself. We'll end this exercise when almost all of you have been able to work on their anger and change it to a healthy feeling of annoyance or disappointment. Please raise your hand after you've been able to change your feeling. (Wait until a number of hands are up; then end the exercise.)

EXERCISE NO. 2:

Make yourself feel as angry as you can feel at some person, some group, some injustice, or some thing or event that you really loathe. Get in touch with your feelings of anger and really feel them. Make your body react to these feelings by clenching your fists, banging your hands, breathing hard, screaming, or otherwise feel very tense and uptight.

Now relax your whole body by taking a few slow, deep breaths. Let your slow breaths go throughout your whole body and reach your toes and feet and your face and head. Breathe easily and freely and really, really relax.

When you are relaxed, let go of your anger. Think of some good aspects of the person or thing you hate. Think of all people as human and fallible, and as deserving of complete forgiveness. Let yourself forgive and accept the hated person or object. Feel relaxed and good. Feel that you have done a fine thing, particularly for yourself, by relaxing and letting go of your anger.

Did you really let yourself feel very angry? Were you able to breathe and relax? Did you let go of your anger? Were you able to feel forgiving and accepting of the person, thing, or event that you hated? Let us hear from you about this.

SHARING: We invite you now to share your experiences of this session on anger with the whole group. How do you feel about what you went through and how you were able to work on your beliefs and your feelings? Do the rational beliefs that you produced to change some of your feelings of anger now feel like a part of you? Do you think you will be able to use these techniques to work on your rage by yourself? What other feelings and ideas do you have about this talk and these exercises on anger?

4:30 p.m. GOAL-SETTING AND HOMEWORK

Advantages of goal-setting

- Maximizes chances of achieving goal – 'If you don't know where you're going, you'll wind up somewhere else!"
- Provides guide for choosing activities and making plans.
- Lets you see you're not only living others' goals.
- Lets you see you aren't locked in forever – you can reassess your goals regularly and change your goals at certain times in your life.
- Allows room for spontaneity.

How to clarify your goals

- Ask yourself: 'What do I want more in my life?'
- Set your goals as positives rather than negatives.
- Plan what you would do if you weren't fearful – and then force yourself to do these things.

- Try to be specific about your goals. Not, 'I want to be happy,' but 'I want to play tennis well' or 'I want to get a specific kind of a job."
- Think about the subgoals that are required for a particular goal: 'If I really want to become a physician, I had better find out about the educational requisites, apply for the medical boards, figure out my finances etc.'

Identifying blocks to your goals

- What are your fears of failure?
- What are your fears of rejection?
- What is your discomfort disturbance or low frustration tolerance?
- How perfectionistic are you?
- What are the main practical blocks:
  - Necessary skills?
  - Required financing?
  - Physical handicaps?
  - Poor conditions in the field you have selected?
  - Educational handicaps?
  - Age handicaps?

Cognitive techniques for tackling emotional blocks to goal achievement

- Identify and dispute irrational Beliefs (iBs) – **'I must do well!'** 'I must do perfectly well!' 'I must not get rejected!' 'Achieving my goals must not be too hard!' 'I'll fix my parents or my mate by *not* achieving what they want me to achieve!'
- Challenge your unrealistic expectations about your goals and about people and life. 'I must make a million before I am forty!' 'I must write the greatest novel ever written!' 'I must have at least three wonderful children!"
- Focus on your strengths. 'Because I am bright and hardworking I think that I can become a physician.' 'I am patient and caring and therefore can be a good parent.'
- Write down and go over the advantages of goal-setting and the disadvantages of not setting goals for yourself
- Figure out how the disadvantages of working for goals that you desire have good points about them and reframe some of them as advantages.
- Point out to yourself some of the ironies of not setting distinct goals – such as the irony that you very much want the results of the goal-setting but don't want the work of setting goals.

Emotive methods for enhancing your goal-setting

- Practice imagining yourself setting distinct goals and achieving them and receive great pleasure in this achievement.
- Use Rational Emotive Imagery to imagine your failing to set goals, let yourself be anxious or depressed or guilty about this, and then change your feeling to appropriate feelings of sorrow and disappointment.
- Forcefully tell yourself some rational self-statements, such as 'I can set useful goals for myself and will work at achieving them!' 'No matter how hard it is for me to set and achieve valuable goals, it's much harder when I don't!' 'Tis much better to have tried and failed at achieving useful goals than never to have tried at all!"
- If you keep blocking in your goal-setting and in your working to achieve the goals that you set, have a dialogue with yourself on tape, in the course of which you vehemently argue yourself out of the irrational beliefs (iBs) that sabotage your goal-setting: such as, 'What's the use of setting goals for myself when I'll never succeed at most of them, anyway?'
- Shamelessly confess to some of your close friends or relatives how you are goofing at goal-setting and goal-achievement, and work on feeling unashamed about their knowing this lack on your part.

Behavioral methods for enhancing your goal-setting

- Collect good information that will help you set goals and achieve them – such as getting useful information from books, people and other sources.
- Set yourself a minimum of, say, a half hour a day to work at setting goals and doing something to achieve them; and force yourself, no matter how uncomfortable you are, to work for that period of time.
- Reinforce yourself for spending time doing goal-setting and goal achievement.
- Penalize yourself for not spending time doing goal-setting and goal achievement.
- When you have set goals, do some things as soon as possible to test when they are practical; and if not, realistically give them up.
- Try many ways of setting and achieving your goals. Don't stick to one or a few ways.
- Get others' ideas on trying many different ways.
- Get some skill training that will help you set and achieve goals, such as assertion training, public speaking training, study skills training, sex information and training, etc.
- Don't wait till you get perfect training or perfect skills to help you with your goals.

- Plunge in and get some skills by your own work and practice.
- Getting support from other individuals or groups sometimes helps you to do goal-setting and goal-achieving with these individuals and by yourself.
- Don't wait until you are comfortable or unanxious to work on your goals. Work on them, at first, uncomfortably!
- Take risks of failure, and sometimes deliberately fail at some goals and tasks – to show yourself that you can accept yourself while failing.
- Persist at your goal achievement, in spite of many possible failures. Don't give up too quickly and wrongly conclude that the goal is impossible for you to achieve.

EXERCISE NO. 1:

We've just given you a number of suggestions for working on your own to carry on some of the things that you would like to do and that you may have started thinking about doing today. Just about all the techniques that we've presented to you today – all the cognitive, all the emotive and all the behavioral methods – can be effectively practiced in your regular life, on a day to day basis. And the more you practice them, the easier they will tend to become and the more 'natural' they will appear to you.

To give you some practice right now in some of these suggested methods, let's turn to the self-help report form that we just gave you. It is included in the packet of homework materials that you are to take home with you and to keep using on your own. If you have a pen or pencil with you, take that out, too; but you can fill out the form in your head right now, without a pen or pencil.

Notice that the form follows the ABCs of REBT that we have been discussing with you all day. Let's start filling out the form – either with a pen or pencil or in your head – by starting with A (Activating Events, thoughts, or feelings that happened just before you felt emotionally disturbed or acted self-defeatingly). Write down (or mentally write in) a situation that you may be now making yourself upset about. For example, you may be sitting there right now, and may be thinking, 'Oh shit! What am I supposed to do with this goddamned form? I'm so tired right now I can hardly see.' If so, fill in section A by writing: 'Getting this form to fill out.'

Those of you who don't have a pencil or a pen just 'write' this in mentally.

Now some of you may be feeling pretty anxious about doing the right thing with this form and may be even more anxious about whether you'll be able to use the REBT we've been teaching you today to help yourself with your problems. So those of you feeling any kind of anxiety will now write 'feeling anxious' in the next section of the form, which is labeled (C) Consequences or Condition – disturbed feeling or self-defeating behavior – that you produced and would like to change. Others of you may feel some other emotion, instead of anxiety – such as anger! You may be pissed off at getting this form to fill out. So you would write in 'feeling angry' in the C section of the form.

Now let's go to the B section of the REBT self-help form. Because if you were feeling anxious or angry or any other disturbed feeling about being asked to fill out the form or if you were procrastinating or goofing about filling it out, you would be producing this feeling or this self-defeating behavior by some irrational Beliefs (iBs) you were telling yourself about the form. Remember, now, that according to REBT you, getting the form to fill out will not produce your anxiety or your anger! It is mainly your irrational Beliefs about the form that produces these dysfunctional feelings.

If you are anxious or have feelings of inadequacy about filling out the form, you probably are saying to yourself, and irrationally believing, that you must do well or very well in filling it out, and that perhaps you are a bad or worthless person if you act weakly or stupidly in filling it out. If this is true, and you have these irrational Beliefs, circle No. 1 in the beliefs or irrational Beliefs column on the self-help form: namely, 'I must do well or very well!' And you may also circle No. 2 in the beliefs column: 'I am a bad or worthless person when I act weakly or stupidly.'

If, however, you feel angry about our giving you this form to do right now, you probably would be thinking that we treated you unfairly by giving you the self-help form at this point in the Intensive, and you would circle No. 5 under the beliefs section of the form: namely, 'People must treat me fairly and give me what I need!' You might also circle irrational Belief No. 7: 'People must live up to my expectations or it is terrible!' and you might also circle irrational Belief no. 9: 'I can't stand really bad things or very difficult people!'

When you have finished circling the irrational Beliefs on the self-help form that are leading to your upsetting yourself about having to fill out the form, you may add some additional irrational Beliefs. For example, you might add under irrational Belief No. 14 another belief that you hold that is making you anxious, such as: 'I must understand this form perfectly and fill it out outstandingly!' And if you are angry, you might add under irrational Belief No. 15: 'Whenever I have many things to do, people should be exceptionally considerate of me and not give me anything extra to perform!'

When you have finished circling the irrational Beliefs that you are holding to make yourself anxious, angry or lazy, you then go on to column D (disputes for each circled irrational Belief) that is included in the next column on the self-help form. Let's do that now. In column D you dispute, question and challenge each of your irrational Beliefs that you have circled in column B. For example, you write down questions such as: 'Why must I do well or very well on this self-help form?' And in the next column, column E (effective rational beliefs to replace my irrational Beliefs), you would answer this question or dispute by writing down a rational Belief or effective philosophy, such as: 'There is no reason why I must do well or very well on this self-help form, though it would be nice if I did well in filling it out.' Again, in column D, you might take your irrational Belief that you wrote down in column B, 'People must treat me fairly and give me what I need!' and in column C, you would dispute it or question or challenge it, as follows: 'Where is it written that people must treat me fairly and give me what I need?' And in column E, effective rational Beliefs, you might answer your own question by stating: 'It is only written in my head! People never have to treat me fairly and give me what I need, though I would greatly prefer that they did so!'

Every single time, then, that you have written down or circled an irrational Belief in column B, you dispute it, question it, challenge it in column D. You ask yourself questions, such as 'Why is this irrational Belief true?' 'Where is the evidence to support it?' 'Prove that it really is so.' And in column E, you give the answer to your own questions and write down some effective rational Beliefs that will help you change your disturbed feeling and will help you to change your self-defeating behavior that you listed under C, consequence or condition – disturbed feeling or self-defeating behavior that I produced and would like to change.

You finally go on to section F of the self-help form: Feelings and behaviors I experienced after arriving at my effective rational Beliefs. In this section you write down the appropriate feelings you experienced after doing the disputing of your irrational Beliefs: Instead of anxiety, you might write down 'Concern' or 'Disappointment' or 'Regret'. Instead of 'Anger' you might write down, 'Annoyance', 'Irritation' or 'Frustration'. And under appropriate new behaviors you might write down, in place of 'Procrastination' or 'Goofing', 'Determination to fill out this form right now and action to fill it out.'

Any questions right now about filling out this REBT self-help form? (Take and answer questions at this point.) All right, now that you know how to fill it out, take it home with you and use it, and some of our other self-help forms in your daily life. Use them regularly for your cognitive homework, until you get to know them by heart and can pretty well use them in your heads, often without actually having them in front of you. But from time to time actually fill out the entire form in writing, and keep writing, and keep working at it until you change your unhealthy and disturbed feelings to healthy and undisturbed ones and until you change your self-defeating and dysfunctional behaviors to sensible and self-helping behaviors. You can use the forms we've given you in this packet; and you may want to stock up on new blank forms from time to time and to keep using them.

EXERCISE NO. 2: GOAL-SETTING

How about each of you now setting one main goal for yourself, a goal that you will try to reach over the next few months, and a goal that REBT can help you reach. It is often best for you to put this goal in positive terms – that is, in terms of something you want to do more. Even if it's a goal like dieting or giving up smoking, try to think of it in terms of taking positive steps to lose pounds or stick to a diet or taking positive steps to give up smoking. Try to pick a goal that is realistic and specific, so that you will have a good chance of reaching it, and so that you will know when you have accomplished it. It can be a goal of improving your emotional states, a goal of doing something that you normally would like to do but don't do (such as regular exercise), finishing a course you would like to finish, looking for a new job, or almost anything else that you would like to work on. And pick a goal of changing your thinking, changing your emotions, or changing your behavior – or all three!

Who would like to share with the whole group now the goal that you have set? (Take about five volunteers and let them state the goals that they have set.)

OK, now. Make a decision, all of you, on at least one important goal that you're going to try to reach. Now each of you strongly and vividly imagine yourself on the path to that goal. Especially imagine yourself thinking the kind of rational thoughts that will help you stick to and reach your goal. Use the rational-emotive-behavioral ways of thinking and feeling that you have been developing throughout this Intensive today and strongly work on thinking and feeling the kind of ideas that will help you melt away the barriers to your goal-setting and your achieving the goals that you set. Keep imagining your progress toward your goals – and enjoying this progress. (Allow one minute for reflection.)

Think of how satisfying it will be to keep making progress toward your goal. You may experience setbacks, but you can help yourself get back on your course by using your rational thinking and by feeling healthy feelings. See yourself getting closer and closer to your goal. Let yourself say, 'Wow! I can really go after what I want in life and often get it!'

SHARING: How did you feel about this talk and these exercises? Who wants to reveal his or her feeling? What did you learn? How can you use this learning in your future life? Who will express himself or herself about this?

INSTRUCTIONS FOR CONTINUED HOMEWORK

Now be sure to keep this packet of homework material that we have given to each of you. It includes: 1. Blank REBT self-help forms that you can keep using, preferably at least once a week. 2. A list of REBT exercises that you can do at home and that you can keep practicing. 3. A supplementary reading list of books, pamphlets, and cassette recordings that you can purchase at our reception desk or order by phone or mail and that you can keep using to help you with your emotional and behavioral problems. The more you use these homework materials the more you are likely to overcome your problems and to achieve what we shall refer to in our next session of this Intensive as the elegant solution to them.

Finale

As we have been emphasizing during this REBT Intensive, you had better take many things in life seriously and work hard to accomplish what you want to accomplish and to build the relationships you want to build. But you never – yes, never – have to lose your sense of humor and take things too seriously. To help you close this workshop in a lighter vein and go on to the rest of your life with a humorous outlook, we have included in your homework packet a double-faced sheet of some of the famous rational humorous songs that are often used in REBT. Turn to this song sheet now and let us all loudly – and shamelessly! – sing some of these rational humorous songs. I'll start you off and you all sing out at the top of your lungs and join me as soon as I start.

Okay, turn first to: (Get the whole audience to sing a few of the rational humorous songs, especially such songs as **Whine, Whine, Whine, Perfect Rationality, I'm Depressed, Depressed!**, and **I Wish I Were Not Crazy**!)

RATIONAL HUMOROUS SONGS, by Albert Ellis, Ph.D.
Copyright @ Albert Ellis Institute, 45 East 65th Street, New York, NY 10021

WHINE, WHINE, WHINE!
Tune: Yale Whiffenproof Song,
composed by a Harvard man in 1896!)

I cannot have all my wishes filled—
Whine, whine, whine!
I cannot have every frustration stilled—
Whine, whine, whine!
Life really owes me the things that I miss,
Fate has to grant me eternal bliss!
And since I must settle for less than this—
Whine, whine, whine!

PERFECT RATIONALITY
(Tune: Funiculi, Funicula by Luigi Denza)

Some think the world must have a right
    direction
And so do I — and so do I!
Some think that, with the slightest imper-
    fection
They can't get by — and so do I!
For I, I have to prove I'm superhuman,
And better far than people are!
To show I have miraculous acumen—
And always rate among the Great!

Perfect, perfect rationality
Is, of course, the only thing for me!
How can I ever think of being
If I must live fallibly?
Rationality must be a perfect thing for me!

I'M DEPRESSED, DEPRESSED!
(Tune: The Band Played On
by Ward)

When anything slightly goes wrong with my life
I'm depressed, depressed!
Whenever I'm stricken with chicken shit strife,
I feel most distressed!
When life isn't fated to be consecrated
I can't tolerate it at all!
When anything slightly goes wrong with my life,
I just bawl, bawl, bawl!

I WISH I WERE NOT CRAZY!
(Tune: Dixie by Dan Emmett)

Oh, I wish I were really put together—
Smooth and fine as patent leather!
Oh, how great to be rated innately sedate!
But I'm afraid that I was fated
To be rather aberrated—
Oh, how sad to be mad as my Mom
    and my Dad!

Oh, I wish I were not crazy! Hooray! Hooray!
I wish my mind were less inclined
To be the kind that's hazy!
I could, you see, agree to be less crazy—
But I, alas, am just too goddamned lazy!

References

Ellis A (1958) Rational psychotherapy. Journal of General Psychology 59: 35–49.
Ellis A (1962) Reason and Emotion in Psychotherapy. New York: Citadel.
Ellis A (1994) Reason and Emotion in Psychotherapy. Updated and revised. New York: Kensington Publishers.
Ellis A, Sichel J, Leaf R, Maas R (1989) Countering perfectionism in research on clinical practice. Journal of Rational-Emotive and Cognitive-Behavior Therapy 1: 197–218.

CHAPTER 8

Problems in Living: The Friday Night Workshop

WINDY DRYDEN, WOUTER BACKX AND ALBERT ELLIS

Introduction

The role of the counselling psychologist as remedial counsellor/psychotherapist is well defined in the literature, even in Britain where the debate concerning the professional status of counselling psychology continues to rage. But, the role of the counselling psychologist as psychological educator is less well defined. As Nelson-Jones (1982) has argued, psychological education is not a unitary phenomenon and he lists six activities that fall under this general heading. One of the activities concerns educating the public in psychological matters.

In this chapter, we will describe an event pioneered by Albert Ellis that has run continuously for the last 37 years or so. It combines both remedial counselling and that aspect of psychological education which endeavours to educate the public in the rational-emotive view of the nature of psychological disturbance, how people perpetuate their emotional and behavioural problems and how they can overcome them. This event has come to be known as 'The Friday night workshop'.

The Friday Night Workshop

Every Friday night (except when he is 'out of town'), Albert Ellis demonstrates the rational-emotive-behavioral approach to counselling and psychotherapy by interviewing separately two volunteers from an audience of up to a hundred and fifty people at the Albert Ellis Institute for REBT in New York. Each volunteer is interviewed for about 30 minutes on a specific psychological problem (or problems), after which the members of the audience who wish to do so are actively encouraged to speak to the volunteer and to the therapist concerning aspects of the volunteer's problem(s)

176

and the interview that they have witnessed. The workshop lasts for about $1^1/_2$ hours and is followed by a coffee hour. Ellis conducts therapy in this format in a very similar manner to how he would conduct therapy in his private office, with the possible exception that he uses more humour in these public demonstrations.

Rational Emotive Behavior Therapy (REBT)

REBT is well suited to this form of public workshop. It is a non-mystical type of therapy where the therapist is very open about his or her interventions. It is also an educational form of therapy which strives to teach both the volunteer and the members of the audience the ABCs of REBT, i.e. it is not 'A' (the event, or the person's inferences about the event) that determines the client's psychological problems (emotional and/or behavioural) at 'C', but rather it is 'B' (the client's irrational beliefs about the event) that seems to account more adequately for the presence of these problems. In the course of the public demonstration, the volunteers are helped to identify, challenge and change their irrational beliefs which take the form of dogmatic musts (shoulds, oughts or have to's) and one of three irrational derivatives. These derivatives take the form of (1) *awfulizing* (rating an event as more than 100% bad – an evaluation which stems from the belief: 'This bad event must not be as bad as it is'; (2) *I-can't-stand-it-itis* (believing that one cannot tolerate an event and/or that one cannot be happy again as long as the event exists); and (3) *depreciation* (giving oneself, other people or the world in general a negative, global rating). It is a feature of the Friday night workshop that while Ellis is working intensively with a particular volunteer, the audience is simultaneously being educated concerning the cognitive underpinnings of their emotional and behavioural problems, and how these underpinnings can be identified, challenged and changed.

The Process of a Public Demonstration with a Volunteer

Both Wouter Backx and I [WD] have witnessed dozens of Ellis's interviews conducted in the Friday night workshop and have identified a discernible process to such interviews. First, Ellis elicits the client's major emotional and/or behavioural problem at C. He then links this to a relevant activating event at A. From there he proceeds to identify the chent's major irrational beliefs and starts to dispute these in a strong, evocative and often humorous manner (here it is the client's beliefs that are ridiculed, not the client). During this process, Ellis often uses self-disclosure to illustrate a number of points (as is shown in the transcript to be presented later in this chapter). Then, Ellis instructs the client how to use rational emotive imagery (REI) – a technique whereby the client vividly imagines the troublesome event at A, is instructed to make him- or herself disturbed at C and then is asked to change this unhealthy negative emotion (e.g. depression, anxiety, guilt or anger) to a healthy negative emotion (e.g. sadness, concern, regret or annoyance).

When the client is successful in using this technique, he or she is practising spontaneously changing irrational beliefs to rational beliefs (which are expressed in the form of non-dogmatic desires and preferences). The client is then asked to practise REI for a few minutes a day for 30 days and is given what Ellis calls 'operant conditioning' to motivate him or her to carry out this task. In 'operant conditioning', the client forgoes an enjoyable activity until he or she has practised REI and penalized him- or herself if he or she forgoes such practice (e.g. carries out an unpleasant task such as cleaning the toilet). At the end of the counselling session, the audience is invited to ask questions and the client is given a tape of the session for later review. Listening to the tapes of their sessions has two major benefits for clients. First, they often gain increased understanding of issues that were discussed in the public session. This is valuable because talking about one's problems in a public setting can be distracting for some clients. Secondly, clients often learn how to challenge their irrational beliefs more effectively after listening to Ellis's disputing interventions on tape.

We now present a verbatim transcript of an interview conducted by Ellis with Wouter Backx in the setting of the Friday night workshop to show this approach in action.

A Public Therapy Session Conducted by Albert Ellis

(Friday Night Workshop, 19 July 1985, in front of an audience of 100 people.)

Therapist: [to the audience]: Please be as compulsively quiet as you can be right now. Later you will get into the act and be able to say anything, but not right now. So shut your big mouths right now or else you'll have to listen in the john, which is a nice place to listen but not as good as in the auditorium. So quiet now and then later you'll be able to talk up and to say practically anything you want.

Therapist: [to client]: OK. Do you want to give me your first name?

Client: Wouter.

Therapist: Woulter, Wouter?

Client: Yes say Walter.

Therapist: Yeah, we would say Walter in English, but W-O-U-T-E-R in your language, right? OK Walter or Wouter, what problem would you like to start with?

Client: Well, I have a problem about doing things on time, especially when I have to take an examination or something like that, and er ...

Therapist: So in plain English you procrastinate, is that right? We call it procrastination; I don't know what you call it in Holland or Germany but we call it procrastination. Right?

Client: That is possible.

Therapist: Give us an example recently when you sat on your ass and procrastinated ...

Client: Oh well when I came to the United States I had to finish an essay about the philosophy of science; and er ... well, I had to finish it and I did not make it, I did not get it ready.

Audience: [murmurs to client]

Client: Sorry?

Audience: [says something about the microphone that the client is using not being turned correctly]

Client: Like this?

Therapist: No, no. When you turn to me, it does not turn with you. If you turn around that way, then you face me. But it does not turn your way. We haven't trained it properly yet. We are training it to turn properly, we are giving it therapy every week on how to turn. But so far we have failed and we may have to give up and kill ourselves. Unless we become rational and stop depressing ourselves about the goddamned mike! Anyway, so this time you could have done the paper ...

Client: Yes that is right.

Therapist: And you delayed, you procrastinated. Because when you were about to do it and you didn't, what did you say to yourself? What negative self-statement?

Client: Oh, 'I have a lot of time. I'll do that easily.'

Therapist: That's what we call a rationalization, which means horseshit in English. That is horseshit, because you did not have that much time. You lied to yourself.

Client: That's right.

Therapist: But what was the *reason* underneath the *rationalization*? You said something about the *hardship* of doing it. What do you think that was?

Client: Well, it could be that I had delayed so much that I did not have sufficient time to do it. So I was afraid to find out. Or realized that it was very difficult, instead of what I originally thought, that it was easy.

Therapist: Yeah ...

Client: I was a little bit afraid of not having enough time left in which to do it after I first delayed.

Therapist: Alright, but let us try the issue of difficultness first. Because your not having time enough was *after* you had already delayed. When you started delaying instead of doing it, you were saying, 'It may be difficult to do.' But if you didn't do it, that would be difficult too. Right?

Client: That seems to be – yeah, that is right.

Therapist: Yeah. So therefore you would probably do it. But what were you saying in addition to 'It may be or will be difficult'? You were saying something in addition to that. And what is that?

Client: 'If I fail I'll feel worse, I'll feel bad. I'll feel like a bad person.'

Therapist: So you were putting yourself down in case you failed.

Client: That's right.

Therapist: Alright, we'll start with your fear of failing first. I'll then get back to the difficulty of the task because that is usually important with procrastination – the difficulty of doing it and your reluctance to deal with that. But let us say, let us suppose you do the task quickly and immediately and it is not so hot and you fail. Why would *that* be terrible? Why would you be a bad person, a failure with a capital F for failing?

Client: Well, er ...

Therapist: Yes?

Client: ... that's difficult. Well, I should, must be able to do that!

Therapist: Oh you *should*! That is right: you *should* do it. But why *should* or *must* you?

Client: And it was my fault not to arrange it in a way that I could do it.

Therapist: That is correct it was your fault. Let us assume that. Nobody made you, put a gun to your head, and made you procrastinate. But since it was your fault, your failure, how does it make *you* a failure, a shit, a no goodnick for having that failing?

Client: Now I cannot find a good reason, but ...

Therapist: You believe it. You still believe you *must* not fail and are no good if you do.

Client: Yes I do believe it, really. That is ...

Therapist: And as long as you *believe* it you are going to procrastinate.

Client: That is right.

Therapist: You see. Now how can you give up that nutty idea? Not the idea that 'It is my fault if I fail,' but the idea that 'I am then a total failure.' How can you *give up* that horseshit?

Client: By telling myself something different.

Therapist: Exactly! What? 'I am a real failure?'

Client: No, 'I am not a real failure, but I am just failing at this moment'. Or 'I am about to fail this time'.

Therapist: 'If I do it badly' – which you may not, you may do well – 'and I fail, I'll be failing *at this moment with this essay*. But I am never a *failing person*. I am never a rotten *individual*.' Right. Now you said the right thing, but you do not really *believe* it? That you could fail at this essay but are not a real failure?

Client: Well, the problem is when I try to tell myself this it is very difficult. I don't make it. I am thinking, 'Well it is not that bad to put it off at this moment.'

Therapist: Yeah.

Client: So I go on delaying it ...

Therapist: Yeah, but that is for the other reason; we'll get to that in a minute, the hardness of it. But could you *really* believe that if you did it steadily and you kept failing, didn't do as well as you could do, do you really believe you would not be a failure, you would not be a worm? Do you *really* believe that?

Client: I think so, to some extent.

Therapist: Yeah to some extent! But how could you believe it *stronger*? Like all

these people in the audience. They believe it about you, but not about themselves. How could you believe it *stronger*? 'I am *never* a failure, a louse, a worm, *even* when I try my best and still fail.' How can you believe that?

Client: Well, I can stop making global evaluations about myself. That's right.

Therapist: Well, er ...

Client: Because after I fail I can still do very many good things. So it is impossible to say what will be any final or global evaluations or rating of me by the time I die.

Therapist: Once you fail, you have the possibility to do many successful things in the future.

Client: That is right.

Therapist: That is correct. So you are never *a failure*. If you were a failure, that would mean that you always deserve to fail and will fail because you failed this time. Is that correct?

Client: That's right, yeah. That's right, I would deserve punishment or whatever.

Therapist: But why *do* you deserve punishment if you fail? If you try your best and you fail this time?

Client: But I did not try my best.

Therapist: But suppose you did try to do your best. Why would you deserve punishment for failing? Why would you?

Client: No, I don't deserve it. That is right.

Therapist: Even if you did *not* try, you don't. Suppose you tried very little and you fell on your face. Why would you still *not* deserve punishment for failing?

Client: Well, I have freedom of choice. I can choose.

Therapist: You could choose *not* to rate yourself and *not* to consider yourself undeserving. Right. And the universe does not give a shit if you fail. It really does not care.

Client: Really?

Therapist: Yeah really. Don't be surprised that the powers up there and the powers down there really don't give a fuck whether you succeed or not. They have their *own* quaint ideas. They are only interested in their own navels, not in your bellybutton. So if you really thought about it you could convince yourself that 'It is bad to fail, it is unfortunate, it is poor behaviour. But I am not a *failure* and I don't *deserve* punishment or anything like that. I just deserve whatever I can get: such as good things in life. And when I get bad things I can live with them.' But now let us go right back to the hardness of doing the essay. You said rightly before that it is easy to put it off till later and to pretend: 'I'll do it later, I'll do it soon. I'll do it when it is easier.' Because it is *hard* to do it right now, right? But it is hard if you *don't* do it right now. In fact it is harder. Is it not?

Client: Well, sometimes it comes out that it is easier to do it later.

Therapist: Yeah, *how many* times?

Client: Yes, well ...

Therapist: Well, what percentage of times is it *easier* if you put it off?

Client: Well, I don't ... Ja ...

Therapist: Yeah, yeah! Out of a hundred times you put it off, how many times does it *really* become easier and a rare delight?

Client: Ja, that's right. But on the short term it is. That is the problem.

Therapist: Aah, yeah. That *is* the point. That is what we want you to see. It is easier *in the short run*.

Client: That's right.

Therapist: If you would really believe that, and would remind yourself how hard it is in the long run. If you write down on a piece of paper or a card the disadvantages of putting it off instead of the advantages of putting it off, which you have solidly instilled in your head, then you would tend not to put essays and things like that off. Now could you do that? Really write down on a piece of paper the disadvantages of putting it off, of doing it later and the advantages of doing it right now?

Client: I can do that.

Therapist: And would that not help you?

Client: I think so, ja.

Therapist: Is there any other reason which we may have omitted for your not doing the essay? Can you think of any other reason why you don't do it quickly, get it over with and that is that, which is what sensible people like me do?

Client: Well, sometimes I think something like, 'Why do they bother me with this kind of stuff?'

Therapist: 'Ooooooh, ooooooh! Those lousy bastards! How could they give a nice guy like me that crummy paper to do?' Right?

Client: That is right!

Therapist: And what is the answer to that question? How *can* they give a nice guy like you that crummy paper to do? How can they?

Client: They are a little bit stupid. They don't know better.

Therapist: They can *easily* do what they do! They have *no trouble* giving you those stupid papers! Do they?

Client: No they don't.

Therapist: And they are surviving very well!

Client: That is right.

Therapist: So you are rebelling and saying to yourself, 'Because it is such a pain in the ass and such a stupid assignment, such a stupid paper to write, there-fore they *should* not give it to me!'. But they *should* give it to you! Do you know why they *should* give it to you, that stupid paper?

Client: Because they choose to give it.

Therapist: Yes. Because *that is their nature*, to give out stupid papers! Do you expect them to give out intelligent papers to do or give you sensible things to do? How ridiculous! So you see you have got three major musts to produce your procrastination: One, 'I *must* do it very well and if I don't that would be terrible! I would be no good.' Two, 'They must not give me that goddamned stupid paper! So I'll fix their wagon by not doing it or by doing it later, when I feel like doing it.' And three, 'It is too goddamned hard to do! It *should not* be so, hard! Therefore I'll put it off and I hope and pray to God almighty that it becomes easier some day.'

Client: That's right. I do say these things.

Therapist: But that is not working. And you see that your irrational beliefs are all *musts*. 'I must do well! They must treat me well! And conditions, the work itself must be easy!' You are demanding and commanding that things *must* be your way. Now that is very unlikely!

Let me say how I did the opposite, when I was in college. I realized that they gave us term papers, especially in English which was really my major because I took more courses in English than in anything else. So the first day of the term they gave us a list of topics to write a term paper on and everybody else would fart around like you did, till the last day of the term or the day after the last day. But I did my paper immediately. I went to the library to work on it right away. First of all, nobody else was in the library and all the books were there, so that was good. Secondly, I could take any length of time I wanted to do the paper and finish it at my leisure. Thirdly, my professor almost dropped dead when he got the paper the second week of the term, was very grateful to get it so soon and thought I was a very noble person and a scholar. It was the first time in his or her history that that had ever happened and I could coast for the rest of term, having nothing hanging over my head. No worry, no problems. So I figured out that it was much more advantageous for me to do my term papers that way. So I did them immediately. But you are not figuring what I figured out. You are deluding yourself that it is advantageous to delay your essays. And it very very rarely, practically never, is.

Let us try you with rational emotive imagery. We have up to now been doing disputing and asking 'Why *must* it be easy and where is it written that you *have to* do a perfect paper?' And 'Who says that those bastards *must* not give you stupid papers?' So we have been questioning and challenging your irrational beliefs and you had better keep doing that. But let us also give you rational emotive imagery. Close your eyes and imagine that the bastards give you another lousy, crummy paper to do which they probably will; and imagine that this paper is really a pain in the ass, it is very stupid that they give it to you, and it is hanging over your head to do. Can you vividly imagine that happening?

Client: Yes.

Therapist: How do you feel in your gut as you imagine that paper hanging over your head, the days passing, and you keep telling yourself 'Tomorrow, tomorrow, mañana, mañana.' How do you feel?

Client: I feel anger at those people who gave it to me.

Therapist: Now get in touch with your anger and really make yourself feel very angry at those idiots for giving you this stupid paper. Make yourself feel very angry. Are you feeling very angry with them?

Client: Right.

Therapist: All right. Now they are still making you do it, your image is still the same. But make yourself feel only sorry, only disappointed at what they are doing to you. Not angry at them. Tell me when you feel sorry and disappointed, not angry.

Client: I do.

Therapist: Open your eyes. That was quick, really quick. Tell us how you changed your feelings. How did you change?

Client: I er first of all turned away from those stupid people and secondly by telling myself, 'Well it is not nice to have to do that paper, but OK I'll do it and I will certainly not die whatever bad things may happen in the world, I can stand it. And when I pass it is OK.'

Therapist: Alright. Now that was really good. Now all you have to do if you follow this, is every day for the next 30 days you imagine the worst you can think of, make yourself very angry or depressed or anything like that – anger is one of the things that shows how you feel, so that is OK – change it into being sorry and being disappointed the way you did and other ways that may occur to you. Now will you do that for the next 30 days at least once a day? You may do it 10 times a day but do it at least once. Would you really want to do that?

Client: Let us say before I go to bed?

Therapist: Well any time in 24 hours once a day, do you want to do it?

Client: Oh, whether I want to do it, I thought you asked when.

Therapist: Yeah. No, no, I am not telling you that. You can do it any time once a day. Now in case you don't we are going to give you reinforcement – operant conditioning. What do you like to do that you do almost every day in the week? What do you really enjoy doing? You enjoy something you do almost every day. What is it?

Client: Well, reading a book.

Therapist: Alright. No reading for the next 30 days until *after* you do that one or two minutes' rational emotive imagery because that is all it takes you. What do you hate to do that normally you avoid doing because you hate it?

Client: Doing the laundry and things like that.

Therapist: Alright. For the next 30 days if bedtime arrives and you have not yet done your rational emotive imagery you are to stay up another hour to do the laundry. But if you do the rational emotive imagery you don't have to do the laundry. And if your laundry gets too clean, you can then do your neighbour's laundry!

Client: I am working at a youth camp, so that won't be difficult to arrange.

Therapist: That is right! At a youth camp there is plenty of laundry to do! Now, is there anything else about this problem that we may have omitted?

Client: Well, sometimes I do just the reverse of what you now tell me. When I feel depressed, I do things I like instead of trying to do things ...

Therapist: ... that you don't like?

Client: Yeah. I do the things that I have to do or that I want to do.

Therapist: Yeah, that would be all right temporarily, just temporarily for a while. But you could make sure that you later do the things that you don't like to do, in case you avoid performing the rational emotive imagery. But it would even be better when you are depressed, to do the goddamned things you don't like. They would preoccupy you, help you get distracted from your depression. Also you can then do work at eliminating the depression. Now another thing when you don't do the work, don't write your essays, how do you feel about yourself for procrastinating, for not doing it?

Client: Well very bad. Shit, shit.
Therapist: Alright. So some of your depression stems from your self-downing. And you could ask yourself not 'Why am I not doing the work?', but 'Why am I a shit for not doing this work?'. And your answer would be what?
Client: There is no reason.
Therapist: Yes, there is no reason. 'I am a fallible fucked up human being who is not doing the work right now. So I'd better move my ass and do it!'
              Let us now get the audience's comments and discussion about this problem.

Audience Participation

We have noticed that the types of issues/questions raised by the audience can be placed into a number of categories.

Practical advice

A number of participants offer practical suggestions or advice concerning what the volunteer can do about his or her problem. Thus, good suggestions concerning how to overcome procrastination and how to approach members of the opposite sex, for example, are often put forward. Ellis endorses those practical suggestions that he considers of merit and points out problems with other pieces of advice. However, he generally urges the volunteers (and thus indirectly teaches the audience) to change irrational beliefs before attempting to solve the practical aspects of their problems. In doing so, Ellis highlights an important point in rational emotive behavior theory that when people are disturbed by holding irrational beliefs about an event, this impedes them from thinking clearly and thus from implementing effective solutions to change the event or to adjust to it.

Challenging inferences

One feature of REBT that distinguishes it from other forms of cognitive-behaviour therapy is that REBT therapists in general first encourage their clients to assume that their inferences about a situation are true (in order to identify latent irrational beliefs) before challenging these inferences at a later stage. Members of the audience often ask volunteers questions which are directed to the truth or falsity of the latter's negative inferences. Ellis generally endorses such interventions but stresses why it is important to first challenge irrational beliefs before challenging negative inferences.

Assessing the impact of self on others

A number of questions and points are addressed to volunteers concerning the possible impact that their behaviour has on others. These often prove to be valuable interventions because Ellis does not frequently address himself to such material in the course of the 30-minute public demonstration interviews. Thus, volunteers who present with problems of maintaining or developing interpersonal relationships are asked to reflect on the possibility that some aspects of their behaviour impede the quality of their relationships. Some members of the audience are quite astute at picking up cues from the demeanour of volunteers that are worthy of consideration.

Anti-REBT viewpoints

Some members of the audience ask questions which are based on therapeutic philosophies that are antithetical to REBT. Here Ellis is quick to show the questioner, the volunteer and the rest of the audience the problems which are inherent in such viewpoints. In doing so, Ellis is quite vigorous in his criticisms of opposing viewpoints, for example, labelling them as 'psychoanalytical horseshit' etc. He does this to stress to the audience the dangers, he sees in such positions. While some claim that Ellis is dogmatic in his expressed views on these subjects, Ellis defends himself by distinguishing between dogma (which he denies) and strongly held viewpoints (which are non-dogmatically expressed in a powerful manner). After voicing his criticisms, Ellis proceeds to offer the REBT position on these issues.

Catching Ellis out

A few members of the audience are extremely knowledgeable in REBT theory and practice and delight in pointing out to Ellis that he has omitted some aspect of REBT theory and practice in his presentation. Ellis takes these points in very good spirit and uses them to teach the audience the neglected aspect of the rational-emotive-behavioral approach.

While no systematic research has been done on the effect of the Friday night workshop on audience learning, Ellis claims that members of the audience are often helped by observing such interviews to solve their own problems by using the same methods that they have watched Ellis employ. This would certainly be a fruitful area for future research.

Further Issues

It can be seen from the presented interview that Ellis's approach reflects his New York origins. Several writers have made the point that one does not have to sound like Albert Ellis in order to practise REBT effectively (e.g. Meichenbaum, 1977). Indeed, one reason why we believe that REBT has not attracted a large following among British counsellors and psychotherapists is that these practitioners equate the practice of REBT with Ellis's forthright and earthy style. So if a British version of the Friday night workshop were ever to be held, a less forthright and earthy approach may have to be adopted to obviate such negative effects. However, it may be that the British public are less sensitive about such matters than British counsellors and psychotherapists!

Such workshops obviously raise issues concerning confidentiality. Our preference would be to announce at the beginning of such workshops that client material should be respected as confidential and should not be discussed with other people outside the workshop other than in general terms. Certainly no names should be linked to discussions of client material. That Ellis does not make such an announcement is something we would criticize.

It is interesting to observe that disclosing their problems before an audience of strangers does not seem to inhibit the volunteers who choose to discuss their problems in New York. Obviously some material might not be disclosed and it is important to stress at this point that such demonstrations are not designed to replace individual therapy. Indeed, a number of volunteers at Ellis's Friday night workshops later seek help from Ellis himself or from one of the other therapists at the Albert Ellis Institute. Whether British people would feel as free to volunteer to discuss their problems in public in such interviews, and whether they will show the same lack of inhibition in their disclosures, remains to be seen.

References

Meichenbaum D (1977) Cognitive-Behavior Modification. New York: Plenum.
Nelson-Jones R (1982) The Theory and Practice of Counselling Psychology. London: Holt, Reinhart & Winston.

CHAPTER 9

The Use of the Group in REBT Training and Supervision

MICHAEL NEENAN

Dryden and Thorne (1991) suggest that counselling training courses should provide trainees with learning opportunities in four main areas: (1) counselling theory and relevant academic material; (2) the acquisition of counselling skills; (3) self-exploration; and (4) supervised work with clients. In this chapter, we look at ways in which a group setting can be used to enhance training and supervision in REBT as well as deal with the blocks encountered in this learning process.

The Role of the Trainer

REBT trainers are role models for REBT trainees, i.e. they should ideally reflect the manner and style of REBT therapists. Therefore they are very active and directive in running a training programme, developing productive working alliances that assist trainees to engage in the tasks (both in-session and for homework) to achieve their training goals, encouraging active participation and feedback from all group members, preventing the group sidetracking into issues that are not pertinent to REBT training, monitoring group dynamics and disputing trainees' irrational beliefs that inhibit or block group cohesion and learning (Ellis and Dryden, 1997). The trainer eschews lengthy and/or elaborate procedures for developing group cohesion and, instead, makes an early start in teaching the principles and practice of REBT. While much of the course content is predetermined, additional items for study can be collaboratively agreed.

Trainers should be aware of some learning theory models in order to create an effective learning environment (Fennell, 1999; Honey and Mumford, 1986; Kolb, 1984). For example, Honey and Mumford (1986) describe four learning styles: (1) activists – their philosophy is 'I'll try anything once'; (2) reflectors – these individuals require lots of time to ponder before coming to a decision: 'I really need time to think this through';

(3) theorists – they prize rationality and logic and like to analyse and synthe-size: 'How does this fit with that?'; and (4) pragmatists – these are keen on trying out ideas in practice to see if they work: 'If it works it's good.' REBT trainers should preferably assist their trainees 'to capitalize on strengths and acquire the other capacities so that all four styles can be comfortably accommodated within his or her repertoire' (Clarkson and Gilbert, 1991, p. 158).

Getting Started

Probably most members of a training group will not be known to each other and therefore the group can begin with individuals introducing themselves and speaking briefly about their professional backgrounds. Further 'loosening up' can follow with small group discussions for about twenty minutes based on what the students hope to gain from the course, what they like, have favourably heard or read about REBT (which presumably drew them to the course) and what they dislike about REBT (the latter may be based on misconceptions such as 'REBT doesn't deal with feelings' or 'REBT teaches selfishness'). At the end of the twenty-minute period, each small group reports back to the main group on their expectations, likes and dislikes. After this discussion, group members usually feel more relaxed and better acquainted with each other and thus more receptive to the first teaching segment.

Status within the Group

One of the problems associated with the dynamics of a training group is the development of a hierarchy based on who appears to be the most knowl-edgeable about REBT, speaks with authority about various issues or has a 'presence' that attracts others. Group members lacking such knowledge and attributes may seem to have been 'left on the shelf' when small discussion groups are formed and therefore band together because 'there is nowhere else to go'. Instead of each group having a balance of abilities, some are 'top heavy' with individuals who can, for example, stimulate discussion or keep to the time constraints of each exercise while other groups may contain individuals who are unassertive, procrastinate or feel resentful at not being in the 'right group'. As a training programme has to go at the pace of the least able small group or individuals, other groups may feel frustrated at this 'slow coach' pace. The trainer can ask the group to sort out the difficulties that this hierarchical arrangement has produced:

Trainer: In some of the groups we are over-represented in certain things like knowledge about REBT or being task-focused. Now, in order to maximize our training effectiveness, we need a better balance of abilities

	in each group. How are we going to achieve this?
John:	What's wrong with the ways things are? I'm happy with the group I'm in.
Trainer:	Well, for the reasons I've just said. I have to think about the training needs of the whole group rather than just one individual.
Janet:	But aren't the groups now fixed?
Trainer:	Well let's see: is there a law of the universe or of this training course which says so?
Paula:	Of course not. Why don't we frequently change the composition of the groups so we get a better skills mix? I'd prefer it that way because you get to know what everybody else has to offer.
Simon:	I agree with that because it seems so much fairer and also adds variety to the training.
Sarah:	It will also help to stop cliques forming, you know, them and us sort of thing.
Mary:	Let's face it: that group over there seems to know a lot about REBT and what they're supposed to be doing while we in this group are really struggling, groping in the dark. We could do with one of them joining our group.
Trainer:	Okay. Do you all agree to change frequently the composition of the small groups so a better balance is achieved? (nods and murmurs of agreement). Okay, swap round at the next small group activity.

Talking: Too Much, Not Enough or Not Interested

Another problem is those individuals who always remain silent in the group. The trainer can ask questions in order to encourage them to participate (e.g. 'David, why do you always look at the floor when I ask for group feedback?' or 'Sandra, you seem to visibly tense when I say "Who hasn't spoken yet?" I wonder what's going through your mind at that moment?'). Alternatively, the trainer can involve the group in analysing this problem, according to the ABC model of REBT, by writing on the whiteboard his hypothesis:

> A = reluctant to talk in case they say the wrong thing and appear stupid in the eyes of the group

and then asking the group what the B and C components of this problem might be (this exercise can sometimes prompt one or two of the silent trainees to speak up and identify their own B and C elements). The usual replies from the group are that the C (emotional consequence) is anxiety and/or shame and the iBs (irrational beliefs) something like 'I must not say the wrong thing and appear stupid in the eyes of the group' and/or 'If I say something stupid, which I absolutely should not have done, I am exposed as a complete idiot.' The silent group members can then be asked if these are the beliefs they subscribe to (which is usually the case). The trainer prods the group for ways of challenging these beliefs cognitively (e.g. learning self-acceptance in the face of possible criticism from others for saying something stupid) and behaviourally (e.g. asking questions and making comments on what others have said). Such methods help silent members to take risks by speaking up and allowing themselves to evaluate more accurately the reactions of others. Eventually, every trainee makes a contribution to group discussion.

On the other hand, one or two individuals may dominate group discussion, continually interrupt or intimidate others with their putative authority when challenged (e.g. 'I've attended some of Albert Ellis's workshops, so I know what I'm talking about!'). REBT trainers prevent certain individuals from 'hijacking' the discussion and do not believe that asking someone to talk less will cause him/her psychological damage (Wessler and Wessler, 1980).

As well as asking someone to talk less, the trainer will also be interested in why others are not talking more, e.g. 'What prevents the rest of the group from participating more and telling Peter and Maureen to stay quiet for a while?' Replies usually include avoidance of interpersonal conflict, fear of losing the approval of the dominant group members, becoming the centre of attention, not having confidence in their own contributions (which usually comes back to looking foolish in the group). By the trainer directly addressing these issues and eliciting and challenging the irrational beliefs underpinning them (e.g. 'In what way could you not stand the discomfort of disagreeing with Peter or Maureen?'), he hopes to achieve a more balanced participation in group discussion.

Alternatively, if the group as a whole appears uninterested, dull, sluggish, taciturn, the trainer can comment on this unresponsiveness, probe for the reasons underlying it and encourage the group to suggest ways of injecting some vitality into the proceedings – in other words, to lead themselves out of their own torpor.

Get Me to the Group on Time

Group members can become irritated or angry by the persistent lateness of one of their number. This can be viewed by the group as a sign of disrespect for them as they are punctual and a lack of commitment to the course (the latecomer may also want to keep borrowing others' notes in order to catch up on the missed learning or is inserted into small group activities and has to be informed by the others about the assigned tasks). Ellis (1997, p. 146) suggests that lateness becomes an issue for the group to focus on: 'We determine, for instance, why he comes late, what core philosophies encourage him to do so, how he defeats himself and the other members by his lateness, how he can change, and what kind of homework assignment in this respect he will agree to carry out.' It is important that group discussion is critical only of his lateness and its effects on the group (e.g. interfering with group cohesiveness), not of the individual himself. In the final analysis, if these strategies fail, then we recommend that the trainer unangrily refuses entry to the trainee when he arrives late. We regard persistent latecoming in both trainee and trainer as unprofessional behaviour.

1. Counselling theory and relevant academic material

Lengthy didactic presentations of REBT (e.g. the ABCDE model of emotional disturbance and change, unhealthy v. healthy negative emotions, ego and discomfort disturbance, and the differences between feeling better and getting better) can encourage students to 'switch off', drift away, feel tired, yearn for the coffee break, etc. as the 'expert' drones on. As Wessler and Wessler (1980, p. 219) point out: 'one of our tasks as therapists [or trainers] is to encourage the group to participate. If the therapist [or trainer] does too much of the talking during the first session, he or she may induce a set of expectations that will be hard to change'. In other words, group members may expect to be spoon-fed REBT principles rather than encouraged to think for themselves about them. To achieve this end, didactic presentations can be kept relatively short to reduce or avoid 'switching off' and questions can be sought or asked by the trainer in order to stimulate group discussion.

For example, what often ignites such a discussion is REBT's hypothesis that emotional disturbance is largely self-induced rather than directly caused by others or external events: 'Let's take a specific case of a person who becomes depressed over the end of a relationship. Now REBT argues that the end of the relationship is unfortunate but the depression is largely determined by the rigid beliefs the person holds about the end of the relationship, not by the end of the relationship itself.' Even if most group members generally agree with this proposition, they also offer exceptions to it, e.g. serious accident, violent assault, death of a loved one. So what could have been a dry-as-dust lecture on REBT theory usually turns into a lively discussion on the perceived limits of REBT's theory of emotional disturbance.

At the end of a didactic presentation, tests can be administered to determine how much information has been absorbed, e.g. 'What are the three main derivatives from an irrational premise and the three main derivatives from a rational premise?' As Dryden (1999, p. 60) observes: 'Remember the maxim: "There is no good course without a test".' Members can form into small groups to take a collective test rather than an individual one as this helps to remind each other of what has been taught.

To deepen their understanding of REBT theory, each student can be assigned, as a homework task, to read about and critique one aspect of it such as REBT's emphasis on how emotional problems are maintained rather than on how they were acquired. The student can present her findings to the group and then lead a question and answer session. In this way, the students help to educate each other and themselves about REBT theory as well as being open to criticisms made about it (Bernard and DiGiuseppe, 1989).

Learning styles

As mentioned earlier, it is important for the trainer to encourage trainees to incorporate other learning styles into their intellectual development rather than rely on their preferred styles. To this end, the trainer will need to construct exercises that provide the trainees with opportunities in experiencing all four learning styles. For example, teaching the ABC model of emotional disturbance (activist) is followed by discussion and observations about the exercise such as 'The principle of emotional responsibility can be very frightening for some people to accept' (reflector); these reflections or observations are internalized as an analysis of what has been learned begins, e.g. 'People are more likely to accept emotional responsibility if it is dissociated from any suggestion of blame for one's problems' (theorist); and putting the new learning into practice in order to find better ways of encouraging clients to accept and act on the principle of emotional responsibility (pragmatist).

Fennell (1999) suggests self-development activities so trainees become familiar with all four styles: for example, do something new at least once a week (activist); keep a diary and reflect on what you write (reflector); practice spotting weaknesses in others' line of argument (theorist); and collect techniques (pragmatist). Trainee learning can become a continual process of change and modification through exploring and analysing experiences; in other words, training relies more on self-direction than a pedagogic approach as trainees attach greater significance to what they experience rather than what they are told (Knowles, 1990).

2. Acquisition of counselling skills

The practice of REBT has been described in 13 counselling steps (Dryden and DiGiuseppe, 1990) and, more recently, has been increased to 18 steps (Dryden, Neenan and Yankura, 1999). The skills required for the successful execution of each step (see Figure 9.1) can be provided in written form through transcripts of therapy, watching videos of skilled REBTers in action, demonstrations by the trainer (which in our experience trainees are always eager to observe), and through small group practice.

In this last exercise, triads are formed whereby one member of the triad plays the client (choosing a personal problem that is appropriate for a training course), another plays the therapist and the last member plays the observer who comments constructively on the therapist's attempt to apply some REBT skills as well as keeping the exercise on track and on time (some trainees may start discussing issues irrelevant to the exercise or may want

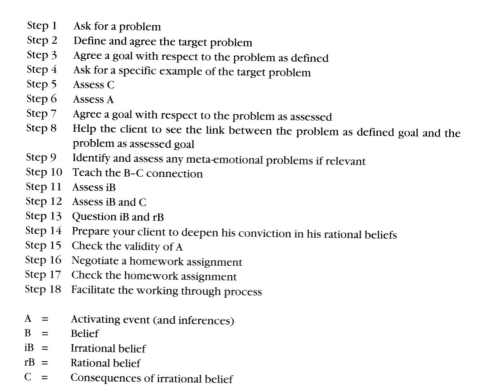

Step 1   Ask for a problem
Step 2   Define and agree the target problem
Step 3   Agree a goal with respect to the problem as defined
Step 4   Ask for a specific example of the target problem
Step 5   Assess C
Step 6   Assess A
Step 7   Agree a goal with respect to the problem as assessed
Step 8   Help the client to see the link between the problem as defined goal and the problem as assessed goal
Step 9   Identify and assess any meta-emotional problems if relevant
Step 10   Teach the B–C connection
Step 11   Assess iB
Step 12   Assess iB and C
Step 13   Question iB and rB
Step 14   Prepare your client to deepen his conviction in his rational beliefs
Step 15   Check the validity of A
Step 16   Negotiate a homework assignment
Step 17   Check the homework assignment
Step 18   Facilitate the working through process

A =   Activating event (and inferences)
B =   Belief
iB =   Irrational belief
rB =   Rational belief
C =   Consequences of irrational belief

Figure 9.1. The Rational Emotive Behavioral Counselling Sequence.

several minutes to feel comfortable before starting it). Each participant in the triad gets to play each role once.

Grieger and Boyd (1980, p. 229) state that 'roleplaying is a training technique with enormous utility because it can tap so many learning avenues. By playing a client's role, trainees get closer to client dynamics, diagnostic understanding of the client is enhanced by acting out the ABC's. When playing the therapist's role the objective of roleplaying is skill practice. Trainees can perform newly learned skills in a lifelike but non-threatening situation.' The observer can enhance his/her own understanding of the skills required by making suggestions to the therapist when he/she is stuck. Feedback from such exercises can uncover problems and possible solutions to them:

Simon: The hardest thing for me was knowing when to intervene. When I asked my client for a problem she just kept on talking.
Trainer: What prevented you from interrupting tactfully?
Simon: I thought it would be rude to interrupt.
Janet: I had the same problem.

Mary:	So did I.
Trainer:	Okay. Who had an overly talkative client but managed to interrupt tactfully?
David:	I said to my client 'May I interrupt you there as I need to ask some questions to clarify in my mind what the problem is?' He didn't seem to mind.
Trainer:	Let's see then. Who was David's client?
Peter:	I was. I didn't feel his interruptions were rude or insensitive. If he doesn't ask questions how is he going to find out about my problems?
Trainer:	So how do we tackle this general reluctance to interrupt overly talkative clients?
Julie:	Make that the next exercise so we can get more practice at interrupting tactfully.
Trainer:	Let's do that then.

When triads or other small group activities are underway, the trainer visits each group to monitor that it is keeping to the designated task such as carrying out the first six steps of the counselling sequence. Usual complaints from trainees include that following the counselling sequence is the same as wearing a straitjacket, makes them feel psychologically uncomfortable because of the concentrated focus required in performing the skills for the successful execution of each step, and that it is easier and more comfortable to revert to a previously learnt counselling approach (e.g. person centred).

The trainer can ask the group what will happen if they escape from their 'straitjackets' too early (frequent reply: 'We won't learn REBT which is what we're here for - put us back in our straitjackets!'). The trainer can point out that flexibility in following the sequence such as omitting some steps or only applying a basic ABC model comes with greater experience as REBTers. The psychological discomfort in carrying out each step requires the trainees to tackle their low frustration toleration ideas (e.g. 'It's too uncomfortable. The steps should be made simpler'). The group can list the benefits of acquiring higher frustration tolerance: e.g. the focus will be on the task rather than on how they feel; the skills will be learnt quicker; they are using REBT on themselves while learning to apply it to others; there is no gain without pain.

Reverting to a counselling orientation that the trainee is already skilled in can be seen as a protective manoeuvre which the group can suggest hypotheses for: trainees can reassure themselves that they are professionally competent whereas struggling to learn REBT can expose them as 'incompetent'; anger at feeling de-skilled or back in a 'situation of dependence' (Perris, 1994), e.g. 'I've been a successful psychodynamic therapist for ten years and I feel as if I'm in nappies again with this REBT stuff'; and REBT does not 'go deep enough in understanding the roots of the client's problems, so that's why I went back to my usual way of working'.

Through discussion, group members usually see that labels like 'incompetent' reside in their minds and are not inherent in the tasks themselves; that the tasks are not deskilling or dependence forming but, instead, are seen through the distorting lens of trainees' irrational beliefs (e.g. 'I must get it right at the first attempt in order to prove I'm a good therapist and not rely on the trainer to help me'); and that REBT does go 'deep' but trainees need to learn how to get there using REBT maps and how to work therapeutically with core-disturbance-producing beliefs once they are uncovered. By avoiding self-labelling, challenging irrational beliefs and not rushing to judgement about REBT's apparent lack of depth-centredness, trainees are able to focus more of their time and energy on skills acquisition.

Disputing or questioning clients' irrational beliefs is a major activity of REBT therapists. Trainees often equate disputing with verbally attacking clients or trying to 'brainwash' them into accepting REBT's view of rationality. The trainer can point out that 'attacking' or 'brainwashing' clients would be counterproductive if actually practised; however, the group can form into dyads and see for themselves the effects of these 'disputing' methods. Feedback can then be elicited:

Sonia: When my therapist started attacking my beliefs I got very defensive. I know some of my beliefs are unhelpful but being attacked made me defend them more than I would normally do.

Jane: I felt the same. When somebody attacks you, you immediately protect yourself.

John: Such disputing doesn't help you to open up at all to examine your thinking.

Paula: If this had been proper therapy, I would have walked out there and then. The therapist needed a bloody good slap!

Simon: I wouldn't have come back for a second session.

Raymond: My therapist tried to brainwash me into thinking rationally. I thought to myself 'You're not interested in me as a person. You just want me to say what you want to hear.' I was having none of it.

Trainer: Right. For all those reasons and more, REBTers do not attack their clients or their beliefs or attempt to brainwash them. You want to engage clients in the disputing process, not alienate them from it. You are encouraging your clients to decide if some of their beliefs are self-helping or self-defeating. We can watch a video which demonstrates constructive disputing and afterwards you can try it the proper way. Okay? (murmurs and nods of agreement).

3. Self-exploration

If trainees hope to be competent REBTers with their clients then it is important that they apply REBT to their own problems in order to increase their self-awareness and self-knowledge. As Thorne and Dryden (1991, pp. 3–4) point out, 'an unaware counsellor leading an unexamined life is likely to be a liability rather than an asset'. For this part of their training, students are required to take part in group psychotherapy. This group is led by an REBTer who does not play any part in the training sections of the course or academic evaluation of the students.

REBT is a robust approach to emotional problem-solving but students can be very reluctant to apply this approach to themselves or others in a group setting. Group discussion can be initiated by the trainer asking each member to say something complimentary about the person sitting next to them and then something critical about them (this latter task starts to increase the emotional temperature in the room). Individuals' reactions to being criticized (e.g. hurt, angry, anxious) can be discussed as well as some members' reluctance to make criticisms of others (e.g. fear of being disliked, being ostracized from the group). Such an exercise helps each group member to uncover their own irrationalities and gain the help of the group in disputing them (e.g. 'Being disliked is unfortunate but not the end of the world').

On the other hand, a group norm or unwritten rule may emerge not to criticize or challenge each other. Wessler and Wessler (1980, p. 226) suggest that when this occurs, 'the therapist would do well to take measures to expose it. For example, the therapist can discuss the norm and point out to the group members how their behavior has conformed to this unwritten rule, or she can create an experiential exercise in which norm breaking is a featured part of the activity'. For example, to get members 'in the mood', the therapist may say 'I want each one of you to say something critical about me.' Through therapist modelling of accepting and responding to criticism non-defensively and in a non-disturbed way, group members learn that it is not an 'awful' experience to be challenged:

John: Didn't you get angry when we criticized you?

Therapist: No. There is no reason why you cannot criticize me. Of course, I don't have to like or agree with some or even all of the criticisms you make. The point is to listen to them in an open-minded way. I might learn something from you.

Paula: But don't you think you must have our respect instead of our criticism?

Therapist: Well, if I started saying things like 'You absolutely should respect me' or 'You mustn't criticize me' then I would be irrational in the REBT sense and my ideas would not stand up to examination.

Julie: I liked the way you handled criticism from us (nods of approval from other group members). But you are used to it.

Therapist: But how did I get used to it?

Simon: By asking for criticism.

Therapist: Asking for it but with what attitude in mind?

Mary: Listening open-mindedly and acting non-defensively.

Therapist: Exactly. And what are we trying to communicate to our clients with
              regard to criticism?
Peter: We accept them unconditionally but not necessarily their behaviour.
Therapist: That's the spirit in which we challenge each other. If you condemned
              the person and the action, what might be the outcome then?
Jane: The person would probably spend more time defending themself or
              putting themself down rather than listening to the criticisms of their
              behaviour.
Therapist: Okay, so let's deal with this group norm by you saying one thing that
              irritates you about someone else in the group.

As Hauck (1980, p. 186) points out: 'Clients are intensely curious to see
whether these fantastic [REBT] statements which the counselor is making
can actually work, and whether they work in the life of the counselor. To
provide an in vivo experience for them in the management of hostility or
depression gives an invaluable demonstration of the veracity of the teachings'. Therapist modelling provides a stimulus for trainees to explore for
themselves 'the veracity of the teachings' and be thereafter less inclined to
follow unproductive group norms.

Self-exploration in REBT is primarily through the use of the ABC model
where irrational beliefs (B) about events (A) lead to dysfunctional cognitive, emotional and behavioural consequences (C). Each group member
can take a turn at applying the model to their own emotional problems;
other members can help the individual to assess the problem, dispute any
irrational beliefs that emerge (e.g. 'Why must you always get it right?'; 'How
does failing at something make you a failure as a person?') and suggest
suitable homework tasks if she is unable to think of any herself (e.g. tell her
work colleague that she does not know the answer to a question she has
been asked).

Once group members become more comfortable with discussing their
problems, those individuals who never disclose their own difficulties and/or
only take part in exploring others' problems usually become the focus of
group scrutiny, e.g. 'Why do you never bring up a problem but are always
quick to jump in and talk about someone else's problem?' The group norm
now becomes that everyone should preferably 'open up' and contribute;
silence will be frowned on. Therefore, it is important that this new group
norm does not become an intolerant one in that silent members will be
damned and/or ostracized – the antithesis of REBT teaching. The aim is to
develop constructive peer pressure in order to encourage everyone to
contribute personal problems for discussion and discover the reasons for
those still reluctant to do so. Group members urge non-disclosing individuals
to 'test the waters' in the safety of the group (e.g. 'We've all spoken up,
gained some insight and help with our problems and nothing terrible has

happened yet'); in this way, the group becomes a laboratory where new behaviours and beliefs can be tried out.

REBT is primarily about emotional problem-solving; therefore REBTers look for emotional solutions to problems (e.g. feeling concerned instead of anxious about possible failure). Practical solutions can be pursued after the emotional solution has been achieved (e.g. improving presentational skills). The therapist can quickly determine if the group is only providing practical solutions to an individual's problems (e.g. 'Why don't you just try harder next time?'), reassurance (e.g. 'I'm sure everyone really enjoyed the workshop') or positive thinking (e.g. 'Your presentation is going to be brilliant next time!'). By pointing out that the emotional solution through cognitive restructuring and action assignments is usually the enduring solution, the therapist can sensitize the group to make discriminations between these different types of solutions. Group members quickly become adept at spotting non-emotional solutions (e.g. 'Sally, why are suggesting to Jane that she change jobs rather than deal with her anger towards her colleague?'; 'Peter is always trying to make us feel better rather than help us deal with the grim reality of events').

As the group becomes more cohesive and skilful in applying REBT to each other's problems, the therapist 'can move more and more into a coaching role ...' and 'move to the sidelines, observe and correct when necessary, and guide the discussion rather than conduct the discussion' (Wessler and Wessler, 1980, pp. 220–1).

4. Supervised work with clients

Beal and DiGiuseppe (1998, p. 128) state that 'the purpose of supervision is to teach and supervise REBT theory and techniques so that practitioners can master REBT approaches to psychotherapy and apply them effectively to a wide variety of people with emotional problems'. Supervision is where students offer their work with clients for analysis and are understandably apprehensive about how their work will be evaluated by the supervisor or seen by other group members (e.g. 'The supervisor will think the audiotape is crap!'; 'The others will see me as a hopeless therapist'). The supervisor strives to develop a learning alliance that will promote supervisees' professional development (Friedberg and Taylor, 1994, 147). Dryden (1987) suggests that this learning alliance can be fostered by, among other things:

- *Unconditional acceptance* – supervisees' skills or behaviours may be rated but not the person. As Woods and Ellis (1996, p. 149) point out: 'Evaluation of performance is best conducted in an atmosphere of acceptance and tolerance for mistakes, by the supervisor for the supervisee, by the supervisee for her/himself, and by the supervisee for the supervisor.'

- *Supervisor self-disclosure* – the supervisor reveals that he struggled to learn REBT in similar ways to his students and that he continues to make mistakes. The supervisor has never been, is or will be an infallible therapist or supervisor.
- *Explaining the nature of human learning* – that making mistakes is part of the learning process for without mistakes progress cannot be made. As Hauck (1982, p. 47) observes: 'Even if you are trying something and do not see improvement, you are still entitled to say that you are improving, because the benefits of practice will show up later.'
- *Employing the judicious use of humour* – Ellis (1977) argues that one major source of emotional disturbance is when individuals take themselves and their ideas too seriously and humour can be employed to diffuse this overseriousness. Therefore, humour can be directed at the supervisor as well as at the supervisees within the context of unconditional acceptance. Wessler and Wessler (1980, p. 227) warn that 'boring leaders can be hazardous to group effectiveness. Groups are probably more successful, and certainly more interesting, if the therapist has a lively, stimulating manner.'
- *Giving balanced feedback* – this means both positive and constructive negative feedback. Too much of the former can create the illusion that the student is making more progress that she actually is while focusing excessively on counselling errors can help to demoralize and demotivate her.

This learning alliance is optimally effective when all members of a supervision group are interested in each other's work with clients rather than just their own. Through listening to other members' case presentations, supervisees can gain some understanding of how to deal with problems (e.g. obsessive-compulsive disorder, panic attacks) that are not on their present caseload but may be encountered at a later date. Also, other group members can, at times, take a supervisory role by suggesting methods of tackling clinical problems a particular supervisee is struggling with.

Supervision comprises a number of activities: developing the clinical skills of supervisees; tackling the emotional problems they develop while working with clients (e.g. anger at clients 'for not working hard in therapy'); focusing on the interpersonal difficulties that arise between supervisor and supervisee (e.g. the supervisor's anger with her supervisee's excuses for not presenting an audiotape).

'Who would like to present first?'

This 'blood-curdling' request can create a palpable sense of unease in the group. In the mind of the group, who is going to be the first one to have their 'incompetence' exposed publicly? In order to prod group members into offering some of their audiotapes for critique, the supervisor can explain the difference between a teaching or supervising responsibility and a learning responsibility:

Supervisor: My responsibility is to help you develop your skills as competent REBTers and assist you in overcoming blocks in this process. Your learning responsibility is to make a commitment to become competent REBTers and part of this commitment is to present me with tapes, among other things, so I can critique them. So who is going to be first one to get this learning partnership going?

Supervisees are often galvanized into action by spelling out their responsibilities in this fashion because they see the self-defeating nature of withholding their tapes. Those who are still reluctant to offer a tape can be urged to reveal their irrational beliefs about audiotaped supervision (e.g. 'My tape's so awful that I can't bear to listen to it or others to hear it'). Humour is often the best vehicle to overcome this reluctance as we have discovered in our supervision groups (e.g. 'John, we can bear listening to your tape if you can'; 'If it's that awful, we'll put our hands over our ears while it is being played'). Such humour 'loosens up' anxious students and tapes are handed over for supervision. Feedback is elicited to discover post-supervision reactions (e.g. 'I can bear it after all and I learnt a few things to help me be more confident with my clients').

For students to receive a qualification in REBT, a specified number of their audiotapes have to be presented for analysis. One or two students may continually offer excuses as to why they did not bring tapes to supervision such as: 'I forgot to turn on the tape recorder'; 'The batteries had worn out'; 'I'm waiting for the right client'; 'I was worried about the client's reaction to being taped.' Group members can become irritated that one or two of their group 'are getting away with it [not presenting tapes]' while they always make presentations. The supervisor can lead group discussion in uncovering the anxiogenic beliefs that the recalcitrant student(s) holds and ways to dispute them (e.g. 'You are making your worth as a therapist conditional upon presenting a perfect tape. A "perfect" tape may be achieved after presenting quite a few imperfect ones').

Each group member can suggest practical problem-solving measures to 'wear down' the student's excuses: e.g. 'Put a Post-it note on the tape recorder to remind you to turn it on'; 'Check the batteries well before the session and have a spare set handy just in case'; 'The next client you see is the right client – so get on with it!'; 'Deal with the client's possible worries about being taped by explaining the rationale for taping and the context in which the tape will be heard.' The student usually concedes that he has no more excuses to offer and will bring in a tape (not try to) at the next session.

Listening to a succession of tapes can become tedious for students and they may 'drift off' when not listening to their own tape. The supervisor can point out that the collective attention of the group is required, not just his, in responding to each tape. To combat this ennui, the supervisor allots a specific amount of time for group discussion of each tape and then each person is asked to make constructive comments about it. If a particular student continually says 'It's all been said, really', the group usually suggests that he should be the first to offer his comments on the next few tapes.

Students sometimes complain that listening to 'endless' tapes just keeps on repeating the same mistakes they are all making (e.g. asking questions that reinforce A–C thinking instead of teaching B–C thinking; an unhealthy negative emotion is not clearly pinpointed for examination; an agenda is not set). The supervisor can suggest that each member practises therapy live and he will pinpoint and remediate through skill demonstration mistakes as they occur:

Supervisor: Live demonstrations are an excellent means of improving your REBT skills.
Simon: It's pretty scary doing it out there in the middle of the room in front of everyone.
Supervisor: Because ... ?
Simon: Well, you're going to make a big fool of yourself in front of everyone.
Supervisor: The usual fear in other words [nods of agreement]. Look, REBT is a robust form of psychotherapy – we encourage clients to take risks if they want change in their lives. You should preferably be doing the same thing in your own lives and in your training. How much REBT you're going to learn and how good a practitioner you will become depends on how much you're going to push yourself. Any takers?
Mary: I'll be the therapist.
Peter: I'll be the client.
Supervisor: And I'll be pointing out your mistakes and showing you how to correct them. Now if someone could write down everyone's name on the whiteboard as we need to keep track that everyone plays the therapist and client role once.
Simon: I'll do that.

Group members can be asked to comment on any interpersonal difficulties that arise between the supervisor and a focal supervisee. These difficulties can be processed by the group in order to uncover the cognitive dynamics at work and suggest ways to tackle them:

David: Raymond, you appeared to be angry when Michael [supervisor] was evaluating your tape. What was going through your mind?
Raymond: I felt he was saying I wasn't much good as a therapist.
Paula: You may have felt it but did he actually say it?
Raymond: No, he didn't actually say it.

Mary:	How do you link Michael's evaluation of some of your REBT skills with your competence as a therapist?
Raymond:	[sighs] I know it's my problem. As soon as I think someone is being critical I immediately start putting myself down.
Maureen:	How could you begin to learn not to condemn yourself because someone else is critical of you or an aspect of you?
Raymond:	Well, I suppose my anger could alert me to what I'm doing and then I could try to get on top of it as quickly as possible.
Mary:	Did your anger help or hinder your supervision session?
Raymond:	It got completely in the way – I didn't hear Michael's comments which I'm sure were very helpful.
Paula:	Now Michael, we can't let you off the hook, can we? There seemed to be a rising impatience in you at times. So what was going on with you?
Michael:	Well, I could hear myself saying 'Stop bridling with indignation every time I make a comment about your tape.' So at times I distracted myself from supervising Raymond's tape.
Paula:	So what will you do to stop distracting yourself?
Michael:	Remind myself that Raymond, or any other student that I'm supervising, should be acting the way they are acting at any given moment rather than not be acting that way. Of course, I can't guarantee that I never will be distracted again!
Paula:	[smiles] We'll be keeping an eye on your progress.

Similarly, group members can help each other to challenge the disturbance-producing beliefs that surface in their supervision tapes (e.g. 'Your client is not doing his homework tasks at the moment and you're getting angry because you're demanding he must do them. Now why must he do what you want him to do?'). As supervisees gain more competence and confidence in applying REBT, they take more responsibility for acting as co-supervisors of others' tapes. Of course, the supervisor monitors their feedback to ensure that it is constructive, problem focused and clinically accurate.

In this chapter, I have described some ways of using the group to help students fully engage in REBT training and supervision. This engagement not only creates a stimulating learning environment, but also draws from students methods for resolving the interpersonal difficulties and other problems that invariably arise in a group setting.

References

Beal D, DiGiuseppe R (1998) Training supervisors in rational emotive behavior therapy. Journal of Cognitive Psychotherapy 12(2): 127–37.

Bernard ME, DiGiuseppe R (eds) (1989) Inside Rational-Emotive Therapy: A Critical Appraisal of the Theory and Therapy of Albert Ellis. San Diego, CA: Academic Press.

Clarkson P, Gilbert M (1991) The training of counsellor trainers and supervisors. In W Dryden, B Thorne (eds) Training and Supervision for Counselling in Action. London: Sage.

Dryden W (1987) Current Issues in Rational-Emotive Therapy. London: Croom Helm.

Dryden W (1999) Rational Emotive Behavioural Counselling in Action, 2nd edn. London: Sage.

Dryden W, DiGiuseppe R. (1990) A Primer on Rational-Emotive Therapy. Champaign, IL: Research Press.

Dryden W, Thorne B (1991) Approaches to the Training of Counsellors. In: W Dryden, B Thorne (eds) Training and Supervision for Counselling in Action. London: Sage Publications.

Dryden W, Neenan M, Yankura J (1999) Counselling Individuals: A Rational Emotive Behavioural Handbook, 3rd edn. London: Whurr.

Ellis A (1977) Fun as psychotherapy. Rational Living 12(1): 26.

Ellis A (1997) REBT and its application to group therapy. In J Yankura, W Dryden (eds) Special Applications of REBT: A Therapist's Casebook. New York: Springer.

Ellis A, Dryden W (1997) The Practice of Rational Emotive Behavior Therapy, 2nd edn. New York: Springer.

Fennell MJV (1999) (workshop) Maximising training effectiveness in cognitive therapy. British Association for Behavioural and Cognitive Psychotherapies Annual Conference, Bristol.

Friedberg RD, Taylor LA (1994) Perspectives on supervision in cognitive therapy. Journal of Rational-Emotive and Cognitive-Behavior Therapy 12(3): 147–61.

Grieger R, Boyd J (1980) Rational-emotive Therapy: A Skills-Based Approach. New York: Van Nostrand Reinhold.

Hauck P (1980) Brief Counseling with RET. Philadelphia, PA: Westminster Press.

Hauck P (1982) How to Do What You Want to Do. London: Sheldon Press.

Honey P, Mumford A (1986) Learning to Learn Resource: Putting Learning into Action. MCB University Press.

Knowles M (1990) The Adult Learner: A Neglected Species. London: Gulf Publishing.

Kolb DA (1984) Experiential Learning. New Jersey: Prentice-Hall.

Perris C (1994) Supervising cognitive psychotherapy and training supervisors. Journal of Cognitive Psychotherapy 8(2): 83–103.

Thorne B, Dryden W (1991) Key issues in the training of counsellors. In W Dryden, B Thorne (eds) Training and Supervision for Counselling in Action. London: Sage.

Wessler RA, Wessler RL (1980) The Principles and Practice of Rational-Emotive Therapy. San Francisco, CA: Jossey-Bass.

Woods PJ, Ellis A (1996) Supervision in rational emotive behavior therapy. Journal of Rational-Emotive and Cognitive-Behavior Therapy 14(2): 135–52.

Index

ABC framework, 20
  attacks by group on therapist, 64–65
  cognitive techniques of REBT, 34, 35
  deep disclosure near session
    termination, 82, 83–84
  Florence Nightingale Hospital CBT
    programme, 114–115
  Friday night workshops, 177
  initial session, 58
  Intensives, 146–147, 148–149
    self-help forms, 170, 171
  leaving the group, 74
  mass group denial, 70
  research into effectiveness, 26
  training groups, 190, 198
  unconditional self-acceptance groups,
    134–135
acceptance beliefs, 9–10
active disputing, 34
activist learning style, 188, 193
activity of therapist and group members,
  47–48
administration issues, Florence
  Nightingale Hospital CBT
  programme, 119
advice giving, 23
aftercare support group, Florence
  Nightingale Hospital CBT
  programme, 117
Albert Ellis Institute (AEI), New York
  assessment for group therapy, 17, 32
  assistant leaders, 44
  Ellis's role, 4
  Friday night workshops, 176

historical development of REBT, 3
humour, use of, 37
Intensives, 38, 142
  supplementary programmes and
    materials, 143–144, 145
Journal of Rational-Emotive and
  Cognitive-Behavior Therapy, 23
kinds of REBT groups, 32
  women's groups, 91, 93, 95, 101–102
always/never thinking, 21
anger, 126
  Intensives, 163–167
anti-awfulizing beliefs, 8
anxiety, 126
approval, need for, 154–157
assertiveness problems
  case presentation, 49–51
  Florence Nightingale Hospital CBT
    programme, 117
  women's groups, 92, 96
assessment for REBT group therapy,
  16–17, 32–33
  exclusion criteria, *see* exclusion criteria
    for group therapy
  Florence Nightingale Hospital CBT
    programme, 110–112
  inclusion criteria, see inclusion criteria
    for group therapy
assistant leaders, 44
  women's groups, 93
attacks by group on therapist, 60–66
audience participation, Friday night
  workshops, 185–186

awfulizing beliefs, 8
  deep disclosure near session
    termination, 82
  Friday night workshops, 177

Beal, D., 199
Beck, Aaron T., 2
behavioural-cognitive homework, 21
behavioural REBT techniques, 38–39
beliefs, *see* irrational beliefs; rational
    beliefs
bibliotherapy, 21
  Florence Nightingale Hospital CBT
    programme, 109
  unconditional self-acceptance groups,
    134, 137
Borderline Personality Disorder, 92
Boyd, J., 194

closed groups, 4–5
  assessment for, 17
  unconditional self-acceptance, 131–132
cognitive behaviour therapy (CBT), 51–52
  development of REBT, 1, 2, 3
  effectiveness, research, 25–26
  women's groups, 92
  see also Florence Nightingale Hospital
    CBT programme
cognitive distortions, correcting, 21–22
  see also overgeneralization
cognitive homework, 21, 35
cognitive REBT techniques, 34–35
co-leaders, 44
  women's groups, 93
'compare and despair' cycle, 98
confidentiality issues
  breaches, 33
  Friday night workshops, 187
  unconditional self-acceptance groups,
    133
consciousness raising, women's groups, 94
constructive action, and unconditional
    self-acceptance, 130
constructivist approach to psychotherapy,
    3
consultant psychiatrists, problems with,
    121–122

coping self-statements
  forceful, 35–36
    Intensives, 159–160
  rational, 34
cost-benefit analysis, 34–35
  Intensives, 143
counselling skills, acquisition of, 193–196
countertransference, 41
criticisms of REBT
  historical development of REBT, 2, 4
  training groups, 195–196

'Dealing with Specific Problems' group,
    Florence Nightingale Hospital CBT
    programme, 115–116
deep disclosure near session termination,
    78–86
demands, 7
  ego disturbance, 125–126
denial, mass group, 66–72
depreciation beliefs, 9
  Friday night workshops, 177
depression, 125
desensitization, in vivo, 38
  leaving the group, 75
  women's groups, 100
'Developing Self-acceptance' group,
    Florence Nightingale Hospital CBT
    programme, 116
development of REBT, 1–4
  group therapy, 4–6
didactic teaching methods, 14
DiGiuseppe, Ray
  disputing, 20, 135
  Intensives, 142
  supervision, 199
disclosure near session termination, 78–86
discomfort disturbance, 125
  see also low frustration tolerance
disputing, 20
  active, 34
  attacks by group on therapist, 65
  case presentation, 49
  deep disclosure near session
    termination, 84
  forceful taped, 36
  group therapy, 31
  initial session, 58

Intensives, 143, 147-148, 149-150, 161-162
   self-help forms, 172
procedure of group sessions, 33
training groups, 196
unconditional self-acceptance groups, 135, 136, 137
women's groups, 96, 100
Dryden, Windy, 192, 196-197, 199

educational emphasis, REBT
   Florence Nightingale Hospital CBT programme, 109, 112, 116-117
   Friday night workshops, 177
effectiveness
   of REBT, 25-26
   of therapists, Florence Nightingale Hospital CBT programme, 117-118
ego disturbance, 124-127
Ellis, Albert
   effectiveness of REBT, research, 25, 26
   fallibility of humans, 128
   Friday night workshops, 6, 176-178, 185-187
      example, 178-185
   history of REBT, 1-2, 3-4, 107
      group therapy, 4
   musturbatory beliefs, 129
   specific and general REBT, 106, 108
   supervision, 199, 200
   theoretical constructs of REBT, 7, 14
   training groups, 191
   women's groups, 91, 93
   worth, rational use of human, 129
emotive homework, 21
emotive REBT techniques, 35-38
empowerment exercises, women's groups, 103-104
encounter groups, 3
   marathon, 3, 5, 32, 38, 144
   see also Intensives
encouragement of group members, 38
environmental resources, focus on, 94
envy, 126
Epictetus, 1, 7
Erhard, Werner, 142
exclusion criteria for group therapy, 18-19, 32-33

Florence Nightingale Hospital CBT programme, 111-112
women's groups, 92

fallibility of humans, 128
feedback
   from group members, 31
      Florence Nightingale Hospital CBT programme, 114, 116
      skill training and role play methods, 22
      supervision groups, 201
      to therapists, 110, 141
      training groups, 196
      unconditional self-acceptance groups, 141
      women's groups, 92, 100-101
   from supervisor, 200
Fennell, M. J. V., 193
flexibility
   Florence Nightingale Hospital CBT programme, 109-110
   unconditional self-acceptance groups, 129
Florence Nightingale Hospital CBT programme, 106-107
   assessment of patient suitability, 110-112
   core elements, 108-110
   description, 112-117
   difficulties, 120-122
   effective leaders, qualities, 117-118
   management issues, 118-120
   REBT, 107-108
Fodor, Iris, 5
forceful coping self-statements, 35-36
   Intensives, 159-160
forceful taped disputing, 36
Friday night workshops, 6, 32, 144-145, 176-177, 186-187
   audience participation, 185-186
   public demonstration with volunteer, 177-185
friendships, encouraging female, 94
full preferences, 7

gate-keeping skills, group leaders, 118
general REBT, 106, 107

Florence Nightingale Hospital CBT
    programme, 107–108
global ratings, illegitimacy of, 127–128
goal setting
    Intensives, 167–174
    unconditional self-acceptance groups,
        134
    women's groups, 94
goal sheets, women's groups, 93, 105
Grieger, R., 194
group processes
    focusing on, 42–45
    leaving the group, 77–78
guilt, 126

habit, unconditional self-acceptance as,
    130
Harper, Robert, 2
Hauck, Paul
    Hold Your Head Up High, 134, 137
    self-esteem, 127
    supervision, 200
    training groups, 198
healthy negative emotions, 11
    Florence Nightingale Hospital CBT
        programme, 115
high frustration tolerance (HFT), 9
    training groups, 195
history of REBT, 1–4
    group therapy, 4–6
holding back by group members, 86–90
homework assignments, 20–21, 31
    attacks by group on therapist, 64
    cognitive, 21, 35
    deep disclosure near session
        termination, 85
    initial session, 59
    Intensives, 144, 174–175
    leaving the group, 75
    mass group denial, 71
    reviews, 33
    training groups, 192–193
    unconditional self-acceptance groups,
        133–134, 135, 136, 137–138,
        139–140
    unfulfilled, 46
    women's groups, 92, 93–94, 100,
        102–104

Honey, P., 188
hospital-based group programmes, 5–6
    unconditional self-acceptance groups,
        132
    see also Florence Nightingale Hospital
        CBT programme
humanity, equality of humans in, 128
humour, use of, 37
    Intensives, 174–175
    supervision groups, 200, 201
    women's groups, 96
hurt, 126

I-can't-stand-it-itis, 177
'I'm Depressed, Depressed!', 175
inclusion criteria for group therapy,
    17–18, 32
    Florence Nightingale Hospital CBT
        programme, 110–111
    women's groups, 92
    unconditional self-acceptance groups,
        132
informed consent, Florence Nightingale
    Hospital CBT programme, 109, 112
initial session, 55–59
    training groups, 189
    unconditional self-acceptance groups,
        132–134
Institute for Rational Living, 5
integrative psychotherapy movement, 3
intensive nature, Florence Nightingale
    Hospital CBT programme, 109
Intensives, 6, 38, 142–145
    historical development of REBT, 3
    Manual, 145–146
        ABC framework and disputing,
            146–150
        anger, overcoming, 163–167
        approval, need for, and love
            slobbism, 154–157
        finale, 174–175
        goal-setting and homework,
            167–174
        low frustration tolerance, 157–163
        perfectionism and self-acceptance,
            150–153
internal consistency, Florence Nightingale
    Hospital CBT programme, 108, 121

internalizing unconditional
  self-acceptance, 130–131
interruptions by members, 45
interventions, 19–20
  ABC framework analysis, 20
  advice giving and problem-solving, 23
  correcting cognitive distortions, 21–22
  disputing, 20
  homework assignments, 20–21
  skill training and role play methods,
    22–23
in vivo desensitization, 38
  leaving the group, 75
  women's groups, 100
irrational beliefs (IBs)
  attack by group on therapist, 65
  cognitive distortions, 22
  cognitive REBT techniques, 34
  deep disclosure near session termina-
    tion, 81
  disputing, see disputing
  ego disturbance, 125
  emotive REBT techniques, 36, 37
  Florence Nightingale Hospital CBT
    programme, 107, 115
  Friday night workshops, 177, 183, 185
  Intensives, 143, 147, 148–149
    anger, 163
    low frustration tolerance, 161–162
    self-help forms, 171–172
  mass group denial, 70
  practice of therapy, 14
  procedure of group sessions, 33
  psychological disturbance, 7–11
  psychotherapeutic change, 11–13
  skill practice and role play scenarios, 22
  training groups, 196
  women's groups, 94, 95, 96, 97–99,
    100–101
    homework assignments, 102–103
  see also awfulizing beliefs; demands;
    depreciation beliefs; low frustration
    tolerance
'I Wish I Were Not Crazy!', 175

jealousy, 126
Journal Club, Florence Nightingale
  Hospital CBT programme, 119

Journal of Rational-Emotive and Cognitive-
  Behavior Therapy, 23, 24–25
Journal of Rational-Emotive Therapy, 23, 24

Kellogg, Peggy, 5

lateness, 42–43
  see also group punctuality
learning styles, 188–189, 193
leaving the group, 72–78
'Love Me, Love Me, Only Me!', 37
love slobbism
  case presentation, 49–50
  Intensives, 154–157
low frustration tolerance (LFT), 8
  Florence Nightingale Hospital CBT
    programme, 116
  Intensives, 157–163
  training groups, 195

magnification, 21
marathon encounter groups, 3, 5, 32, 38,
  144
  see also Intensives
mass group denial, 66–72
Maultsby, Maxie, Jr
  fallibility of humans, 128
  rational emotive imagery, 36
meta-emotions, 115
mixed therapeutic regimes, 121
modelling, 35
  Intensives, 143
  training groups, 198
  women's groups, 94, 95
monitoring patient progress, Florence
  Nightingale Hospital CBT
  programme, 119–120
Mumford, A., 188
musturbatory beliefs
  deep disclosure near session
    termination, 82
  ego disturbance, 126–127, 129
  Friday night workshops, 183
  initial session, 57
  relapse prevention, 39

Nelson-Jones, R., 176
never/always thinking, 21

non-participative members, 46–47
    see also reserved and shy members
obnoxious events, avoiding running away
        from, 38
open groups, 4
    assessment for, 17–18
    unconditional self-acceptance,
        131–132
operant conditioning, 178, 184
orientation to Florence Nightingale
        Hospital CBT programme, 112–113
overgeneralization, 22
    deep disclosure near session termina-
        tion, 82
    and unconditional self-acceptance, 129

part-whole errors, see overgeneralization
passive members, 46–47
    see also reserved and shy members
patient liaison workers, Florence
        Nightingale Hospital CBT
        programme, 120
penalties, use of, 39, 184
perfectionism
    Intensives, 150–151
    women's groups, 98
'Perfect Rationality', 37, 175
polite members, 46–47
    see also reserved and shy members
post-modernism, 3
post-traumatic stress disorder (PTSD), 19
    in vivo desensitization, 38
pragmatic learning style, 189, 193
preferential beliefs, 129
problems and goals sheets, Florence
        Nightingale Hospital CBT
        programme, 115
problem solving, 23
    women's groups, 96, 98–99
'problems of living' workshops, see Friday
        night workshops
problems treated using REBT group
        therapy, 23–25
processes of therapy
    activity of therapist and group
        members, 47–48
    countertransference, 41

difficult group members, working with,
        45–47
    group processes, focusing on, 42–45
    intervention methods, 41–42
    transference, 39–40
procrastination
    Friday night workshops, 179–185
    Intensives, 161–162
    see also low frustration tolerance
proselytizing, 35
psychodynamic group therapy, 16
psychoeducational techniques, 35
psychotherapeutic change, 11–13
psychotherapy integration movement, 3
punctuality
    Florence Nightingale Hospital CBT
        programme, 121
    Intensives, 146
    training groups, 191–192
    see also lateness

'Raising Frustration Tolerance' group,
        Florence Nightingale Hospital CBT
        programme, 116
rational, definition, 146
rational beliefs (RBs)
    attacks by group on therapist, 65
    cognitive techniques of REBT, 34
    Florence Nightingale Hospital CBT
        programme, 107, 115
    Intensives, 143, 148–149, 161–162
    mass group denial, 71
    practice of therapy, 14
    psychological disturbance, 7–11
    psychotherapeutic change, 12–13
    role play methods, 23
    unconditional self-acceptance groups,
        135, 137
    see also high frustration tolerance
rational coping self-statements, 34
rational emotive imagery (REI), 36
    case presentation, 50
    Friday night workshops, 178, 183–184,
        185
    Intensives, 155–156, 159
        anger, overcoming, 165, 166
        goal-setting, 169
    leaving the group, 77

mass group denial, 71
unconditional self-acceptance groups,
        138–139
Rational Living, 23–24
rational portfolio method, 136
recording therapy sessions, *see* tape
        recording
reflective learning style, 188, 193
reframing, 35
reinforcement, use of, 39
relapse prevention, 39
relationships techniques of REBT, 38
relaxation groups, Florence Nightingale
        Hospital CBT programme, 117
research into REBT
    effectiveness of REBT, 25–26
        Friday night workshops, 186
    historical development of REBT, 2–3
reserved and shy members
    case presentation, 49–51
    group process, 43
    training groups, 190–191
resource sharing, women's groups,
        103–104
reverse role-playing, 36
rewards, use of, 39, 184
Richman, Diana, 142
role modelling, *see* modelling
role-playing
    reverse, 36
    training groups, 193–195
    women's groups, 92, 99–100
running away, avoiding, 38

self-acceptance
    Intensives, 151–152
    quiz, 140
    unconditional, *see* unconditional self-
        acceptance
self-care, women's groups, 94
self-disclosure
    exercises, 89
    by supervisors, 200
self-downing
    ego disturbance, 125–126, 129
    forceful and energetic challenging of,
        131
    Friday night workshops, 185

as habit, 130
    Intensives, 152–153
    women's groups, 91, 92, 95, 97–98
self-esteem
    and global ratings, 127–128
    unconditional self-acceptance groups,
        133
self-exploration, training groups, 196–199
self-help forms, Intensives, 170–173, 174
self-pleasuring assignments, women's
        groups, 94, 102–103
self-statements
    forceful, 35–36
        Intensives, 159–160
    positive, 94, 103
    rational coping, 34
shame, 126
    Intensives, 152
shame-attacking exercises
    deep disclosure near session termina-
        tion, 85
    holding back by group members, 89
    Intensives, 152–153
    unconditional self-acceptance groups,
        139–140
shyness, *see* reserved and shy members
skills-oriented nature, Florence
        Nightingale Hospital CBT
        programme, 109
skill training, 22, 39
social anxiety problems, 49–51
societal change, focus on, 94
Society for the Exploration of
        Psychotherapy Integration (SEPI), 3
Socratic teaching methods, 14
songs, humorous, 37, 175
specific REBT, 106, 170
    Florence Nightingale Hospital CBT
        programme, 107–108
Stoicism, 1, 7
structured nature, Florence Nightingale
        Hospital CBT programme, 108
style of therapist, 14, 186–187
    Ellis, 40, 43–44
        Friday night workshops, 177–178,
        186
supervision, 199–203
    Florence Nightingale Hospital CBT
        programme, 120

support system, women's groups as,
    101–102
syndromes and symptoms treated using
    REBT group therapy, 23–25

talkative members
    group process, 43
    training groups, 192
tape recording, 35
    disputing, 36, 137
    Friday night workshops, 178
    supervision groups, 201–203
team management, Florence Nightingale
    Hospital CBT programme, 119
theoretical coherence, Florence
    Nightingale Hospital CBT
    programme, 108
theoretical constructs, 6
    practice of therapy, 13–16
    psychological disturbance, 7–11
    psychotherapeutic change, 11–13
theoretical learning style, 189, 193
therapeutic relationship, 13–14
Thorne, B., 196–197
time spans of groups
    Florence Nightingale Hospital CBT
        programme, 120–121
    unconditional self-acceptance groups,
        132
    women's groups, 94
training groups, 188
    acquisition of counselling skills,
        193–196
    counselling theory and relevant
        academic material, 192–193
    punctuality, 191–192
    self-exploration, 196–199
    starting the group, 189
    status within the group, 189–190
    supervised work with clients, 199–203
    talkative and silent members, 190–191
    trainer's role, 188–189
transference, 39–40
transpersonal psychotherapy, 3

unassertiveness
    case presentation, 49–51

Florence Nightingale Hospital CBT
    programme, 117
women's groups, 92, 96
unconditional other-acceptance (UOA), 38
    case presentation, 50
    training groups, 199
    transference, 40
    women's groups, 94, 101
unconditional self-acceptance (USA), 47,
    124, 126–131
    case presentation, 50
    ego disturbance, 124–126
    Florence Nightingale Hospital CBT
        programme, 116
    groups for, 131–132
    training groups, 199
    women's groups, 98, 101
unfair comparisons, 98
unhealthy negative emotions, 10
    Florence Nightingale Hospital CBT
        programme, 115

Watson, John L., 1
Wessler, R. A.
    supervision, 200
    training groups, 192, 197, 199
Wessler, R. L.
    supervision, 200
    training groups, 192, 197, 199
'Whine, Whine, Whine!', 175
Wolfe, Janet
    Intensives, 142
    women's groups, 5, 91, 94
women's groups, 5, 91–94, 104
    exercises, 99–101
    goal sheets, 93, 105
    homework assignments, 102–104
    irrational beliefs, 97–99
    myths about, 94–97
    as support system, 101–102
Woods, P. J., 199
worth, rational use of human, 128–129

yoga groups, Florence Nightingale
    Hospital CBT programme, 117

zigzag technique, 136–137